CONTENTS

PART I
History

We begin with an overview of the visible church, the architectural complex, and the pastors who guided its many stages of development. Subsequent chapters focus on individual aspects of the history of the Catholic community in Harvard Square:

> • the mainly Irish immigrant community which built the great Church of St. Paul,
>
> • the mature and confident parish which produced great missionaries like Maryknoll founder James Walsh,
>
> • the liturgical traditions of St. Paul Church and the founding of the Boston Archdiocesan Choir School,
>
> • the growth of Catholic students and scholars at Harvard and Radcliffe and their contributions to the church at large.

Parishioner and Harvard graduate, Edward T.P. Graham designed the "Lombardic" church in 1915.

Introduction:
Building the Church in Harvard Square

Catholics in Early Cambridge

The denizens of Harvard Square uniformly worshipped in the New England Puritan tradition until the middle of the eighteenth century, when Rev. East Apthorp established a mission for the Church of England. The first gathering of a more diverse nature was the encampment in 1775 in Harvard College and on the Cambridge Commons of the Continental Army, a force including Catholics from Maryland, Pennsylvania and Canada. When George Washington was informed of the plans for the annual Guy Fawkes procession ("for the observance of that ridiculous and childish custom of burning the Effigy of the Pope"), he halted the event, expressing his surprise at the lack of common sense and propriety in such an activity.

For decades after its completion in 1803, the old Cathedral of the Holy Cross on Franklin Street was the only Catholic church in the Boston area. That building, designed by Bulfinch, was hardly convenient for Cambridge Catholics but their number was miniscule. A collection of small villages—the Old Village (now Harvard Square), East Cambridge, and Cambridgeport—Cambridge continued to be almost uniformly Protestant and English speaking. The 481 names on the 1822 voter list included only four that sounded "foreign."[1] When the parish of St. Mary's, Charlestown, was created in 1828, it ranged over the large area north of the Charles River.

Then came the Irish immigration of the 1830's and 40's. At first just a few families, with men working in factories, women employed as domestics, and children occupied in an array of tasks, they moved across the bridges into East Cambridge. At this time, the parts of Cambridge were so separated, both physically and psychologically, that no one at Harvard had to pay much attention to the new Catholics in East Cambridge. The attention they did pay was divided. The morning after Protestants burned the Ursuline Convent in Charlestown in 1834, Royal Morse, an auctioneer, roused the citizenry of the Old Village to guard Harvard against anticipated Catholic retaliation and

about fifty graduates of the college spent the night there, armed with muskets and ball cartridges, prepared to fight the imaginary danger. On the other hand, typical of the intellectuals concerned for civil liberties, Judge Story led a meeting to protest the outrage in Charlestown and to affirm the rights of "our Catholic brethren."

Soon the immigrants overwhelmed the natives, with over a thousand Irish living in East Cambridge in 1840. Through the zealous efforts of the convert Daniel H. Southwick, a Sunday-school was organized there and money was raised for a church. When constituted in 1842, the "St. John's Church," later to become Sacred Heart Parish, comprised the entire towns of Cambridge and Somerville and much to the west. The pastor there, the Rev. John B. Fitzpatrick, was made coadjutor-bishop of the diocese in 1844 and two years later this man, the first priest of the first parish in Cambridge, succeeded Bishop Fenwick as the Bishop of Boston. The Rev. Manasses P. Dougherty was appointed pastor of St. John's.[2]

Fr. Manasses Dougherty

The name of Manasses Dougherty dominates the expansion of Catholicism in this area for the next thirty years. Seeing the necessity for a church in the western part of Cambridge, he built St. Peter's on Concord Avenue in 1848. As one of the frontier churches of Boston, St. Peter's extended over much of the northwest metropolitan area. The original parish limits enclosed Belmont, Lincoln, Lexington, Bedford, Medford, Malden, and Somerville west of Dane Street.[3] Out of St. Peter's, Fr. Dougherty built so many parishes, the last of which was St. Paul, that he received the sobriquet "Founder of Churches."

The continuing arrival and integration of immigrants was not always easy. What was perceived as an Irish flood completely changed the landscape of those who had known the village of Old Cambridge. "Paddy Jokes" appeared in some newspapers and differences between "natives" and "foreign-born" were obvious. Conservatives in the Old Village were petitioning to withdraw from the rest of Cambridge, as were the residents of East Cambridge.[4] But Catholic growth was so rapid, that Fr. Dougherty planned to erect a church in Harvard's own neighborhood. John Langdon Sibley, longtime Harvard librarian and historian, noted in his journal in 1846:[5]

> The Catholics within a few years have erected a church at East Cambridge and have just purchased five acres to build another church about one mile west from the University buildings. They are very quiet but zealous in all their movements and the time will come when many of the old battles, the theological at least, must be fought over again, and that too in this country. It is incidentally remarked in the paper today that one-quarter of the population of Boston is Catholic.

Zealous, to be sure, but Sibley would hardly have called Catholics quiet once Manasses Dougherty arrived in the Old Village. A classic, energetic pioneer priest, Father Dougherty started his fund drive for St. Peter's in January, 1848 by celebrating Mass

When built in 1848, St. Peter's Church on Concord Avenue served a parish that reached from Cambridge to Lincoln and Malden.

in Lyceum Hall (the site of the present Coop) and appealing for subscriptions for the new building on Concord Avenue—the *Pilot* reported that sixteen thousand dollars were raised.[6] Bishop Fitzpatrick officiated at the laying of St. Peter's cornerstone in July, 1848.

It can hardly be coincidental that in this neighborhood, there were two Harvard alumni among the priests present, George F. Haskins, Class of 1826 and Joseph Coolidge Shaw, S.J., Class of 1840, who preached the cornerstone sermon. Fr. Haskins, whose major work was the establishment of the first Catholic reform school in New England, also served as a temporary pastor at St. John's and at St. Peter's during the illnesses of their administrators. One evening in 1859 during Fr. Dougherty's poor health, it was Fr. Haskins who brought him a note from the parishioners with the sum of a thousand dollars for a recuperative vacation in Ireland. No doubt, the mixture of Yankees like Shaw and Haskins into the heavily Irish parish was curious—but the local clergy at this time was mainly foreign Jesuits and local converts. As Catholics were beginning to surround the college, Catholics were also beginning to emerge from within it. So, after years of anti-Popery, Harvard in fact provided some of the clergy who welcomed the first Catholic Church to Harvard Square.

After twenty-five years, the Catholics in the vicinity of Harvard University had grown so much that a "chapel of ease" was needed for their use, and in 1873 the meeting house of the Shepherd Congregational Society (including organ) was purchased at $20,000 for this purpose. The Congregationalists had erected this small wooden structure on the northwest corner of Mt. Auburn and Holyoke Streets (the present site of Holyoke Center) in 1830 and had twice enlarged it. The appropriate alterations were quickly effected and two days before Christmas the building was opened for the worship of the 1200 Catholics in the area. References to the St. Paul church in its first fifty years regularly name the famed Fr. Manasses Dougherty as the founder, and tablets in the vestibule of both St. Peter's and old St. Paul's marked the memory of the pioneer priest whose funeral in 1877 drew three thousand mourners.[7]

On the site of the Harvard Coop, Fr. Manasses Dougherty, "Founder of Churches," celebrated the first Mass in Harvard Square.

The First Pastor

Fr. Dougherty retained charge of the St. Paul Church until October, 1875, when the district was created a parish and the fiery Rev. William Orr was appointed pastor. The sacramental registers were opened on October 26th with the christening of Alice Callaghan of Flagg Street and the marriage of William Russell of Charles River Street to Catharine Sullivan of Brattle Street. The parish confirmations that year took place at St. Peter's, but two years later Archbishop Williams confirmed 120 young Catholics at St. Paul's, as 100 received their first communion that day.[8]

Fr. Orr was born in the North of Ireland on August 1, 1830. His early education was in the schools there, but he took his classical and theological courses in Maryland. After ordination in 1864, he was appointed assistant at the Church of the Immaculate Conception, Lawrence. After two years as pastor in Templeton, where he had eighteen townships to attend, he returned to Lawrence as pastor until 1875. Large-hearted and energetic, Fr. Orr was a popular clergyman devoted to his homeland. His strong North-of-Ireland accent endeared him to a largely Irish flock, many of whom had come to America in the same generation as he. A contemporary account describes him, "Being an Irishman by birth and having such a broad, sympathetic disposition it is only natural that the land of his birth has always had his warmest sympathy and also financial assistance in her struggle for legislative and national independence."[9]

To the Harvard crowd, Fr. Orr's vigorous style was less endearing. It was perhaps natural that he did not share President Eliot's vision of Harvard Square, but he did not even answer correspondence from the coordinator of student religious clubs. One student, John LaFarge of the Class of 1901, was distinctly embarrassed by Orr, as he explains in a later reminiscence of the relationship between Orr and the local character John the Orangeman:[10]

If John the Orangeman meant anarchy on a humble plane, Father Orr spelled anarchy on a lofty scale. It was just conceivable that some being like John might lurk in one of the discreet pews of the Appleton Chapel or even be found loitering momentarily in the corridor of the Fogg Art Museum. But by no stretch of the imagination could anything like Father Orr's sermons be conjectured in Appleton's pulpit nor would its staid walls ever echo to anything like his lurid descriptions of what he saw by night and sometimes by day occurring around his rectory in the rooming houses of Mt. Auburn St., not to speak of his hygienic discussion as to the effect that the taking of a "blue pull" (to rhyme with *dull*) is apt to have upon a pastor's health. One would have to go back to the early days of the Massachusetts Colony when pulpits were pulpits to find anything resembling the

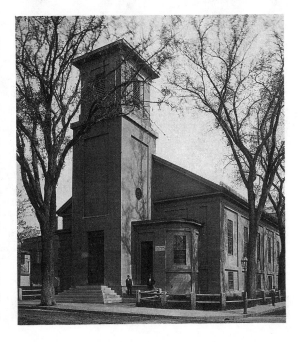

In 1873, Fr. Dougherty bought the Shephard Congregational Church on the corner of Mt. Auburn and Holyoke Streets.

aspersions uttered by Father Orr upon the personal character of John the Orangeman when the latter presented his bewhiskered self for his Easter Duty in a state of general good will but of somewhat uncertain stance and step.

The relationship between church leaders, however, was apparently quite civil— Catholics contributed to the recasting of the bells of Christ Church and Fr. Orr offered a polite congratulations to the two congregations of the First Church celebrating their 250th anniversary in 1886. Catholic and Protestant clergymen united particularly in the "No-license" movement which banished saloons from Cambridge. By the end of the century, civic leaders took pride in "The Cambridge Idea," a blessing of religious tolerance and public goodwill.

After an initial decade of growth and expansion, the parish undertook its first burst of development in the 1880's, acquiring the cemetery on the Arlington line, building a school and substantially renovating the second-hand church. In accord with the instructions of the Third Plenary Council of Baltimore, many parishes were then building schools. In early 1889, the Archdiocese paid $17,000 for the estate of the late Gordon McKay, a wealthy sewing-machine manufacturer and Harvard benefactor, on the large sloping lot between Arrow and Mount Auburn. The *Cambridge Chronicle* reported on April 13 of that year that there was some doubt as to the disposition of the property:

> At the time of the sale it was understood that a parochial school was to be erected. Later an idea has gone forth that it would be wiser to erect a new church building. The society has outgrown the present building at the corner of Mount Auburn and Holyoke streets, and at the present date a new church will be imperative shortly. If a new church is built on the McKay estate it is probable that a school will be erected in connection with it.

The school went ahead. The house along Arrow Street, built for William Winthrop in 1811, was immediately converted to a convent and temporary classrooms for young children while a proper school was erected on the site. The new construction was built by the firms of Driscoll and O'Brien from the plans of Patrick W. Ford, an Irish architect who came to the United States just after the Civil War. He is credited with a large number of Catholic churches, schools and convents including Sacred Heart in East Cambridge and the old St. John's church and school in North Cambridge (originally built for St. Peter's in 1891). The school stood for a century, but its twelve class-

Before the Catholic renovation, the Shephard Church was a plain Protestant meeting house.

rooms, two large meeting-rooms and first floor hall for 800 were soon insufficient and had to be augmented by an adjacent brick building, known most recently as the Catholic Student Center.[11] On the McKay estate, Fr. Orr apparently still intended to build a new church and for that reason the school building had been set back in the block leaving open the site where in fact the current church stands.

Parish resources must have been restricted, however, so Fr. Orr settled on expanding the church at Mt. Auburn and Holyoke Streets at the same time the school was rising. Thus in 1890 the capacity of the lower church was enlarged by 200 and in 1891 a new front and tower were finished as part of a plan that lengthened the church by twenty-five feet, replaced the pews and improved the heating. After so many changes, the church was even thought worthy of rededication, accomplished that October by Archbishop Williams—an occasion for which Orr's friend Bishop John J. Keane of Catholic University preached the sermon. The plan of the church, converted from a simple New England meeting house, somewhat resembled the basilica design of the old Cathedral. Doric columns, surmounted by Corinthian capitals, divided the nave into aisles. A large cross was the principal design of the vault and the front of the altar displayed a lamb, which survives today.[12] A de-

Lively Fr. William Orr, St. Paul's first pastor, was devoted to Irish causes.

cade later, in 1903, Fr. Orr initiated a second effort at a new church on the McKay estate and obtained a building permit for a church 75 feet by 125 feet with a pitched roof.

Meanwhile Harvard had started to invade the neighborhood. As part of the 1890's civic movement for attractive and healthy public spaces, the coal and lumber yards along the river were purchased by the park commissions and developed into the Charles River

After the Catholic renovation. The altar seen here was later used in the lower church of the new St. Paul on Bow Street.

Parkway (the present Memorial Drive). The subsequent damming of the river completed the beautification project. While several grand plans for new quadrangles and boulevards stretching down from Harvard Yard circulated, a group of Harvard alumni under the leadership of Edward Waldo Forbes saw the opportunities as early as 1902 and began to acquire properties between Mount Auburn Street and the Charles River. The question of a boulevard widening and extending De Wolfe Street to Harvard Yard particularly concerned the parish lands. Prof. J.D.M. Ford, the only Catholic member of the faculty, was an occasional intermediary between President Eliot and Fr. Orr and even between the landscaper Frederick Law Olmstead, Jr., and Mayor McNamee, a St. Paul's man.[13]

These purchases and the resultant

Harvard houses have been lauded as successes in city planning, but the rapid changes shook the parish. While recognizing the civic improvements and "positive transformation of the locality," an assistant pastor later noted that "More than a half dozen streets with the dwellings of a Catholic population estimated at 1200-1500 souls were taken over. These people were compelled to seek homes elsewhere outside the parish boundaries. The movement which swept through the center of the parish involved the church and rectory and even threatened the property where stood the schools and convent."[14] One can see why Fr. Orr stalled his building plans on the McKay property and decided instead that the church should follow the parishioners' emigration. Shortly before his death on Dec. 30, 1906, he bought an expensive piece of property at the

In 1903, the river area south of Mt. Auburn St. was still occupied by small residences.

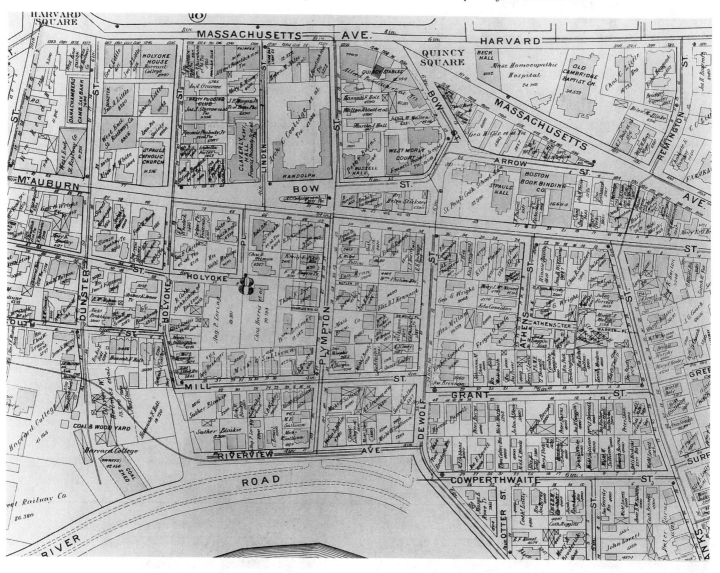

Children used to play on the steps of the old Rectory on Holyoke Street, now the site of Harvard's Lowell House.

corner of Massachusetts Avenue and Ellery Street with the intention of building the new church there.

Pastor for thirty years, Fr. Orr was a shepherd who knew his flock. A lively character, he took St.Paul's from its creation as a offshoot of St. Peter's to its status at the turn of the century as a self-sufficient parish with its own rectory, school and convent—and still growing population.

Fr. Ryan's New Church

Fr. Orr was succeeded as pastor by his long-time assistant, the prudent Rev. John J. Ryan. A native of Roxbury, Ryan had been editor of the *Stylus*, head of the student sodality, and prominent in debating, dramatics and athletics at Boston College. Later in life, he continued to write frequently (for the *Pilot* and religious magazines) and developed some reputation as a lecturer. He studied for the priesthood in Boston and was ordained by Archbishop Williams at the Cathedral in 1889. The following week he was assigned to St. Paul's where he spent his entire priestly life, first as Assistant and then as Rector when he succeeded Fr. Orr in March, 1907.

Since the church had established herself in Harvard Square rather late, her choice of suitable property was constrained. Accordingly, Ryan inherited a scattered collection of buildings: a church on Mt. Auburn and Holyoke, two school buildings and a convent several blocks east, a rectory two blocks south

(where Lowell House B-C-D entries now stand) in which baptisms and marriages were performed, and within another year there would also be the Newman House at 34 Mt. Auburn St., given by the Archbishop to the Harvard Catholic Club. Most pressing, however, was the new property further east on Massachusetts Avenue with its heavy mortgage—the site for the proposed church.

After much reflection Ryan returned to Orr's original plan—to build the new church where it stands today, on the former McKay estate. In July 1915, the convent was torn down and the priests each dug a shovel of earth to break ground for the new church. When the cornerstone of this Italian Romanesque monument to Catholic faith, arts and education was laid on November 12, 1916, the church was already partly under roof. Before the afternoon Mass and dedication, the Cardinal was met on Putnam Avenue by an escort of the Knights of Columbus, the Holy Name Society, and the Harvard Catholic Club.[15] The pastor's sermon that day spoke of the dangers of the time, and Cardinal O'Connell made the reference explicit, "There is very grave danger, not far distant from this sacred edifice. It is the growing tendency to separate science from faith and spiritual from material forces. Prominent educators are striving to undermine the foundation of all truth, the source of all knowledge, of all life—Christian faith."[16]

The siting and the design of that incredible building reflect Ryan's clear and so-

9

FR. RYAN'S AUTOMOBILE

In a mobile, immigrant community, twenty-five years is a long time. When Fr. Ryan celebrated his Silver Jubilee in 1914, he had probably been a Harvard Square resident longer than most of his flock. For his anniversary reception on June 14, the parish pulled out all the stops. They lit the school yard (the site of the present church) with electric lights and scheduled speeches and music into the night. As tokens of appreciation, they presented the pastor with the hefty sum of five thousand dollars and something special—an automobile.

The relative importance of the pastor's new auto is evident from its juxtaposition with another item in the convent day book that same summer:

> August 20—The Holy Father died at 1:20 a.m. The choir boys had an outing. Fr. Ryan took fifteen of them for an auto ride to Concord, Lexington and the surrounding towns. They had a grand time and returned about 4:30 p.m.

The automobile was still a novelty and the pastor knew how to put it to good use. The machine's potential for ill was also soon apparent—that November Anna and Bridie Conroy, two children on their way to the parish school, were run over by an auto on Putnam Avenue and Anna died from injuries.[17]

Fr. Ryan quickly recognized the automobile's ability to combine pleasure and ecclesiastical business. In an official 1925 volume surveying the progress of the archdiocese under Cardinal O'Connell are found sections on diocesan charities, property, missions, etc. Half the book in fact is the property section, actually entitled, "Seeing the Archdiocese by Automobile", by Rev. John J. Ryan.[18] He explains that three or four years earlier a group of about a hundred ministers had convened at Harvard for study and, desiring to learn what other churches were doing, had come to visit St. Paul's. So impressed were they by the management of the Children's Mass and the singing, that they sought out a priest and inquired how the church attendance was secured. After their departure, Fr. Ryan says he realized how little the best informed Catholic knows of the affairs of the archdiocese and asked himself, "Why would it not be most beneficial to see for himself, as the visiting ministers had seen, the work of the parishes and institutions?" So the plan was put into operation with optimal results, and the results of the tour are detailed for a hundred pages. In naming Harvard Protestants as the inspiration of his endeavor, Fr. Ryan shows he has no antipathy to the university. Likewise, he describes the location of St. Agnes Church, Arlington, in a way few other clergymen would, "Massachusetts Avenue is near, and Harvard University may be reached in about fifteen minutes."

One suspects that his position on the diocesan building commission may have required him to make many of these trips, but they are phrased as visits which any interested person might undertake, beginning, of course, with Cardinal O'Connell's birthplace in Lowell. He concludes his introduction by asking a timeless question:

> Possibly a like auto visit might be serviceable to other priests and even the laity who often ride out without any objective. The mountain and seashore have their place in these trips: why not an occasional study of some part of the Archdiocese?

Fr. Ryan's architectural statement to Harvard begins with "The Church of the Living God, the Pillar and Ground of Truth" (I Tim. 3:15).

phisticated vision of the Catholic Church's role in Harvard Square. The new church was the center of that vision and it should stand tall in the center of the parish, next to the university. He worked well with the Harvard Catholics and the university, and he knew the Catholic Church had an educational opportunity in Harvard Square. He determined to make its presence unmistakably visible and audible. In describing the site to the Cardinal, Ryan wrote, "the church will face Quincy Square, opposite Pres. Lowell's house. . .This site is the end of the so called "Gold Coast." As *Veritas* is the motto of Harvard, so the front facade of St. Paul's boldly states the logical priority of "The Church of the living God, the pillar and ground of truth." The tower bell rings out with the inscription from Isaiah, *Vox clamantis in deserto*— a voice crying out in the wilderness of Harvard Square.

It was Edward T.P. Graham, a parishioner, graduate of Harvard and winner of the first Travelling Fellowship to Rome and the Ecole des Beaux Arts, who articulated Fr. Ryan's vision in architectural terms. In a career spanning over fifty years he designed dozens of institutional buildings across New England, of which St. Elizabeth's Hospital was the largest. Locally his work ranged from a hall for St. Peter's parish in 1897 to a hundred units in Jefferson Park on Rindge Avenue in 1949. He had recently completed several buildings for St. Mary's in

Central Square, when in 1913 he received his first commission from Fr. Ryan, an eight hundred dollar alteration of the Harvard Catholic Clubhouse. Soon afterwards he was asked to design the hundred thousand dollar Church of St. Paul, working with his usual contractor John B. Byrne. The sources for the church and tower were Verona's S. Zeno Maggiore and the Torre del Commune. Throughout experts from European universities were consulted, but parishioners were also involved, such as Martin Feeley for the execution of the decorative colors.[19]

It is impossible at this stage to sort out Graham's ideas from those of Ryan, whose obituary gives him credit for the design, but a complex programme of iconography was exploited. The Irish heritage of the parish is prominently displayed by an altar to St. Patrick and a mural of St. Columban, in Ryan's words, "parting with his Irish home and mother, as he and his companions set their faces to the journeys and labors that have immortalized their names." The other characteristic feature of the parish, its aggressive setting beside an expanding secular university, is seen in the choice of the bas-reliefs, St. Paul addressing the philosophers of Athens and inspiring the Ephesians to burn their false books of divination. Moreover, in an appropriate but unusual statement of Catholicism's own scholarly tradition, the stained glass parades the doctors of

11

the church and other intellectual giants: from Athanasius and Ambrose to Bonaventure and Thomas Aquinas. The last window in the cycle is that of Ignatius of Loyola, whose purpose Fr. Ryan stated was "to combat in the universities of his day the rationalism that culminated in the French Revolution"—a broad view of the Enlightenment but a pointed one for the local audience. The Church's two constituencies are brought together not only in the facing statues of St. Peter (given by the Knights of Columbus) and of St. Paul (in memory of the six Harvard Catholics who died in World War I), but also in the unusual mission mural picturing parishioners and Harvard alumni going off to spread the faith, all under the pastor's benevolent watch and the Cardinal's blessing.

While the church was under construction, fundraising continued apace. The annual field day held in the summer of 1918 drew five hundred parishioners and friends. The *Cambridge Chronicle* of June 22 recorded several festive activities:

The parish was divided into four districts and each district had a table and booth in the basement of the new church as well as in the parish school where home made candy, fancy articles, ice cream and soft drinks were for sale, presided over by the women of the parish. During the afternoon, sport and field events were held by the children, and dancing in the evening. Special features were held in the afternoon, and there was a road race, over a course of about a mile and a half on the streets around the church for boys under 18, which was won by John Murphy.... A potato race was held in the basement of the new church, and a three-legged race for boys furnished much amusement.

After beginning the triduum services in the old building, the parish moved its liturgies to this new church for Easter Sunday, April 1, 1923. Five early Masses that morning were followed by the solemn High Mass at 11 a.m. featuring Mozart's 12th Mass but also including works by Schubert, Tozer, Falkenstein and Haydn, with orchestral accompaniment. For a year, while the lower church was being finished, three Sunday Masses were held upstairs with the earlier and weekday liturgies still at the old church. At the dedication of the church of a million bricks on October 13, 1924, Cardinal O'Connell devoted half his sermon to praising the priests and people of the parish and half to the juxtaposition of this Catholic

The parish dramatically opened the new church on Easter Sunday 1923.

Holy Week

and

The First Opening

of

The New

St. Paul's Church

Easter Sunday

1923

Arrow and DeWolfe Sts.

Cambridge

SERVICES AT OLD CHURCH

Palm Sunday, March 25
at 11 A. M.
BLESSING AND DISTRIBUTION OF PALMS
HIGH MASS AND THE PASSION

Wednesday, March 28
at 8 P. M.
LENTEN DEVOTIONS
Sermon . . . . . Rev. Denis A. O'Brien
Benediction

Holy Thursday, March 29
at 8 A. M.
SOLEMN HIGH MASS
PROCESSION OF THE BLESSED SACRAMENT
DIVESTING OF THE ALTAR

at 8 P. M.
DEVOTIONS OF THE HOLY HOUR
Sermon . . . . . . Rev. Wm. W. Gunn
Visitation to Repository till 10 P. M.

Good Friday, March 30
at 8 A. M.
MASS OF THE PRESANCTIFIED
PROCESSION
VENERATION OF THE CROSS

at 3 P. M.
THE WAY OF THE CROSS

at 7.45 P. M.
TENEBRAE
Sermon . . . . . . Rev. John J. Ryan
Prayer

church with "a great temple of learning." While giving credit to "the great influential institution" nearby (which he never called by name), O'Connell reminded his audience that centuries ago Oxford and Cambridge also "forgot their duty to their Mother" and have hence missed the way in their campaign for truth. In contrast, "This sacred edifice, this temple of God, possesses the whole truth, the real truth, the fundamental truth."

It is difficult to evaluate O'Connell's involvement with the building of the church. The oral tradition of the parish claims that the Cardinal was opposed to the building of the church, gave not one cent for it and actively persuaded wealthy Catholic professionals and business people not to support it. Such statements are the natural pride of parishioners in their own work. On the other hand, there is no evidence that O'Connell was anything but helpful. Correspondence shows that he regularly approved the mortgages Fr. Ryan took out on the old church building and appointed Fr. Ryan to important diocesan positions. O'Connell's insistence that the dedication service be a Low Mass, that Fr. Ryan's sermon be short, and that he would not be able to stay for lunch (since he would be tired) were

merely par for the course during the busy archbishop's reign. Whatever it actually thought, the excited parish treated the impatient prince of the church to an escort parade, starting on Putnam Avenue. Great credit clearly goes to these parishioners, many of whom had limited resources, and to Fr. Ryan who organized weekly dime collections as well as field days when the contributions slowed. Although St. Paul's was no longer a very poor parish (the pew rent then totaled twenty-three thousand dollars annually) the ambitious and expensive church tested its limits.

The pastor had not otherwise been idle; he was also developing the property on Massachusetts Avenue. In 1908 one newly acquired house there was rented out to the seven hundred members of the Holy Name Society to give them a headquarters for meetings (and to carry the lot's heavy mortgage). To house the sisters, whose residence on Arrow street was removed for the church, 1033 Massachusetts Avenue (next to the school annex and the Holy Name Society) was altered for a convent of twenty-five bedrooms, chapel, and reception rooms.

With the church now towering over the river area (there were as yet no Harvard

---

Holy Saturday, March 31
at 7 A. M.
BLESSING OF THE FIRE AND FONT
HIGH MASS

The Chancel Choir and the Intermediate Choir will render the musical portion of the services on the mornings of Holy Thursday, Good Friday and Holy Saturday.

NEW CHURCH — FIRST OPENING
ARROW AND DeWOLFE STREETS
EASTER SUNDAY, April 1, 1923
Masses at 6, 7, 8, 9, 10 o'clock

SOLEMN HIGH MASS
at 11 A. M.

Prelude	Schubert
Antiphon, "Vidi Aquam"	Witzka
Processional	Regina Orchestra
Introit, "Resurrexi"	Falkenstein
"Kyrie," "Gloria in Excelsis"	Mozart's 12th Mass
Graduale, "Haec Dies"	Tozer
Sequence, "Victimae Paschali"	Bordonnel
Sermon,	**Rev. Denis F. Murphy**
"Credo"	Mozart's 12th Mass
Offertory, 1. "Terra Tremuit"	Tozer
2. O Filii et Filiae	
"Sanctus, Benedictus, Agnus Dei"	Haydn
"Sanctus Benedictus, Agnus Dei"	Mozart's 12th Mass
Communion, "Pascha Nostrum"	Falkenstein
Recessional, Hallelujah Chorus	Senior Choir

With Orchestral Accompaniment

SOLEMN VESPERS
at 4 P. M.

Combined Choirs (Senior, Intermediate and Junior)

Prelude	Gounod
Antiphons	Singenberger
Psalms	Singenberger
Canticle, Magnificat	Maurzo
Antiphon, "Regina Coeli Laetare"	Lotti
"O Salutaris"	Melvil
"Tantum Ergo" (Male Quartet)	Hammerel
"Adoremus"	

The 11 o'clock Mass will be rendered by the Senior Choir, Chancel Choir and the Regina Orchestra.

The Junior Choir will sing at the 9 o'clock Mass.

The Preparatory Choir will sing festival hymns at the 8 o'clock Mass.

PROF. GEORGE G. McCONNELL,
Organist and Director.

Leaving the church without pews, open in the European style, was the preference of some. The church interior is 65 feet high, 72 feet wide, and 160 feet long.

houses), Fr. Ryan's work was almost done. There remained only the matching rectory to be built. In June 1918 Fr. Ryan, alerted by the owner, had obtained permission to purchase at foreclosure a parcel with two houses on Mt. Auburn Street immediately opposite the rear of the new St. Paul's Church and adjacent to the Newman House, commenting to the Cardinal "this property would make an ideal location for a rectory in keeping with the new Church." Later that summer, however, he came down with pneumonia and was forced to take his first vacation in fifteen years. In the summer of 1924, with the new church open, Fr. Ryan despite failing health determined to finish the building program. He bought another house along De Wolfe Street and sold the old church and rectory to Harvard for $85,000 (through a Catholic alumnus as broker). After payment of a $42,000 mortgage, he had over $40,000 on hand towards the cost of his $70,000 rectory—he had built the new church without resulting debt! Graham had already started on the plans for the new rectory, when on April 7, 1925, a stroke of apoplexy ended John J. Ryan's long ministry on Mount Auburn Street.

When Fr. Ryan arrived at St. Paul's as an assistant in 1889, the parish was just undertaking its first major project, building a school. By the time he died as pastor thirty-five years later, St. Paul's was a powerful sign of the Catholic Church in Harvard Square—not only an extraordinary edifice, but also a thriving parish with active societies and over eight-hundred school children. In the last five years of his life, he served on the Diocesan Building Commission and as Synodal Examiner and Diocesan Consultor. Before 1914 he had been state chaplain of the Knights of Columbus and at the time of his death he was still council chaplain for Cambridge. His relations with Harvard were vastly superior to his predecessor's. He served as chaplain for the students for several years and in regard to university expansion, he and the parish committee chaired by the dry-goods merchant J. H. Corcoran felt that Harvard dealt squarely with their concerns. Most conspicuously, he conceived and executed the Church of St. Paul in a way that now seems inevitable. Thinking back to Harvard's petition for a boulevard to absorb much of the open Church property along De Wolfe St., Fr. Ryan commented in his final days, "The Lord has worked the opposite."[20]

Fr. Hickey and a Changing Parish

The new pastor was the pious and careful Rev. Augustine F. Hickey. Born in Cambridge, he had studied at the North American College in Rome where he acquired a great devotion to Pope Pius X. Ordained in 1906, Fr. Hickey spent many years as arch-diocesan superintendent of schools and was always attentive to that aspect of the parish's work, though the Church's liturgy remained his greatest treasure.

Fr. Hickey proved himself as prudent in real estate as his predecessor. Soon after taking the helm at St. Paul's, he sold two unused lots on Ellery Street (using the same realtor with whom Fr. Orr had purchased them almost twenty years before). In particular, although school enrollment was declining, he purchased additional property in order to provide more school playgrounds. In this way the parish acquired the house east of the school on Mt. Auburn as well as several houses on De Wolfe St., which were later used as a parking lot. He also put permanent windows into the lower church and repaired the convent.

Like Cardinal O'Connell, Fr. Augustine Hickey studied at the North American College in Rome. He is seated third from the left under the flags current in 1906.

The only building he did not improve was the Newman House. After the Rectory displaced its lodging, the Catholic Club used 8 and 10 De Wolfe as addresses. Slowly the Newman House became less active, and what was called the "Clubhouse" became a parish house. In 1939, 10 De Wolfe was razed for a playground without any mention of Harvard students. The diminished campus ministry, never a particular focus of Hickey's, left a vacuum which the St. Benedict Center filled during the next decade. The student chaplaincy was always assigned to an assistant, but Hickey was willing to intercede at the Chancery for Harvard students who needed Catholic letters of reference for research in Europe or who sought permission to read indexed books (like Gibbon's history and the novels of Fielding, Richardson and Sterne)—although he was not always successful.

As the Harvard Summer school grew, a number of clerics and religious took part in the courses and special programs, both as students and teachers. The parish benefited as visiting priests (including Rev. Fulton Sheen of Catholic University in 1927) filled in as summer replacements. Priests who came to do graduate work during the scholastic year helped with the parish Mass schedule, a resource which has continued to assist St. Paul's even today.

Shortly after he was elevated to domestic prelate in 1937, his own attempt to distribute a small parish bulletin was stymied. The monthly bulletin would just have been four pages the size of a holy card, outlining parish activities and important feast days—alerting the faithful to feasts was always part of Hickey's liturgical mission—but O'Connell's chancery refused him permission, telling him emphatically to "concen-

Primum Regnum Dei

Hickey was named a domestic prelate (entitled to be called Monsignor) by Pope Pius XI in 1937. His coat of arms was designed by heraldist Pierre la Rose.

trate all efforts on the *Pilot* which contains all news and sufficient instruction."[21]

Harvard University's expansion did not cease with the building of the Harvard House system in the 1920's and 1930's. Further Houses were added and, as important for the parish, the university acquired apartment houses and other residential property on a large scale. The university cannot be blamed for the demographic shift, since most areas of Boston witnessed a population movement of younger and more affluent families to the suburbs during the post-war period. Harvard Square's distinctive history is that the suburban emigration was accompanied by institutional expansion rather than urban decline or the immigration of new groups.

The parish census numbers show that the community was still growing at the time of World War II, but it was already aging. In fact school enrolments, both parochial and public, had been declining from 1914, just as the new church is being planned. Though baptisms surged during the post-war "baby boom," the number of parishioners peaked in 1947 with 6637 Catholics in the parish boundaries. After 1955, the flight to the suburbs (in many cases no farther than Belmont) acceler-

ated and by 1970 the Church only served half as many parishioners as it had for the first half of the century. Although it is not clear when and whether students were counted in the rolls, the parish certainly regained strength under Fr. Boles in the late seventies and since then the number of "souls" has stayed somewhat over 3000.

During Fr. Hickey's forty-year tenure, he was assisted by a number of fine priests, of whom Rev. William G. Gunn (1918-1937) was one of the longest in residence. A noticeable change came after World War II, when the rectory was filled by a completely new set of assistants: Rev. John E. Kenney (1946-61), Rev. Charles B. Murphy (1947-60), Rev. John J. Sullivan (1946-54), and the eventual successor as pastor, Rev. Joseph I. Collins (1946-71).

Msgr. Hickey retired at age 81 on Jan. 18, 1965 and became the first occupant of Regina Cleri, the archdiocese's home for priests in the West End. A small, devout and proper man, Fr. Hickey was seen as rather intellectual by some parishioners and aloof by some students. He preferred to work quietly, rarely making appeals for funds. However, his formal and introspective nature did not stop him from generously helping those in material need or putting energy into his great love—the liturgy. Although in general his long administration of the parish reflected the nominal stability of the pre-conciliar period, he was an early and active advocate of participation by the laity in liturgy. His greatest legacy to the parish is the work he accomplished with Theodore Marier in building congregational singing and eventually in founding the Boston Archdiocesan Choir School. A founder and original board member of the Cambridge Community Federation, he also served as a member of the Cambridge Housing Authority and a director of the Cambridge Red Cross.

Since the Council

A graduate of the College of the Holy Cross, Rev. Joseph I. Collins was ordained in 1940. After returning from wartime service as a military chaplain, he was assigned to St. Paul's in 1946 and ministered there for the next twenty-five years, first as an assistant and then as pastor from 1965 to 1971. Fr. Collins was an early supporter of the liturgical movement and participated in many "demonstration Masses," non-sacramental explanations of the ritual. As

ST. PAUL'S PARISH[22]

	Families	Souls	Marriages	Baptisms	Parish School	Sunday School
1910	846	5394	47	126	900	346
1915	918	5508	-	-	962	403
1920*	1278	5202	-	-	834	353
1925	1010	5110	72	157	828	413
1930	1106	5355	68	132	700	401
1936	1257	5958	55	130	654	391
1940	1351	5911	97	133	648	371
1945	1357	5778	79	164	514	254
1950	1376	6418	54	157	478	259
1955	1435	5867	52	154	392	284
1960	1026	4843	41	131	315	230
1965	682	2681	57	105	263	178
1970	519	2098	79	64	†93	174

*In 1916, Blessed Sacrament Church, Cambridgeport, was opened with some reduction from St. Paul's.
†By this time the school no longer offered full grades.

pastor, he coordinated the local implementation of Vatican II and dealt with other challenges of the time: the closing of the parish school, the sale of the convent in 1968, the needs of the recently founded Choir School, and reconciling various approaches to campus ministry.

Fr. Collins was spiritual director to the Radcliffe students from his arrival, and, with the merger of the Harvard and Radcliffe chaplaincies in 1960, he became a full-time chaplain, assuming responsibility for the men of the university as well. In the academic year 1963-4 the popular priest served as chairman of the United Ministry at Harvard. Three years after he became pastor, he arranged for the first full-time campus ministry staff for Catholics at the university. Exploiting the energy he first displayed as a Holy Cross cheerleader, Fr. Collins was also active in Cambridge civic groups, including the Unity Commission, the Economic Opportunity Commission, the Boy Scouts, and the American Legion. As a member of the Riverside Neighborhood Association, he helped plan the elderly housing complex at 2 Mt. Auburn St.

In the seventies, migration to the suburbs had changed the parish environs dramatically, university life had been radically altered and St. Paul's too underwent a number of shifts. In 1971, Fr. Collins was succeeded as pastor by Msgr. Edward G. Murray, former rector of St. John's Seminary. Three years later, Rev. John P. Boles, D.D., another priest with wide administrative skills and student experience, was appointed to the combined position of Pastor-Chaplain.

Fr. Boles had been Headmaster of St. Sebastian's Country Day School and Director of Education for the Archdiocese. His goal in 1974 was to bring together the various elements of the Catholic community. Fr. Boles tried to be sensitive to what he called "the reality of the town-gown relationship, staying visible on the campus ministry side and among the community which built the church." Rev. Joseph Fratic, Rev. Paul Hurley, and Rev. Gerald Osterman worked with him to sustain and expand the complex parish ministry. The popular student chaplains of this period were Fr.

Monsignor Edward G. Murray, former Rector of St. John's Seminary, was pastor from 1971 to 1974.

17

Thomas Powers, Sr. Evelyn Ronan, S.N.D., and later Fr. John MacInnis and Sr. Mary Karen Powers, R.S.M. In 1986 the guard also changed at the choir school, when Principal John Dunn succeeded Dr. Marier as Music Director.

In May, 1992, after the completion of a new parish center, Fr. Boles was named titular Bishop of Novasparsa and Auxiliary Bishop of Boston. The new pastor turned out to be Harvard graduate Rev. J. Bryan Hehir, an old friend of the parish and frequent guest speaker in the past. While a counselor for social policy at the United States Catholic Conference, Fr. Hehir assisted the bishops in the development of several pastoral letters on that topic. Reassigned from Georgetown University, where he had been a professor of ethics and associate vice president, Fr. Hehir continued his teaching at Harvard—a visible sign of the degree to which the parish's mission has shifted from the days of Fr. Orr.

In demographic terms, St. Paul's is a young and diverse parish. A well-organized 1983 pew census of 1500 parishioners found that 50% were under 25 years of age, mostly students. Another 35% were between 25 and 45, a certain number of whom lived outside the parish boundaries but are drawn by the quality of liturgies, university association, and parish activities. In a university neighborhood, the parish is naturally quite literate and even literary—when Sally Fitzgerald edited Flannery O'Connor's letters, she took an office in St. Paul's Rectory itself. The increasing diversity of the worshipers at St. Paul's reflects the

Harvard graduate Rev. J. Bryan Hehir became St. Paul's seventh pastor in 1992.

parish's international and ecumenical awareness. St. Paul's continues to attract global visitors—during one month in 1986 celebrants included Cardinal Lustiger of Paris, Cardinal Koenig of Vienna, and Cardinal Law of Boston, whose love of liturgy was nurtured during the four undergraduate years he called this parish home.

In 1989 the deteriorating schoolhouse and student center were removed for the construction of a large complex including parish offices, choir school, student center and rectory. The new building (designed by the firm of Koetter, Kim and Associates and dedicated by Cardinal Law on November 1, 1991) shapes itself physically to the parish's great hall of worship. On top of the new chapel rises the bronze cross which has stood for over a century above the Catholics of Harvard Square.

The consolidation of the parish's scattered properties which Fr. Ryan began at the turn of the century is now achieved—with the brick-patterned church supported by her matching attendants. No one could have foreseen the changes of Harvard Square in the past fifty years, but Fr. Ryan's vision of an enduring landmark has been proved right."It is a monumental structure," he wrote of the church in 1924, "suited for any demand in the way of religious service and adapted by style of architecture to whatever developments or change of surroundings may arise in this vicinity."

John Campbell addressing a 1983 meeting planning for the new parish buildings. Other speakers are Geraldine Gross, Rev. John Boles, Mercedes Evans, and Elizabeth Mahan.

The Immigrant Community:
at Work, at Play, at School
by Marie Daly*

For its first hundred years, the character of the Church in Harvard Square was mainly that of its immigrant worshippers—manual laborers whose grandchildren became mayors. This contribution examines the parish's first generations, the industry which employed many of them (book printing), and the institution which did the most to educate them (the parish school).

Irish Immigration

In addition to the well-documented English immigrants, Irish, Scottish, African and French natives populated Boston from the earliest days of the colony, and continued to arrive in small numbers throughout the seventeenth and eighteenth centuries. Most of the Irish immigrants were indentured servants from the south of Ireland. In the seventeenth century, some were recruited involuntarily, i.e. kidnapped, transported to Massachusetts, and sold as indentured servants. Although originally Catholic, they soon joined the predominant churches of their communities. The practice of Catholicism was proscribed until the late eighteenth century, and the first Catholic Mass was not celebrated in Boston until 1788.[1]

In the nineteenth century, conditions in Ireland caused a dramatic increase in emigration to the New World, with Massachusetts the destination for many. In 1816 and 1817, a volcanic eruption and resultant temperature decline produced major famines in Europe, including Ireland. Prior to 1817, Ireland had profited from the French Revolution and the wars between Great Britain and France. However, a postwar recession precipitated a 50% drop in agricultural prices, and the mechanization of textile production in England ruined Irish textile markets. From 1744 to 1841, the Irish population quadrupled to 8.1 million, with increases greatest in western rural areas.[2] With the rise in population, farms were subdivided, land became scarce and rents rose sharply. A government commission estimated that 2.3 million poeple (25%) were in need of relief. For young Irish men and women facing a declining standard of living, periodic famines and epidemics, and dim future prospects, emigration was believed to be a release from poverty and overpopulation. Consequently, the number of persons emigrating per year rose from 20,000 in 1818 to 100,000 in 1842. Between 1825 and 1830 alone, 125,000 people left Ireland, and 30,000 of these ultimately arrived in Massachusetts.[3]

From 1845 to 1854, the Great Famine fundamentally disrupted the Irish economy, produced a major breakdown of society and family structures, and created an enormous increase in emigration. Most small farmers, cottiers and laborers had subsisted entirely on potatoes, with adult males consuming about fourteen pounds per day. In 1845, a fungus attacked the potato crops, destroying about 30-40% of the harvest. In 1846 and 1848, the entire potato harvest failed, and in 1847, achieved only 10% of the 1844 levels. From 1849 through 1854, the potato harvest remained at less than 50% of the pre-Famine levels.[4] Despite relief efforts, 1.1 to 1.5 million people died of starvation or the associated diseases of typhus, relapsing fever and dysentery. The very young and the elderly suffered disproportionately, and excess deaths were highest in south Ulster, west Munster and Connaught. Compounding the disaster, some landlords availed themselves of the opportunity to rid their estates of unwanted tenants. Evictions of one-half million tenants in Munster and Connaught in 1849-1850 ensured localized high death rates. The Irish population rushed to escape the desolation by emigrating to Great Britain, Canada and the United States. Groups of families commonly pooled their resources to send to America one member, who would then remit passages to those left behind. Fleeing ragged and hungry, many debilitated passengers died at sea or soon after landing. Between 1845 and 1855, 2.1 million people,

---

*Marie Daly combines her work at the New England Historic Genealogical Society with the study of Irish immigrant history in Boston. Her family, the Kellys, emigrated from Prince Edward Island to Saint Paul parish in 1892.

This 1897 view shows the neighborhood around St. Paul Church (left), School (right), and Rectory (three white chimneys in center).

90% of whom were Catholic, left Ireland, and about 1.5 million of these came to America.[5]

With myriads of ill, starved Catholics arriving in Boston, the diocese faced almost overwhelming problems. The population quadrupled from 1790 to 1840, and by 1850 the new Irish comprised 25% of the city's population. The Irish clustered along the waterfront, where they could obtain employment as laborers, longshoremen, and tailors. The new immigrants were most densely situated in the North End, Fort Hill and South Cove districts, where they crammed into hovels, one-room apartments and basements without floors or furniture. Mortality rates climbed steeply, surpassing even the worst of English slums. In the Irish neighborhoods of Boston, deaths were four times higher than on Beacon Hill.

In pre-Famine Ireland, the Catholic church had suffered a dearth of capital and churches. Irish-speaking peasants in the West of Ireland irregularly attended Mass outdoors, with priests using "Mass rocks" for altars. Many of Boston's immigrants originated in these remote, Gaelic communities where religious beliefs were characterized by supersti-

tion, worship at holy wells, wild pattern days and fairs. Thus, the diocese of Boston faced the daunting tasks of rapidly establishing churches, orphanages, aid societies and hospitals and recruiting clergy both to accommodate the burgeoning ranks and to guide the parishioners from a peasant religion to a more orthodox one.

Pinioned by poverty and close family and community connections, the Irish clung to the Northeast in a distribution which remained stable until 1910. More sensitive than other ethnic groups to regional economic disparities, the Irish exhibited intense mobility within the region.[6] They migrated to those areas where the economy was expanding, to where their labor was most needed. The men constructed factories and mills, dug canals, laid railroad tracks and roads, drained swamps, and erected buildings and docks. The women labored in the mills as textile workers and in private homes as servants. "In effect, they occupied the worst seats in the best theatres."[7] The mobility and the occupations of the Irish were exemplified by one group from Bantry, County Cork, who landed at Lechmere Point

20

in the 1840's. Some stayed in Cambridge, others proceeded to Manchester, New Hampshire, and others migrated to the slaughterhouses at Brighton, the Sand Banks at Mount Auburn and the brickyards at North Cambridge.[8]

The Irish in Cambridge

In the first half of the nineteenth century, business developers located in Cambridge small-scale industries that attracted immigrant labor: ice harvesting at Fresh Pond, brickmaking and cattle pens at North Cambridge, and ropewalks, tanneries, glassworks and soapworks in East Cambridge and Cambridgeport.[9] Subsequently, the population of East Cambridge rose from 382 in 1820 to about 4,000 in 1850, 50% of whom were foreign born.[10] A number of the pre-Famine immigrants in East Cambridge originated in the vicinities of Dromore, County Tyrone and Carrickedmond, County Longford. However, very few industries employing immigrant labor located in Old Cambridge where the foriegn born comprised less than a quarter of the population. Consequently, Old Cambridge

retained a bucolic, village setting of small shops, college buildings, and private homes.[11]

In 1860, the Irish people of Ward One, Cambridge occupied the lowest strata of the Ward's society, performed the most menial work and occupied the most undesirable land. The boundaries of the soon-to-be-established parish of St. Paul conformed closely with the boundaries of Ward One, except on the eastern side. In 1860, Irish immigrants comprised 23% of Ward One's population, and of these immigrants, 65% were females whose average age was 29.4 years. 52% of the Irish were employed as servants and another 24% as laborers. In other words, the typical Irish immigrant of Ward One was a 29 year old female servant. At this time, Old Cambridge supported few industries which employed immigrant labor. With a substantial number of middle and upper class homes, the community could offer employment only as servants and laborers. Until the river was dammed in the next century, the Charles River was tidal up to Gerry's Landing, polluted with industrial and human waste, and malodorous. The poorest Irish built ramshackle huts on stilts over the tidal areas,

An adjacent 1897 view shows the residential area alongside the malodorous and industrial Charles River. Both of these photographs were taken from a tall chimney at the foot of the current JFK St.

21

forming "tin villages", and using household wastes as landfill. Irish families clustered near the river along Brighton (JFK) Street, Dunster Street, and the cross streets of South and Winthrop Streets. Not surprisingly, only 5% of the Irish owned real estate, and the value of their property averaged about $1,600 (as compared with the Longfellow-Craigie House valued at $100,000). Among Ward One's Irish residents, only Maurice O'Connor, a soap manufacturer who lived on Bow Street, was listed as a taxpayer. Other families who lived in Harvard Square in 1849 were:

> Malachi Eagan, laborer, h. Dana St. near
>   Harvard
> John Kelley, laborer, h. Dunster
> John Mahan, laborer, h. Dunster
> Jeremiah McCarty, gardener, h. Ellery
> John McCarty, laborer, h. Brighton
> Joseph McFarland, laborer, h. Brighton
> John McGuir (sic), laborer, Brighton
> James McLaughlin, shoemaker, Dunster
> Thomas McMahon, blacksmith, Ellery
> John Powers, laborer, Dunster n. South
> Eugene Sullivan, blacksmith, h. Brattle opp.
>   Brighton
> Eugene Sullivan, laborer, h. Winthrop

Some of the descendants of these early families still live in the parish today.

The journal of John Langdon Sibley, the Harvard historian of the mid-century, gives

In 1884, the parish acquired fourteen acres in Arlington for the St. Paul's cemetery, but all the lots were sold within a few decades.

June 22, 1889 — — June 22, 1914

Silver Jubilee
OF
Rev. John J. Ryan, P.R.

**St. Paul's School Building
and Yard**

Sunday Evening, June 21, 1914

❧

Program

1 OVERTURE ....REGINA ORCHESTRA
2 SELECTION ....ST. PAUL'S CHURCH CHOIR
3 OPENING REMARKS ....HENRY LANG
4 HOLY NAME SOCIETY ....ALBERT E. GOOD
5 PAST PARISHIONERS......................HON. J. H. H. McNAMEE
6 ST. PAUL'S ALUMNI.....................TIMOTHY J. SULLIVAN
7 ST. PAUL'S CATHOLIC CLUB (Harvard).......THOMAS L. O'CONNOR
8 SELECTION ....REGINA ORCHESTRA
9 POEM ....PAUL F. SPAIN
10 SELECTION ....ST. PAUL'S CHOIR
11 OUR PASTOR AND SIR KNIGHT.............CHARLES F. J. McCUE
12 OUR PASTOR AND FATHERLAND..........TIMOTHY F. McCARTHY
13 OUR PASTOR AND ATHLETICS...................J. FRANK FACEY
14 OUR PASTOR AND THE CITY......HIS HONOR, TIMOTHY W. GOOD
15 SELECTION ....REGINA ORCHESTRA
16 THE PARISH TRIBUTE..................GEORGE F. McKELLEGET
17 THE JUBILARIAN ....REV. JOHN J. RYAN, P. R.
18 HOLY GOD ....AUDIENCE

> Holy God, we praise Thy name.
>   Lord of all we bow before Thee;
> All on earth Thy sceptre claim;
>   All in Heaven above adore Thee;
> Infinite Thy vast domain,
> Everlasting is Thy reign!
>
> Hark! the loud celestial hymn
>   Angel choirs above are raising!
> Cherubim and Seraphim
>   In unceasing chorus praising,
> Fill the heav'ns with sweet accord,
> Holy! Holy! Holy! Lord.

*Fr. Ryan's jubilee gives a survey of
the parish activities in 1914.*

the native's viewpoint of the new immigrants. He kept an old Irish gardener named McCrosson out of charity, but he had a less favorable view of the Irish youth he hired at the Harvard library: "Of the four boys who have been employed in the library, only the first, John Maccarty, has been strictly honest. The chief of police says he has the names of 400 young boys in Cambridge who steal. It is almost impossible to find an honest servant of any kind. While the Catholic Irish with which the country abounds are exceptionally conscientious in abstaining from meat on Fridays, they are utterly untrustworthy." When McCarthy's mother died a few years later, he went to her funeral. Although Sibley had once attended a Mass while visiting Montreal a decade earlier, he notes vividly in his journal: "The time must come when the flummary of such funeral services must be regarded as little less than blasphemy."[12] Comments about the character and crime rate of the Irish and complaints about Irish funerals

ELIZA McGOWAN McGLINCHEY:
A Famine Immigrant to Harvard Square

At the time the parish of St. Paul was established (1875), the largest number of the parishioners were single, female servants, and the community lived in dire poverty along the river and the oldest streets of Cambridge. The life of Eliza (McGowan) McGlinchey, whose descendants still live in the parish, is typical of the circumstances and life stories of many.

Eliza was born in 1817 in Buncrana, County Donegal, Ireland. She and her husband Patrick McGlinchey lived in Meendacalliagh, a townland located between Buncrana and Carndonagh. Perched on a mountain, Slieve Snaght, their three-room, thatch-roofed, stone cottage faced heather-covered highland moors. The couple raised potatoes, oats and sheep and handloomed wool, while Patrick cut stone in a local quarry. To augment their diminishing income, Patrick and Eliza travelled seasonally to Greenock, Scotland where many young Irish men and women worked as migrant farm laborers. Subsisting on oatmeal and bread, the migrants slept on cold barn floors and crawled through rain-soaked fields to harvest Scottish potatoes. Working as potato lifters, women often remained in Glasgow after the harvest. Eliza returned home long enough to give birth to her son Andrew on November 10, 1839. Leaving the baby in the care of her parents, she soon returned to Greenock to work. In the next decade, Patrick and Eliza had four more children who survived. Patrick McGlinchey died during the Famine, leaving his family in marginal circumstances. Eliza's sister, Hannah McGowan, had previously emigrated to Old Cambridge, had married Peter McGirr (one of the first marriages in St. Peter's), and probably remitted passages to her family back in Ireland.

On July 11, 1850, Eliza arrived in Boston aboard the ship *Parthian* out of Liverpool and went directly to her distant cousin, Fr. Manasses Dougherty, who helped her become established in Cambridge. Desperate and destitute, Eliza had to leave her children in Ireland for almost two years before she could earn enough money to send for them. (Her brother, William McGowan, also arrived in Cambridge at this time, but travelled separately.) Accompanied by their uncle, Daniel McGowan, her three sons, Andrew (age 11), James (age 9) and Patrick (age 7) sailed out of Liverpool with 632 other passengers, arriving in Boston on May 19, 1852. Eliza McGlinchey established her home on the side of Brighton Street (now John F. Kennedy), on the river front, but later moved the house to the corner of Eliot Street, where the Kennedy School of Government now stands. She set up a school to train young girls as servants, and by cleaning houses, taking in laundry, and renting to boarders, Eliza struggled to raise her five children. Her brother William worked as a laborer for the Cambridge street department.

Eliza and her family's battle to survive, their separation in the flight from Ireland, eventual reunification and valuation of strong family bonds typify the ordeals of the Irish Famine immigrants. Her grandchildren growing up in Cambridge at the end of the century, however, already lived quite different lives. They attended college (boys at Boston College, a girl at Radcliffe) and one, Joseph McGlinchey, would serve St. Paul's as a parish priest.

William McGowan and his family lived at 17 South Street for a century.
Built on a colonial ice house, it is one of the few residences left
in the area near the bridge where the Irish first settled.

were typical of nativist prejudices of that time period. In fact, Cambridge tried to prevent Catholic burials at the Cambridge Catholic Cemetery on Rindge Avenue, termed a "festering plague in our midst," by sponsoring "Paddy Funeral" bills in the state legislature.

Not All Irish

During the 1870's, European emigration to America fell sharply as adverse economic conditions in the United States and relatively prosperous economies in Europe stemmed the outflow of peasants. By 1880, the first generation Irish comprised only 59% of the foreign born and only 17% of Ward One's total population. The Irish were concentrated on the south side of Mount Auburn Street, especially along Cowperthwaite, Grant, Brighton, South and Mill Streets. Thus, development was spreading eastward from Dunster and Holyoke Streets.

Increasingly, other groups arrived to find employment as servants, carpenters, shopkeepers, and in the publishing industries. In Ward One, the most numerous were Maritime Canadians, especially Catholics of Scottish and Irish descent, who made up 22% of the foriegn born, and 6% of the ward's total population. Emigres from Nova Scotia and Prince Edward Island were heavily represented in this group. Among the Nova Scotians were a number of black families who settled along DeWolfe, Plympton and Elmer Streets with West Indian families. Slaves of African descent had

By 1900, many Irish businesses were prospering and expanding.

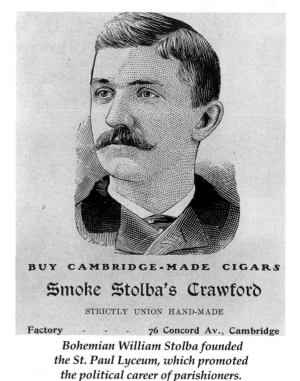

BUY CAMBRIDGE-MADE CIGARS
Smoke Stolba's Crawford
STRICTLY UNION HAND-MADE

Factory - - - 76 Concord Av., Cambridge

Bohemian William Stolba founded the St. Paul Lyceum, which promoted the political career of parishioners.

accompanied the pre-Loyalist and Loyalist migrations from New England to Nova Scotia in the eighteenth century. Once freed from slavery, the blacks had migrated to Halifax where they established one of the largest African communities in Canada. The black Nova Scotian families who lived in the ward presumably came as part of a general migration from the Maritimes.

French, Spanish, Germans and Scandinavians began to arrive by 1880, and comprised about 4% of the ward's foreign born population. Many of the German families, such as the Lerners, originated in Schleswig, Baden and Bavaria. In 1867, Christian Lorensen emigrated from Denmark to Boston and eventually settled on DeWolfe Street and later Ellery Street. His son, William Lorensen, worked for Harvard University for many years. Henry Lang, head usher at St. Paul's Church and resident of Putnam Avenue, emigrated from Le Havre in 1872 at the age of seventeen. Andrew Beluchi, a native of Spain and a cigar manufacturer, lived on Sands Street. William Stolba from Bohemia (an area spanning Austria and the Czech Republic) owned a cigar factory on Concord Avenue but resided near the church on Mount Auburn and Holyoke Streets.

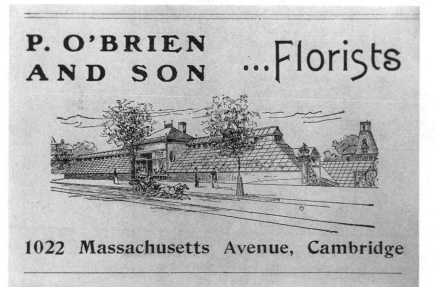

P. O'BRIEN AND SON ...Florists

1022 Massachusetts Avenue, Cambridge

Prosperity and Prominence

After 1880, poor economic conditions in Ireland caused a resurgence of emigration to America, and with cousins, aunts and uncles already in the United States, a new wave of immigrants poured into the existing communities. These post-famine immigrants originated in western and southern Ireland and were mainly farm laborers, younger sons and single, undowried women (more than 50% of post-famine immigrants from Ireland were female). In St. Paul's parish, people with names like O'Connor, Lovett, Sullivan, O'Connell, Sugrue and Downing settled around Flagg, Banks and Cowperthwaite Streets, an area which became known as "Kerry Corner." With the growth of industries such as the Riverside Press, the University Press, the Cambridge Gas Co., and the Boston Elevated Railroad, industries which provided skilled employment to the immigrant community, economic and social conditions improved. Typical occupations changed from servant and unskilled laborer to compositor, electrotyper, pressman, motorman, and shopkeeper.

With the increased economic status of its parishioners, St. Paul's social and fundraising activities began to reflect the new working and middle class interests of the community. A beautiful day in August 1890 drew 850 members and friends to the parish picnic at "Lake Walden":[13]

The dance hall, where Dolan's orchestra rendered excellent dance music during the day, was the central attraction. At the field of sports an enthusiastic audience watched the games and races. The ballgame between the Lindens and the Fairmonts was won by the former by a score of 12 to 10. The married men and the single men played four innings in the afternoon, the single men winning by a score of 16 to 1. The races resulted as follows: Half-mile run for boys under twelve years: J. Sullivan, first, Edward Brown, second; half-mile run for boys under sixteen years, F. Mahady, first, J.C.Good, second; quartermile run for girls, Miss Mamie White; three-legged race, Messrs. Shea and Tobin; half-mile race for married men, Patrolman Tim Corcoran of Station One; a swimming match, Michael Sullivan; Whilehall race, Shaw Shea; putting the shot, J. Reagan, Michael Quill. The prize for the best jig and reeldancer was awarded to Mr. and Mrs. J. O'Brien.

Modeled after the highly successful St. John's Institute, a number of educational societies or "Lyceums" for young men sprung up during the era of Archbishop Williams.[14] In 1883, William Stolba founded St. Paul's Lyceum which met at Lyceum Hall on Brattle Street. This organization offered a broad range of activities including lectures, debates, sacred music concerts, poetry readings, children's plays, banquets and dances, and also indirectly promoted the political careers of parishioners such as John H. H. McNamee (City Councilman and Mayor) and Edward J. Brandon (Cambridge City Clerk, U.S. Attorney, K. of C. Grand Knight).

In 1893, McNamee, Brandon and John T. Shea founded the Cambridge Council No. 74 of the Knights of Columbus, whose best known activity was the operation of the Cambridge Day Nursery. In addition Council No. 74 established the first Memorial Mass, first Communion Sunday, first "feature" nights, and first Council flag. Fr. Ryan, and later Fr. Hickey, was the Council's chaplain.[15]

The working class community of St. Paul's parish reached a peak in numbers, character and closeness between 1900 and 1920. At that time, two and three family houses packed the streets between Mt. Auburn Street and the Charles River, between Western Avenue and Putnam Avenue, between Broadway and Kirkland St. In 1900, for instance, nearly six thousand people lived along the river between Sparks Street extension and Putnam Avenue. With the increased voting

Andrew McGlinchey (center) established his own bookbindery on Washington St. after serving as foreman at the Riverside Bindery. He held a patent for the gold-leafing of marbled paper.

dormitories. With increased affluence, second and third generation young families were moving out to the street car suburbs of Belmont, Watertown and Arlington. The commercial growth of Harvard Square replaced formerly residential lots.

By 1950, it was clear that the parish was changing, a change most apparent in the 50% drop in St. Paul's school population. By 1970, the transformation from a blue-collar immigrant community to a college student community was nearly complete. In 1970, the majority of the Riverside population were college students living in group residences, and the average age was 21 years. Among the working population, about 60% were employed in educational services. In the 1970's and 1980's, new immigrants from Central America and Asia have added to the diversity of population.

Many of the remembrances of St. Paul's parish are nostalgic and may have glazed over any negative aspects. But almost all the people interviewed regretted the loss in the sense of community, the loss of closeness, of being known and cared for by one' neighbors, and the loss of the security and mutual aid neighbors would provide in times of need. "I think we all miss what we knew way back, the closeness of the families, the affection and trust that existed among neighbors," says John Caulfield. "Today everything is business. People next door never meet each other. You don't see people out. You don't go in and sit for a cup of tea anymore. You lock your door."

power of the immigrant community, St. Paul parishioner John H. H. McNamee was able to gather enough votes to score an upset victory over an incumbent mayor in the 1901 election. This feat initiated a long-standing tradition of political leadership from St. Paul's parish in subsequent elections: Mayors Augustine J. Daly, Timothy W. Good, Michael A. Sullivan, Edward Sullivan, and Walter J. Sullivan.

After 1920, the parish population began to dwindle for various reasons. At the turn of the century, the damming of the Charles River improved the waterfront areas, thereby increasing the value of real estate. Harvard University carried out its planned acquisition of land in the riverside area and replaced community housing with mostly

The Riverside Press was established by Henry O. Hougton in 1852.

The Riverside Press

The printing of books with its associated trades was one of the major industries in the Harvard Square area in the nineteenth century. A small establishment, John Wilson and Son (Wilson was a native of Scotland), was located on the corner of Arrow and Main (Mass. Ave.) Street. The University Press, located off Mount Auburn Street at University Place, had been founded in the seventeenth century, and had run continuously since then. Both firms hired immigrant members of St. Paul parish, but it was the Riverside Press, located between Blackstone Street and the Charles River in Cambridgeport, that became one of the largest employers in the parish.

The establishment of The Riverside Press coincided with the arrival of the Famine Irish to Old Cambridge and Cambridgeport, and the expansion of the business contributed significantly to the growth and welfare of the surrounding community. Indeed, the fortunes of the Press were so intertwined with the area that the neighborhood assumed the company's name—Riverside. As a major employer in St. Paul parish, the Press raised the occupational status of many in the parish from servants and laborers to skilled craftsmen. The Riverside recruited young men and women as apprentices, provided them with jobs that required intelligence and skill, and ensured the security of lifetime employment close to home. With the trades they had acquired, some of these young people went on to start their own businesses. The relationship of the Press with the community was symbiotic, since the firm also flourished with the long service of a loyal workforce, comprised of men and women who produced some of the finest books of their time.

The Riverside Press was established by Henry O. Houghton, originally a poor farm-boy from Vermont who had learned the printing business at the Burlington Free Press, attended the University of Vermont, and later developed entrepreneurial skills. Originally located on Remington Street, Houghton's firm moved in 1852 to the old Almshouse estate in Cambridgeport. In the early days, Houghton routinely recruited personnel from Europe, travelling to London and Paris, but especially to Glasgow, a city renowned for its printing industry. By 1867, Houghton had built a large, four-story brick building, purchased ten additional presses, and employed three hundred people, half of whom were women. Among the occupations at the Press were pressmen, bookbinders, compositors, sewers, stampers, clerks and bookkeepers.[16]

Winning numerous gold medals for its book design and manufacture, The Riverside Press has a worldwide reputation as an originator in features of paper and type, binding and execution. Even among the more routine productions, books manufactured at the Riverside Press had a uniform excellence and dignity of design and execution. Some of its earliest publications were the *Atlantic Monthly*, Merriam-Webster's *Unabridged Dictionary*, and household editions of Charles Dickens. In the late nineteenth century, the Press's great accomplishments were the ten volumes of English and Scottish Ballads by Francis James Child, and Edward Fitzgerald's translation of

In 1896 The Riverside Press employed over 600 people who worked a 52-hour week.

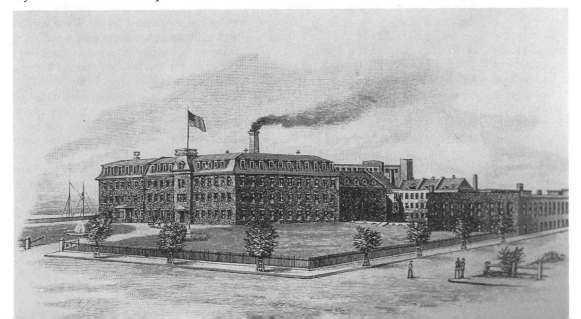

The Rubaiyat by Omar Khayam, illustrated by Elihu Vedder. When Houghton bought out the publisher Ticknor and Fields, it thereby acquired the publishing rights to works by Henry Thoreau, Oliver Wendell Holmes, John Greenleaf Whittier, Nathaniel Hawthorne, James Russell Lowell, Harriet Beecher Stowe, Sarah Orne Jewett, Samuel Clemens, Henry Wadsworth Longfellow, William Dean Howells and Stephen Crane. By the twentieth century, Houghton-Mifflin Company (The Riverside Press was the printing division of the publisher) expanded its educational textbook business, which eventually became a mainstay over the years.

One of the most well-known artists associated with the Press was Bruce Rogers, a typographical genius who preferred to use older, less commercial methods. In a small, bare studio Rogers worked side-by-side with an elderly, senior pressman, Dan Sullivan, whom Rogers found indispensable to his work. Parishioners of St. Paul's, the Sullivan family of Green Street had long been associated with The Riverside Press. Together Rogers and Sullivan printed on a handpress the famous Riverside Press Editions, which were "truly extraordinary works..., designed and executed with imagination, taste and brilliance."[17]

By 1886 the workforce had grown to six hundred employees, who ran thirty-three presses and seven sewing machines. The company had initiated a number of employee welfare plans in advance of other printing businesses: an employee savings plan that consistently maintained a good interest rate, and a Mutual Benefit Association that provided short-term disability benefits and death appropriations. Even though the employees worked 52 hours a week with Saturday afternoons off, the workweek was shorter than that in other companies. The Riverside Press had a long history of good employee relations and worker loyalty that spanned generations of families. In 1899, the force included seven hundred people. "Nearly every branch of the work requires a high degree of intelligence and education; a spirit of sympathy and assistance in time of trouble and distress...result in good feeling which contributes to the happiness of those connected with the business. Rarely does anyone give up his position except for reasons that make such a step unavoidable. Loyalty to Riverside on the part of employers and employed is a characteristic feature, conducive to good work and the comfort of all."[18]

By 1905, the Riverside operated 60 presses which used 2,000-3,000 tons of paper annually. Employees belonged to the International Typographical Union, which, with 642 locals in 1906, led a drive to the eight-hour day and closed shop. When the Boston locals went out on strike, the Cambridge Typographical Union (which included employees from The Riverside Press, the

JACK HANNON

A graduate of St. Paul's School, Mr. Hannon has worked in the publishing business for over forty years.

I started working at The Riverside Press the year I graduated from high school in 1947. Mr. Murphy's job in the high school in those days was to try and find a place of employment for all the people who were not going on to college, and they had this thing with the Riverside personnel department. I went to the shipping department. I was there a year and a half, and then I went back into the service for a year, the Korean conflict. I went back to the Riverside in 1949. I stayed and worked up from the shipping department to traffic manager. When they sold and a company called Rand McNally came in and bought out the rights to the printing that

Riverside was doing and all the existing equipment, they opened a plant south of Boston, Taunton, Massachusetts, nineteen years ago. They offered fourteen people at Riverside Press fourteen bosses jobs, and we went down there and have been down there ever since.

[The effect of the plant's closing on the community was] devastating, devastating. You're talking about people who had long longevity at the plant. It was like home to them. It was close to their houses and homes. More than one generation worked there. There were fathers and sons who worked there over the course of the years that we knew of. There was the McNeil family; there were three brothers and one sister that worked there for years...When you look back over the years, I think it was the convenience more than that they liked working there. I'm not saying the wages were the best around, but they were equal to what was in the city

they were paying. There was something about walking back and forth to work. They had no transportation. Even in the bad days, you could walk to work in snowstorms.

They worked in the pressroom; of course, we printed things. They worked in the lithoroom making plates up. They worked in the bindery, and in those days we did a lot of what they called indexing and gilding, gilding gold leaf on books. That was kind of a special job that six or eight people had. There were casemakers, that you cased the book. There was sewing, stampers, that stamped the cover of a book. Of course in those days it was not like the covers you have today that are preprinted. Mostly everything had to be stamped with the title on it. The backbones had to be stamped. There was a process that you had to wait two days sometimes for the ink to dry to go back and put another kind of stamping on it.

University Press and the Atheneum Press) held a mass meeting. Capitulating to the threat of a strike, the three employers agreed to the eight-hour day, but retained the open shop. That some of the union meetings were held at St. Paul's parish hall is one measure of the extent of involvement Riverside employees had in the parish.

In 1921, the Typothetae union struck all the plants in Boston for a forty-four hour week, but this time The Riverside Press fought the strike and kept the plant open. The strike was eventually broken, and many of the striking workers never returned to work. During the worst of the Depression of the 1930's, the plant paid its workers for only three days every other week. With the Wagner Act recently passed, in 1941 the union bargained for the forty-hour week and this time their demands were unopposed.[19]

Until 1971, The Riverside Press exerted a stable, benevolent influence in the community of Cambridgeport by providing secure, long-term employment, and teaching young men and women highly marketable skills in occupations that required intelligence and education. With the success and the expansion of the Press, the living standards of the whole community were raised. Former servants and laborers who lived in tin-roofed shanties progressed to compositors, pressmen and bookbinders who lived in the two and three-family houses still evident today. Likewise, the presence of a long-term, stable and devoted workforce enabled The Riverside Press to maintain its reputation for high-quality production. However, by 1971 the old brick buildings on Blackstone Street were hopelessly inadequate for the volume of production. The business was flourishing, but the Press increasingly had to find storage facilities off the premises. Furthermore, the multi-storied layout of the buildings inhibited the smooth flow of production. The Riverside Press was merged with Rand McNally and moved its operation to Taunton, Massachusetts. The 500 employees of the Riverside (80% were unionized) were given a choice to go to Rand's plant in Taunton, which was a non-union open shop. Only a handful of supervisory and management staff transferred to Taunton. The Cambridge plant was demolished in 1973.[20]

The closing of the Press after 122 years of operation in Cambridge shocked the people of the community. Those who had worked all their lives at the Riverside, preceded by their parents and grandparents, people who walked to work and who lived and worked in the same close-knit community, were devastated by the imposition of change. With the closing of other manufacturing plants, such as Lever Brothers, Boston Woven Hose, Blake and Knowles Steam Pump, Simplex Wire and J. P. Squire among others, a large portion of the workforce in Cambridge and in the Riverside community shifted from blue-collar to white-collar.

There were a lot of different kinds of jobs that you had that had to do with the making of a book: working on a gathering line, feeding signatures into sewers, casing the book, packing the book, shipping the book, picking pack operations in the shipping room to get orders out to customers. Of course in those days, we used to do a lot of work to the schools, a lot of shipments to the New York area, to all the public schools in New York, and a lot of shipments to bookstores in Boston and the surrounding area. They printed educational textbooks, dictionaries, encyclopedias, and at one time, they got into a lot of Bible work.

The place was all unionized, but each department had separate unions. The pressroom had their own union, the bindery had their own union, and the shipping room had their own union. It was Local 27 I think. I remember going to a union hall, a hall right in back of Prospect Street.

Lots of people from Saint Paul's parish worked at the Riverside. I don't know what the total employment of the Riverside was, at one time it was running pretty good. We ran two shifts in the bindery all year round; and we ran two shifts in the pressroom all year round. In the shipping department, when they got busy we used to go on overtime and work twelve hours out of the twenty-four hours in a day. We never had a night shift in the shipping department. But when you got behind in your work and you had to fill orders, especially in the months of July and August when you had to get the books out to the depositories for the schools, so they could have books in the schools in September when the kids came to class, you had to go on overtime. Of course in those days, if you went on overtime, it was what everybody looked forward to. When you had kids going to school, you had to get clothes and things like that for the kids, people would work four nights, five nights a week and Saturdays, and be thankful they got it. They looked forward to that. It was almost like it was part of your income. You knew it was coming every year, and you hoped it came in the summer months before the school opened up. You were hoping it would come back, which it did a lot in November and the beginning of December before Christmas, so you could have extra money for Christmas. In those days, the big book that we used to do in October and November was a book called *The Robe*. That was a big, big seller in those days, and that lasted for about two years. The demand for that book was so high that we had to work overtime to get it out to the customers.

Saint Paul's School

Under the direction of St. Paul's first pastor, Rev. William Orr, a parish school was established in 1889.[21] The Sisters of Saint Joseph began their long tenure of exemplary service at Saint Paul's by assisting at Mass on the Feast of the Assumption, August 15, 1889. By September, they opened the school for grades one through nine in an old mansion, formerly owned by inventor Gordon McKay, at the corner of Bow and Arrow Streets. The mansion, in which the Sisters made their residence as well their school, had been furnished with great elegance, with inlaid floors, heavy crystal chandeliers and high oak wainscotting. Two years later, on September 2, 1891, the new school, a symmetrical brick building between Arrow and Mount Auburn Streets, was opened. Three Sisters began instruction in the first year with an enrollment of 198, and within a short time were joined by two more nuns.

At the time it was built in 1889, the sixteen-room parish school was not large enough to accommodate all the classes.

These first teachers were Sister Margaret Mary, the Superior, Sister M. Genevieve, Sister Mary Angela, Sister M. Angela, and Sister M. Coletta.

Establishing Catholic schools, as many parishes were doing in accord with the instructions of the Third Plenary Council of Baltimore, was often a challenge. Since many New Englanders regarded the instillation of "American values" as the primary function of public schools, the Protestant community reacted with great prejudice to the establishment of the parochial school system in Boston. Their reaction was exemplified in the East Boston "Little Red Schoolhouse" parade of 1895, in which marchers, dressed in derogatory costumes as priests and nuns, carried a model of a schoolhouse through the Catholic areas of East Boston. In this environment, a parish school, while a stimulus for bigotry, was felt all the more necessary to protect the parish's young people.

St. Paul's School, like the parish in general, felt a special challenge from its large neighbor, Harvard University. Aware of the academic achievement of both Harvard and the Cambridge public schools, Fr. Orr set a high standard of education at St. Paul's School. The class of 1895, the first class to graduate from a full tenure at St. Paul's, fulfilled this expectation in a very decisive manner, when it reported for the entrance examination to the public high school. Of the twenty-three students who took the examination, twenty passed unconditionally. After five years of similar performance by St. Paul's graduates, the School Board at the recommendation of the Superintendent of Schools, voted to accept St. Paul students on the sole basis of their diplomas.

The Harvard environment, educationally advanced but morally retrograde, continued to be a source of comparison and an inspiration to produce the best in Catholic education. At the twenty-fifth anniversary of the school, Paul Francis Spain, an early graduate, described St. Paul's as a case study of the fine work of the Sisters of St. Joseph:

> Surrounded on three sides by public schools, and having in its midst the great University of Harvard, it furnishes ample opportunity to try out a plan of Catholic education that is steeped in all those influences

When purchased in 1889, the Gordon McKay mansion was expanded to serve as a convent. This view is taken from Mt. Auburn St. looking uphill towards Arrow Street.

which tend to neutralize, if not undo, the good effect of the principles which are basic to Catholic education. The viewpoint of the University regarding religious matters, certainly not enthusiastically pro-Catholic, or over pro-Christian, cannot be kept from leaking out beyond the walls.

Right in the heart of the parish, on the very street through which the Sisters and children pass every day, is situated the famous "Gold Coast" so named because of the palatial dormitories where the scions of wealthy scions are quartered. Evidences of wealth and the affected superiority which it begets in some of its possessors are apparent on every side, and the open disregard for the rights of the passer-by, a distinguishing mark of some "College Men" is not the best example in the world for the young boy or girl....I mention these things to show the atmosphere in which the Sisters labored....How well they have succeeded has become an historic fact in Cambridge.

Many students remembered the pastor's frequent visitations to their school rooms and his stern exaction of good work. Fr. Orr's dedication to the parish and the education of its young people was memorialized in a poem written in 1907 by Fr. Ryan:

The priest beloved by youthful years,
　　Has vanished from the sight.
In mem'ry's halls his form appears,
　　Aflame with heavenly light.
His grateful children praise bestow,
　　For all the love and care
That aged man, while here below,
　　Gave them as daily fare.

The school became his pride and joy,
　　The solace of his life.
The days to come could ne'er annoy,
　　If, in this earthly strife,
Christ's lessons, herein seen and wrought,
　　Were made the soul's best love —
The polar star to ev'ry thought,
　　Till crowned by Him Above.

[line missing]
　　Have mingled with the dust.
Wise Founder, whose declining day
　　In earnest effort spent
Raised up these walls, whose fondest hope
　　To this one aim was bent.
Read, in these smiling eyes tonight,
　　Your noblest monument.

As much as Fr. Orr and Fr. Ryan had encouraged competition and scholarship among the students of St. Paul's school, it was the Sisters of Saint Joseph who carried out the task of teaching and inspiring their charges. Many students remembered the Sisters with great fondness. Louise Forrest, class of 1904, wrote of the Sisters' good work:

We were given a diploma after eight or nine years' instruction by the Sisters. I ought not say instruction, for what we received was far more reaching and deeply effective than mere instruction. It was part of themselves, their enthusiasm, their ambitions for us, their love, their very life, it was what those good Sisters gave us. And they gave it so that we might go out fully equipped, both morally and mentally to do good work in life.

31

This 1913 orchestra of the Sisters of St. Joseph included St. Paul's teachers Sr. Mary Eugenia Madigan (on bass) and Sr. Mary Camilla O'Connor (front right).

This quality education was achieved in circumstances teachers today would find unbelievable. By the time Louise Forrest was graduating, the enrollment had grown to 786 students, taught by sixteen Sisters of St. Joseph—an average of 49 students per classroom, but still one less than the recommended number. The operating cost per pupil was just under $30 and the school calculated that in 1902 it saved the city $23,316.16.

School enrollment reached its peak in 1914, when the parish celebrated the twenty-fifth anniversary of the school and the new church is being planned. In that year, 990 pupils were registered for the parish school and 412 came for Sunday classes. However, the population of the neighborhood began to decline as residents moved to the suburbs and Harvard purchased land along the Charles River, so that in each subsequent decade the school lost about 150 students.

The parish clergy were active in the school, often visiting classes and consulting with the various Sisters of St. Joseph. Fr. Hickey, in general a fastidious administrator, had been Superintendent of Schools for the archdiocese before assuming the pastorate of St. Paul's and was particularly attentive to the operation of the parish school. Since the new church had greatly reduced the school playground, in replacement he acquired the adjacent house on Mt. Auburn and several behind the rectory as they became available. When the number of sisters being transferred in and out of the school seemed exceptionally high, he felt quite free to make complaints. Under his watchful eye and the Sisters' high standards, students came away as impressed as preceding generations and made remarkably similar observations, such as this statement by Dr. Frank Bane, class of 1943:

We had an awful lot go on to college, for that era, at Saint Paul's. I think the nuns did a marvelous job of educating kiddos who were first generation Irish, products of people who came from Ireland. Their parents did not have a grammar school education. They went to these nuns, and with their parents' will to give them an education, I would say a good 50% went on to college. It was a tremendous background to have. They stimulated you to learn, to want to learn, to want to achieve, not for the sake of doing better monetarily. There was no mention of that. It was to do better for your faith, your family and your heritage. They instituted the idea that you should want to be an educated person.

The school's impact reached the entire community. "If I can recall anything, its the Saint Paul's Christmas play," says John Caulfield, who attended many of them in the thirties. "We all knew the lines. It was the same play every year. I didn't go to Saint Paul's school, but I'd always go to the play." For the May procession, the children marched out of the school and around the church to enter by the front door. "There were four or

"Erected in loving remembrance of Mother Genevieve by Children of St. Paul's School, Cambridge." Over a dozen Sisters of St. Joseph lie in St. Paul's cemetery.

five hundred people in the street," Caulfield remembers. "It was a big day. You just wore a clean shirt and tie, and the whole thing. I used to be always envious of Saint Paul students because they had red sashes, a different role than the Sunday school kids."

The power of school activities in developing children's spirituality can be seen from Betty Linehan's account of the graduation play and its consequences:

I remember Sister saying, "All those who haven't got a part in the graduation play, please stand up." I didn't, so I stood up. She said, "Elizabeth, sit down. You're going to be the Little Flower." And all the kids in the room screamed, laughing. So she kept me after school, wanting to know why everyone, the kids, laughed so hard at my being the Little Flower. When I was out of school, I did my share of tearing around the streets and everything. When we were in the eighth grade, four or five girls, we would go for a walk down the River. It was the big thing to do on Sunday afternoon. All the kids met down the River. The kids were roaring to think that she picked me. You know I was dressed just like a nun, with the rosary beads, the crucifix, and all that.

Regina Daly, she was the Virgin Mary. For as long as I can remember, she had hair down to her bottom, the most gorgeous hair you ever saw. She was just ladylike and soft and not boisterous, and she was picked, she got the part of the Blessed Mother. As I think of it now, it had to be her face. She was very quiet

and sweet-type. I was the Little Flower. I had a piece to say about her, and dropping her thing of roses on the earth, and I had her rosary beads on. My mother made me the long white cape that Saint Theresa wore, and Sister got me the long brown robe to wear under, and then her black veil and the white. They had Saint Joseph, Saint Francis of Assisi.

There was a novena to Saint Theresa every Tuesday night, and from the time I was little, my mother always took me to that novena on Tuesday. You know, I went with her so she wouldn't be alone. You know, when you're a kid, I used to think she had the most beautiful face, on the statue. Then years and years later, I almost always said novenas to her. I got into the habit. Then over the years, I sort of promised her on her feast day every year, I would put a couple of roses at her shrine, wherever she was. I was in this house, and we were here thirty years. And I'll never forget near the feast day, I went up to Saint Peter's and they had taken her out of there. They had taken all the statues out of there. I got back home and I called Saint Paul's. He said, "That's been gone out of there for years." I always went up to the Shrine, but if I couldn't get in, I would have a back up. I had Jimmy, my youngest drive me into Arch Street. I went in just before they closed the church and did it. So now I go in, and they have an alleyway between the shrine there. There's a florist and I see him all the time, and he'll say, "Is it that time again?" It's just something I decided I'll do in appreciation for all the things.

33

In 1950 there were only half as many students as there had been at the beginning of the century. The baby boom never had a chance to reverse the decline, as many parishioners left the immediate area in the postwar period before their children entered school. By the 1960's, the school faced not only declining attendance but also a shortages of nuns and was relying increasingly on lay teachers. On June 28, 1968 the remaining few Sisters of Saint Joseph vacated their convent. The convent was purchased by Stebbins, La Messurier and Dupree, who replaced the house with a commercial building at 1033 Massachusetts Avenue. In 1974 the last class of the St. Paul's parish school graduated, but in a reduced form the enthusiasm and standards of excellence of the Sisters of Saint Joseph continues today in their association with the Boston Archdiocesan Choir School.

Seven hundred students were attending St. Paul's School in 1931.

SCHOOL NOTES FROM 1912

In the Convent day book are recorded various events and business concerning the sisters and the school, although they also give a glimpse of the wider parish life in which the sisters took part. Following are some extracts from the year 1912, when the sisters were teaching over 900 students in St. Paul's school (in three buildings) and the parish was still using the old church on Mt. Auburn and Holyoke Streets.

Jan. 9—Raining. No school in the forenoon. Very few children came in the afternoon.

Feb. 8—Fr. Ryan spent the day in Sr. Mary Carmel's room, Grade 2. He brought some pictures to the office for Bible History lessons.

Feb. 9—The 7th, 8th, and 9th grades had a mitten examination in music. The Junior Sodality went to confession at 3 p.m.

Feb. 12—Lincoln Day. The Catholic Union of Cambridge had a

Feb. 13—Sr. Mary Lawrence finished the address to the Cardinal.

Feb. 18—The Holy Name Society had a banquet in the evening.

March 21—Snowing all forenoon. A public school teacher visited the third grade.

April 9—Doctor Barnes saw the children who had been absent on account of the measles. All were admitted who had certificates from the Board of Health.

April 25—Two Sisters of Mercy from Worcester came to stay a few days. They went to visit Agassiz Museum and the Germanic.

May 12—Fr. Finn examined the Public School children for confirmation.

May 14—Prof. McConnell took the 6th and 7th grade choir to the hall at 11:15 to rehearse a song for the closing exercise.

May 26—Feast of Pentecost. The Knights of Columbus had their annual breakfast in St. Paul's Hall as usual. After it was over, Father Ryan took the gentlemen on the School Committee to some of the classrooms, where they met the Sisters. He also invited them to the Convent to see the vestments.

May 28—Father Ryan took the 9th grade girls in the Hall for Elocution.

June 8—The children received their First Holy Communion at a High Mass celebrated by Fr. Ryan at 8:15. The 7th grade choir sang the Mass. At 9:15 a.m. there was a rehearsal for the Corpus Christi procession. Everything was over about 11 o'clock. In the afternoon there was an entertainment in the hall for the children in aid of the "Field Day".

June 18—Class Day in Harvard for the first time on Tuesday.

July 21—Sunday. Fr. Corrigan, S.J., said the 9 o'clock. The Intermediate Choir sang. Fr. Ryan introduced him to the people and referred to his youth when he was an Altar Boy in St. Paul's. His mother and sisters were present and received Holy Communion from his hands.

Nov. 27—The choir boys and men of the choir sang the Mass at the dedication of St. Clement's Church, Somerville.

The Columbus Day Nursery

Neither working mothers nor day care centers are novelties of the late twentieth century. On January 17, 1912, the Columbus Day Nursery, Inc., of Cambridge came into existence, under the auspices of the Knights of Columbus (Cambridge Council 74, mostly from St. Paul's). Property at 252 and 254 Green Street was purchased and the day care center started operating there in May, 1912. In 1919, the directors of the Columbus Day Nursery, Inc., of Cambridge gave a report of their work, slightly abbreviated as follows.

The work of the Nursery is non-sectarian and consists chiefly in the care of children of working women, under the school age, during the day time, and the procuring of work for needy women.

The Nursery aims first to help mothers of children, who have become dependent upon their own resources, for whatever reason. The father may have died, or he may have been in poor health and unable to work. At any rate, any respectable mother who has an opportunity to become a wage-earner and shows that it is necessary for her to contribute to the maintenance of her family is always welcome to place her children here during the day time. The welfare of the mother is always in mind, and she is aided and encouraged in every way in her struggle to provide properly for her little ones. Before the child is admitted to the Nursery, a careful investigation is made, not rigid or painful, however, of all the circumstances in connection with the character and habits of the mother. Upon being admitted, the mother is expected to pay the sum of five cents a day for each child, but if for any reason the mother is unable to pay, this does not prevent the admission of the child.

. . . . The children are provided with good, wholesome food, under well regulated conditions, and provision is made for sleeping accommodations for the little ones when they may need rest. Suitable cribs, properly provided with clothing, are furnished for infants and the younger children. During the day, the children seldom have a dull moment, as they find interest in the many little things provided for them.

The work of the Nursery is well within the spiritual atmosphere of Catholic charity, without in the least attempting to question the religion of an applicant, for in our work we know no creed, race or color—all look alike if worthy.

The duty of caring properly for the children is in the care of a very faithful, competent matron, Mrs. Elizabeth A. Madden, herself the mother of three children left fatherless many

"Suitable cribs, properly provided with clothing, are furnished for infants and the younger children."

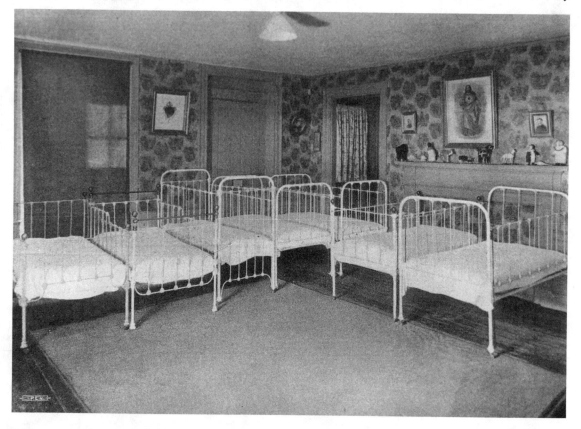

Some Statistics of the Columbus Day Nursery
from January 1, 1918 to December 31, 1918

Days the Nursery has been open to receive children...............271
Total attendance for the year...3731
Actual number of children cared for....................................78
Average number of days per child...48
Families from which the children were received......................56
Days work for needy women 1733
Women who shared in this work...121

years ago. Under her supervision, every want is carefully administered.

We have always taken precaution to avoid sickness and the spread of disease. In this respect we have had the helpful co-operation of the Health Officials of the City of Cambridge, and the generous support of the physicians of the city.

The sum of five cents each day for each child cared for is the only fixed revenue, and of course goes only a short way towards the maintenance of this enterprise. . . . Alone and unaided, the members of the corporation long ago came to realize that they could not continue the work of the Nursery, and Cambridge Council, Knights of Columbus, under whose auspices the undertaking was begun, soon came to our assistance with a fixed yearly contribution.

The good ladies of Cambridge also came to our assistance, and a Ladies' Guild was organized as an auxiliary to our corporation. Since then we have been entirely at ease, all obligations have been readily met, and all fear of success has been removed. The Guild has become as much, if not more, of a necessary adjunct to the Home than the corporation itself. To the untiring efforts of the ladies we are indebted for material assistance in the raising of funds, and in many other ways, without which help we could not long have been expected to succeed.

Since the beginning the Nursery has been opened to receive children for a period of 1,992 days. During this time there have been cared for 940 different children, which is equal to a total attendance of 51,834 children, at a cost of about $12,500 for the entire period, or about 24 cents per day for each child. The number of days work for needy women procured since the opening of the nursery is 11,017.

"The children are provided with good wholesome food."

The Mission Mural in St. Paul's Church shows Cardinal O'Connell sending forth six missionary priests connected with the parish or the college.

The Mission Community: Propagators of the Faith

by Angelyn Dries, O.S.F.*

The parish of St. Paul, which in its very name evokes the great missionary of the Gentiles, has been prominent in the tradition of mission and evangelization. From the parish came two leaders of the mission movement, James A. Walsh, founder of Maryknoll, and Joseph McGlinchey, Walsh's successor at the Society for the Propagation of the Faith. While the symbols which express that mission have changed over the years, the Parish has steeped itself in the commission to "teach all nations."

The west transept of the Church was designed to remind parishioners of that tradition. Fr. Ryan noted in the building's dedicatory pamphlet in 1924, "An oval space over the window lends itself admirably to the symbol of the Propagation of the Faith—the cross surmounting the earth's orbit swinging in the empyrean—constant reminders of the divine commission, 'Go teach all nations.' " Flanking the windows are two murals. One, now concealed by the choir organ, portrays the departure from home of St. Columban the Irish monk, who represents the era of "national" missioners.[1] The second mission theme mural to the left of the first portrays six men who represent parish engagement in home and foreign missions. William Cardinal O'Connell, with the Pastor at his side, is bestowing his blessing on Rev. Celestine Roddan, C.P., Rev. Paul F. Rooney, O.F.M., John J. French, O. Carm., Rev. Robert Carroll, O.P., Bishop James A. Walsh, M.M., and Rev. Henry McGlinchey, S.J. Some of these missioners were natives of St. Paul parish, some were Harvard alumni, some were both. As in other areas, the outreach to missions united the parish and the Catholic students.[2]

From its inception, the United States was the recipient of the mission energy and finances of the Spanish, French and English. Missions toward Indians and ministry toward those who came to explore and colonize this new country continued to develop, but by the nineteenth century, the efforts of priests and bishops tended to concentrate on establishing the Church among the newly arrived Irish and German immigrants. For this, financial aid and personnel was provided by the Society for the Propagation of the Faith and by other European mission-sending organizations.

Archbishop John Williams (1823-1907) of Boston always retained a deep feeling for and a promotion of missions, for he was educated by the mission-motivated Sulpicians in Paris and his diocese had been the recipient of the financial efforts of the Society for the Propagation of the Faith. He engaged the Sulpicians to teach at the diocesan seminary at Brighton, where seminarians such as James A. Walsh, Maryknoll's founder, heard stories from their professors of mission exploits of their classmates in the Far East.

Walsh and McGlinchey Awaken Mission Consciousness

"The Heart of our Master is world-wide;...the commission to the Apostles was unmistakably universal; and from these premises it follows that American Catholics ought to share in the world propaganda."[3] By the time James A. Walsh (1867-1936) spoke these words to the clergy and laity assembled for the 1919 Catholic Education Association, he, along with Thomas F. Price had founded the Catholic Foreign Missions Society (1911) and had sent the first group of Maryknoll priests to Yeungkong, China. This consistent symbol of a world-wide heart captured Walsh's conviction of the need to get the word out to American Catholics of their responsibility as a maturing Church to develop a mission spirit. Though the United States was considered by Rome to be a mission country until 1908, Walsh and Mother Mary Joseph Rogers, foundress of the Maryknoll Sisters, put their energy into providing American Catholics with reading material to engage them in the needs of the missions abroad.[4]

---

*Sr. Angelyn Dries, O.S.F., holds a Ph.D. in Historical Theology from the Graduate Theological Union, Berkeley, California. Assistant Professor at Cardinal Stritch College, she is currently researching a book on U.S. Catholic Mission history for the U.S. Catholic Mission Association.

Thousands gathered at the Cathedral in Boston as part of the American Catholic Missionary Congress of 1913.

In his home on Ellery Street in Cambridge, Walsh had read stories of the foreign missions in *Annals*, a magazine sponsored by the Society for the Propagation of the Faith. His own father was involved in parish evangelization at St. Paul's Sunday School. While a seminarian at St. John's, Brighton, Walsh was greatly influenced by one of his teachers, Father Gabriel André, S.S., who had a vital interest in foreign missions, and by Father John Hogan, S.S., the Superior at the Seminary (1884-1889), a classmate of Blessed Theophane Vénard, a missionary martyr in the far east. Walsh was ordained in 1892 and was sent to St. Patrick's, Roxbury. In 1903, the ailing Father Joseph V. Tracy, diocesan director of the Society for the Propagation of the Faith, suggested Walsh as his replacement. From then until his death, Walsh did all in his power to spread among Catholics the need to develop a habit of thinking about missions and to enkindle in them a zeal that would draw them beyond the concerns of their parochial borders. The crystallization of these efforts resulted in the foundation of the first American seminary for foreign missions. "We must cultivate in all our people...a solicitude for all the Churches; not only for the parish Church or the great Cathedral at our doors, but for the rudest hut or the humblest chapel that some far-off missionary has made the home of the altar, and the Blessed Sacrament and the Gospel of Christ."[5]

When Walsh left Boston for Hawthorne, New York (eventually settling at Ossining, New York) in 1911 to start the seminary, he was replaced at the Propagation of the Faith Office by another St. Paul parishioner, Father Joseph F. McGlinchey (1882-1959) of Athens Street, who also served as an assistant pastor at the Parish from 1907 to 1911. Speaking at the Second American Catholic Missionary Congress held in 1913 in Boston's Symphony Hall, McGlinchey remarked that as the director of the Boston Office, many letters from missionaries came across his desk, the "letters of the modern apostles, who, in answer to the command of Christ, 'Go forth and teach all the nations,' and have gone the whole way."[6]

This Missionary Congress (the first one had been held in Chicago in 1908) was an impressive event in the Diocese. On a crisp October day, thousands gathered in and around Holy Cross Cathedral, its pillars inside festooned with cardinal red, for the opening Congress Mass and sermon preached by Car-

dinal O'Connell. Among the participants at the Congress over the next few days were Pastor John J. Ryan, Paul Hanley Furfey (later priest sociologist at Catholic University) and James A. Furfey, Patrick J. Walsh, Thomas Jennings, Mrs. W. P. Daly and several more parishioners and Catholics from Cambridge.[7] St. Paul also received the honor of being designated one of the Churches in the Archdiocese where sermons on the missions were preached by visiting bishops during the evenings of the Congress.

These Congress participants and those who belonged to the parish Society for the Propagation of the Faith were a significant force which enabled missioners to undertake their work. Many adults will remember the "mite boxes" into which their pennies went as children to rescue the "pagan babies." Through such means, promoted through the school and the home, many gave their "pennies and prayers" and had their eyes opened to a world quite different from theirs in culture, religion, and government.

McGlinchey continued the concern Walsh had—to provide material in English on the Foreign Missions.[8] Toward this end, he translated and published two works by an Italian missionary, Paul Manna, *The Workers are Few* and *The Conversion of the Pagan World*. The former book was affectionately dedicated to Joseph's youngest brother, Henry McGlinchey (1888-1918) a Jesuit missioner who was prefect general of the Jesuit School in Bombay. Henry's great facility with languages enabled him to learn Hindustani as well as several dialects of the tribes in the area. He died in the 1918 flu epidemic.[9]

American Hardiness

In the first quarter of this century, Europeans had the impression that Americans were too "soft" to undertake the rigors of mission life. Both Walsh and McGlinchey strove to counteract this belief. Walsh enlarged on a spirituality of martyrdom and sacrifice, not only for those who were to become members of Maryknoll, but for those thousands of laity, many of them from St. Paul's, who read *The Field Afar* and became "Auxiliary missionaries," whose money and prayers were lines spun across the globe.

Not all missioners would die a martyr's death, and so Walsh commented on the overall life of sacrifice that was the training ground of martyrs:

Rev. James J. Walsh, founder of Maryknoll, started his mission work as director of the Propagation for the Faith in Boston.

The blood is one of the most noble features of the human body, next to the heart. There is a close relation between the spiritual life and the physical flow of blood, a precious element in the human body....The spiritual motive back of [the feast of the Precious Blood] is a lesson of sacrifice....We think of that great army of martyrs registered in the Church, not only of our race, but also of the yellow race....But besides the actual shedding of one's blood for Christ, there is a thinning out of the blood... very few of us will actually shed blood for Christ, but there is not one of us who will not have an opportunity to thin out his blood for Christ....The thinning of the blood for Christ is expressive and symbolic of the desire to go to the limit.[10]

Joseph McGlinchey also took up the theme of America's hardiness and readiness to take on the mission cause. While director of the Society for the Propagation of the Faith, he had written of the life Mother Mary Lawrence, a Franciscan Missionary of Mary who labored in China, and who corresponded with McGlinchey over the years. In the introduction of that work, he described her using traditionally masculine qualities, as a "young and valiant combatant, nobly fallen at her post of duty in the vanguard of the army of Christ," a member of the "armies of Christ [which] have been and are fighting for the material and spiritual betterment of every creature."[11]

American Catholic interest in foreign missions began to surface just after the Spanish-American War, as the U.S. took its place among the top international powers. The Harvard Catholic Club heard a lecture on April 6, 1899 by Father Francis B. Doherty, C.S.P., a member of General Marritt's staff in the Philippines, who conducted negotiations with the Archbishop of Manila to enable the bloodless surrender of the city. His topic, the situation of the Franciscan Friars in the Philippines, was typical of the methodology missioners used to obtain interest and support for their work: personal narrative of first-hand experience.

Fourteen years later, with a changed Church/State relationship in the Islands, Fr. Joseph McGlinchey addressed the Catholic Club of Harvard in 1913 on "The Church in the Philippines." In between these two events, the intrepid James A. Walsh spoke to this group in 1907 hoping to "deepen and widen" the missionary spirit among these young adult American Catholics. Possibly in the audience then was William Howard Bishop, a Harvard student in journalism later destined to found the Glenmary Home Missioners.

Clustered around mission organizations such as McGlinchey's Propagation of the Faith, and Walsh's Catholic Foreign Missions Society were thousands of women who formed "mission circles." Not only did they make make substantial individual and collective financial contributions which enabled priests to build Churches, but these women also "dressed" the Churches with the work of their hands. They sewed altar linens and vestments and sent chalices and silver objects to "set the Lord's Table" in foreign lands. In return, the Radcliffe Catholic Club minutes notes that on Jan. 15, 1911, "Fr. Walsh, the diocesan director of foreign missions, was the speaker of the day, and he supplemented his talk with a display of beautiful embroidery done by Chinese women."

St. Paul's has a unique place in mission history in the United States. It was home for individuals such as Joseph McGlinchey and

James A. Walsh, who provided national leadership in mission work. Through individual participation in the Society for the Propagation of the Faith and other mission groups, and through the financial support of individual missionaries, hundreds of parishioners have lived a mission spirituality which integrates prayer and action. The shadow of the steeple of the local Church fell well beyond the neighborhood. The local Church realized, in a small way, its relationship to other small Church communities throughout the world. This "mission awakening" among the parishioners, focused visually by Fr. John J. Ryan in the murals of the church, relied on the efforts of the laity. The Catholic Action Movement of the 1930's through the 1960's grew out of such efforts of "mission mindedness" and provided leadership experience for Catholic laity. Out of such experiences came *Lumen Gentium*, the Vatican II document on the Church which emphasized the role of the laity in its description of the Church as the People of God. The history of St. Paul's Parish mission experience contributed part of the foundation for such a document.

Mission fundraiser Msgr. Joseph McGlinchey visiting the grave of his brother Henry in India.

FR. JOSEPH McGLINCHEY

(as recalled by his niece Genevieve McGlinchey Mathison)

Fr. Joseph was very bright, because he built up the Propagation of the Faith, when he took it over from Bishop James Anthony Walsh, who had gone to start Maryknoll. My uncle at the time was assistant pastor of St. Paul's in Cambridge under Fr. Ryan. He built the organization from $28,000 a year in 1911 to $2,000,000 a year in 1928. He had written many books, *The Workers are Few, The Conversion of the Pagan World, The Cathechism in Uganda* and numerous others. He travelled around the world a great deal because he was the secretary to Cardinal O'Connell. He would represent Cardinal O'Connell at all the activities. He was also treasurer of every one of the clubs that Cardinal O'Connell was involved in.

He left the Propagation of the Faith to become the pastor of St. Mary's in Lynn. He had been recommended by Cardinal O'Connell to be Bishop of Boston in 1933. But Cardinal Spellman wanted to come back from Rome and didn't want to be in the Boston diocese, but wanted to get back on the east coast. He was a very close friend of Fr. Joseph and had been in charge of the *Boston Pilot*, while Fr. Joseph was in charge of the Propagation of the Faith. Spellman wanted to come back, and he had first choice of course, although he was younger than Fr. Joseph, since he had been in charge of the American College in Rome. So he came back and became Bishop of Boston. He moved right on to become Cardinal of New York. My uncle was very fond of him, and I don't think he cared about being bishop anyway.

Cushing had been selected by my uncle. He had been working over in South Boston. He was a very ardent person and my uncle thought he would make a wonderful priest. My father on one occasion said, "I can't understand why you have that man. He talks so loud, he'll burst your eardrums." And my uncle said, "That's just why I want him; because he can be heard. When I'm trying to get money for the Propagation of the Faith, you've got to be heard. If you're talking to yourself (Cardinal O'Connell didn't have a very loud voice), you can never get the idea across of why you need money. I think he has a wonderful voice!" In those days, there was no amplification in the church. He was very devout and very sincere, so my uncle was fond of him.

St. Paul Choir School outside St. Peter's Basilica, following Pontifical High Mass by Pope Paul VI, July 9, 1967.

The Liturgical Community: Worshipers and Singers

The richness of the music and the dignity of the liturgy at St. Paul's are often remarked, but as remarkable as the Boston Archdiocesan Choir School is the concomitant congregational participation. The parish's high liturgical literacy probably dates to the middle of Fr. Hickey's pastorate over fifty years ago, but it rests on a musical tradition even older.

We know little of nineteenth century liturgy at St. Paul's, although there was an organ in the old St. Paul Church initially played by Louisa Quigley. The parish advertised the music and soloists for its 10:30 High Mass in the Cambridge papers—a rare act among Catholic churches, which suggests a greater than usual emphasis on song. The Easter program for 1890, while Nellie Doherty was organist, featured H.G. Ganss' Second Mass and the Christmas one Millard's Mass in B-flat, with other pieces by Witzka, Bordese, and Dressler. For Sunday Vespers on those days, Gregorian selections were popular, but the congregation also heard Mozart's *Magnificat*, Wiegand's and Mertiam's *O Salutaris,* and Rossi's and Goebs' *Tantum Ergo.*

The first known music director at St. Paul's was the colorful Professor George G. McConnell. An Australian by birth, supposedly from a well-to-do family that had been cheated of an inheritance by its lawyer, McConnell held degrees from the London Academy of Music. A pupil of Wiegand, he came to America with the famous organist for the St. Louis Exposition, and, when Wiegand died in Syracuse, McConnell was persuaded by relatives to take a position there. About 1910, when the parish organist Bardschurl had been secured by the Cathedral, Fr. Ryan heard about McConnell through a Harvard student who said the organist was looking for a better opportunity.[1]

Ryan held a high opinion of the musician, "McConnell is an exceptional organist, can teach voice, play any instrument either in orchestra or band, and is tireless as a worker." Although calling him "a musician of the first class," Ryan thought him a poor organizer. Although calling him "a man of faith", Ryan thought him "quick tempered if he has a drink in him, and outspoken". All this fit into a

When St. Paul Church opened in 1873, it continued to use the organ of the Congregational Church.

Joseph Ecker and the St. Paul's Choir in 1927.

pattern: "He is generous, cares little for money and is always in need of it—in one word, he is an *artist*." Accordingly, Fr. Ryan, who was always organized, began a systematic plan of music in the school and arranged the work program, so that McConnell had only to execute it. We also read in the convent day books of Fr. Ryan explaining "the object and plan of the music in the school" to the sisters. In the early part of the twentieth century, the parish had several choirs and for Fr. Ryan's Silver Jubilee a group called the Regina Orchestra played in public for the first time.

In 1912, the choir (both boys and men) was so distinguished as to be invited to sing at the dedication of St. Clement's Church, Somerville. Some of their programs through that decade were quite ambitious. When the new church opened, the organ from the old St. Paul Church was moved into the gallery and was enlarged. The large parish choir of men and women maintained an equally strong reputation through the twenties and thirties when Mr. Joseph Ecker was choirmaster. The Sisters of St. Joseph, who staffed the school, had a number of musically talented members; the last one to direct the boys' choir was Sr. Agneta (Mary Elizabeth Donovan), music teacher from 1933 to 1952 (see Dr. Francis Bane's reminiscence for more on this period).

A new age in liturgy at St. Paul's comes immediately after World War II and is associated with three hard-working men: Theodore Marier in the choir, and Msgr. Augustine Hickey and Fr. Joseph Collins on the altar. In 1934, Theodore Marier began fifty years of musical service at St. Paul's, first as organist and then from 1947 as choir director. A graduate of Boston College, he was director of band and music there from 1934 to 1942— as well as composer of the music to "Sweep Down the Field for Boston" and "Boston's Out to Win Again." In 1940 he received a master's degree from Harvard, and over the course of the years he was also choir director or lecturer at Emmanuel College, Newton College of the Sacred Heart, and Boston University.

As Marier was taking over the choir, Msgr. Hickey was inspired by the papal encyclical *Mediator Dei* to encourage congregational participation—quite unusual in a time when the choir or altar boys gave all the responses. It was Marier's experience that the Gregorian Chant was ideally suited both to congregational singing and for musical nourishment. Gradually, the parish developed the habit of singing the Ordinary of the Mass (*Kyrie, Gloria, Credo, Sanctus, Agnus Dei*). In 1958, the Vatican's *Instruction on Sacred Music and Sacred Liturgy* continued the directive that every parish should have a boys choir but especially encouraged that "every effort must be made that the faithful of the entire world know how to give the responses in chant."

Few parishes fulfilled Rome's hopes with efforts comparable to St. Paul's. In fact, it was Theodore Marier who spread the gospel of musical participation around the country, addressing the National Liturgical Week on "Organ Design and Placement" and "The Choir and Congregational Participation". To implement participation, the parish had to move two mountains. First, in 1960 the choir was removed from the gallery to a more suitable place near the sanctuary, where a new pipe organ accompanied it. From there, the choir's voice could lead the congregation and serve in its triple role as Marier saw it: taking its own part properly, inspiring the congregation, and teaching the people by establishing the norms to imitate. Secondly, in 1963 the parish undertook to move the music physically into the pews—publishing its own hymnal of suitable songs and service music. The book's goal was clear from its Latin title *Cantus Populi* and its English subtitle *Hymns and Chants for the People's Participation*. In an age when Catholic song books rarely appeared outside benedictions and Marian celebrations, the parishioners of St. Paul's suddenly gained the necessary support for their fuller participation in the Mass. Later versions would be still larger.

In 1960, the parish was featured in an article in *Worship* magazine (see page 49). From this snapshot of the parish's liturgies on the eve of Vatican Council II, one can see why St. Paul's never suffered the crisis of confidence that afflicted much Catholic music in the following decades. Since St. Paul's had been an early innovator in liturgical renewal and congregational participation (both spoken and sung), the further expansion of the role of the people happened fairly smoothly and always rested on a solid foundation. In particular the chant, elsewhere applauded but undeveloped, was recognized as a successful vehicle for communal song. Rather than discard baby and bathwater, as many parishes did with the Catholic tradition of sacred music, St. Paul's continued to embrace the chant and indeed enlarged the resources for it.

The St. Paul's Choir School began in 1963 with twenty-five students chosen from throughout the archdiocese. Under the direction of Theodore Marier, the young musicians sang in the parish choir with members of the Harvard Catholic Club. Harvard students also helped out with the recreation program. The school was designed as a four-year course for students of academic ability and musical talent, assigning two periods of each school day to music, plus an hour after school. The music program included sight reading, tone placement, appreciation, theory and history, and instrumental studies.

A number of factors came together to create the early success of St. Paul's *schola cantorum*. Foremost were the personal expertise of Marier and the support of Frs. Hickey and Collins, not only fiscally but also in educating the parish and providing appropriate liturgical settings for a well-trained choir. Additionally, the rapidly declining enrollment of the parish school provided the occasion for rethinking the dimension and nature of the boys' choir. "Founding the school was really a matter of survival," recalled Marier, who asked the archbishop if he could fill the school's empty seats with choir boys. Also, as Marier often remarked, the opening of the choir school coincided with the first completed document of Vatican Council II, the *Constitution on the Sacred Liturgy*, which contained a long chapter on music strongly encouraging the formation of choir schools. A fourth and related phenomenon was the sudden emergence of ecumenical events, especially at Harvard, which gave the new choir school a broader audience than it might have had a decade before. No small part of the choir school's high reputation has come from interdenominational services and guest appearances with secular orchestras.

The three-day Liturgy-Music Seminar and Workshop held at St. Paul's in March, 1964, exemplifies these combined issues. Sponsored by the archdiocesan Sacramental Apostolate, of which Fr. Joseph Collins was the long-standing Secretary, the program stressed the spirit and directives of the new conciliar document on liturgy. A high point was the annual Mass for Harvard-Radcliffe students on the Feast of St. Thomas Aquinas, which the Cardinal celebrated with Fr. Collins as the choir sang the Gregorian Chant proper for the feast. This event and various Lenten services that weekend gave the choir school exposure in front of area liturgists and several Protestant guests—a phenomenon that would become typical.

Theodore Marier giving advanced organ instruction in 1964 to Leo Abbott, now organist at the Cathedral of the Holy Cross.

Those first years were extraordinary. Between 1963 and 1970, the choir made guest appearances with the Boston Symphony Orchestra at Symphony Hall (Berlioz' *Te Deum* and Xenakis' *Polla ta Dina*) and at Tanglewood (Mahler's *Symphony No. 8*), with the Boston Philharmonia (Monteverdi's *Sancta Maria*), and with the Handel & Haydn Society (Holst's *Hymn of Jesus*). Annually they performed with the Boston Ballet in Tchaikowsky's *Nutcracker Ballet*, with Arthur Fiedler conducting. In 1967 the choir school extended its reputation with its participation in the International Congress of the Pueri Cantatores in Rome, and with performances in Paris, London and Dublin. By 1968, music lovers could hear five records by the thirty-five member boys choir: *When in Rome* (their repertory from the International Congress), three Christmas albums, and *Music for the Sung Liturgy* (in English).

Although the choir, relabeled the Boston Archdiocesan Choir School, was soon invited by area churches of other denominations—and sang for over twenty-five ecumenical services in that first decade—the bulk of their concerts have been in Archdiocesan churches. Special occasions have included the 1970 services for the burial of Cardinal Cushing and the installation of Archbishop Medeiros, and many events for Cardinal Law.

Each year several of the dozen eighth graders are eagerly recruited by the area's best secondary schools. Many alumni sing in church choirs and regional opera companies, and a few have gone on to musical careers. In fact, Leo Abbott, the current organist of the Cathedral of the Holy Cross, was in the choir school's first graduating class. Charles E. Callahan, Jr. '65, has also developed a career as an organist-choirdirector, and Rev. Peter Uglietto '66 still sings but has moved from the choir to the sanctuary.

A recipient of the St. Gregory Medal in 1963, Marier was also honored by Boston College and various organ societies. From 1966 to 1970, he was national president of the Church Music Association of America. In 1984, while celebrating fifty years of service at St. Paul, he was made a Doctor of Music, *honoris causa*, by Catholic University. Since retiring from the choir school, Dr. Marier has been the Justine B. Ward Professor of Music there as well as Director of the Center for Ward Method Studies. He has completed several music textbooks and student workbooks for the Ward Method, the instructional system of rhythmical principles which are the foundation of the Choir School's choral music teaching program. John Dunn, Marier's successor as Music Director, first came to St. Paul's as a Harvard freshman in 1960. While still a student, he played organ for the weekly college Mass and taught part-time in the young choir school. He joined the faculty full-time upon graduation and was named principal a decade later.

After the parish school graduated its last class in 1974, the choir school remained as the sole occupant of the century-old school building. The unimproved condition of the structure was a trial to the choir program but not more so than their temporary moves to St. Joseph, Belmont, and Immaculate Conception, North Cambridge, while their new facility on Mt. Auburn Street was erected. During this transitional period, Music Director and Principal John Dunn cited "the extraordinary support of students, faculty, parents, alumni, benefactors and friends." The space in the 1991 building was designed especially for the contemporary needs of the school.

St. Paul's Liturgy in 1960

As an innovator before Vatican Council II, St. Paul's did not go unnoticed. The parish's liturgical vigor was profiled in Worship, *March, 1960, in an article by Rev. William J. Leonard, S.J., the majority of which follows.*

Saint Paul's Church in Cambridge, Mass., stands a little out of Harvard Square, at the junction of Bow and Arrow Streets. The parish is steadily dwindling in numbers. Harvard's expansion means that more and more land becomes part of the campus, and what is left becomes apartment houses or shops to serve the large academic community. The solidly Irish segment of the parish is increasingly replaced by Negroes, few of whom are Catholics. During the college year, between five hundred and a thousand students assist at Mass. There are some fifty-two hundred souls in all. The parish school in 1946 had some six hundred children; now there are only three hundred and twenty-five.

Thirteen sisters make up the teaching staff, where formerly there were twenty-one.

Since 1925 the pastor of St. Paul's has been the Rt. Rev. Augustine F. Hickey, the vicar general of the archdiocese and for many years previously superintendent of schools. In 1956 Msgr. Hickey celebrated the golden jubilee of his priesthood. His student days in the North American College in Rome are among his dearest memories, and he feels that the influence of St. Pius X, who was pope then, has been very strong in his own life; he tells of going to hear him speak to the people on Sunday afternoons, of listening to the white-clad figure talking about the Good Shepherd on Good Shepherd Sunday.

St. Paul's has always been distinguished for the dignity of its worship; its music director, Mr. Joseph Ecker, was an accomplished musician and a gifted choirmaster. Solemn Mass on Sundays and feasts drew people from great distances, and the parishioners took pride in the reputation of their choir. The liturgy, so far as the priests were concerned, was carried out, as the Monsignor always insisted, "with reverence, punctuality, and concern."

For thirty-five years the Sunday Mass has been the center of parish life, the important act of the parish week. The daily seven o'clock Mass, celebrated by the pastor, has always been the Mass of the day, and requests for Requiems have never been allowed to interfere with this rule.

The 1990 handbell choir, using a four octave set donated by the Fratic family.

Congregational participation in the sung liturgy is fortified by the strong St. Paul adult choir, pictured here in 1991 with John Dunn at the organ.

Children Trained in Participation

The children of the parish school have always sung one of the Masses on holydays in the chant. They have always been urged, too, to bring with them to Mass the same edition of the missal, and Monsignor has himself been present at their Mass to instruct them in its meaning. In this way he anticipated long ago the present function of the "commentator" (in the best sense of that term), indicating unobtrusively the proper page in the missal and giving occasional one-sentence explanations of a rite or a prayer. To inculcate the idea that religion is a seven-days-a-week concern, he announces each Sunday the feasts that will be celebrated during that week.

For many years he gave lectures to his Sisters so that they could better instruct the children in these basic ideas. "Bring the people to God," he says, "by the means that God has given us." The Sisters (of the Boston Sisters of St. Joseph) have cooperated magnificently, teaching the children the pronunciation and meaning of the responses and the ordinary, helping with the training of the boys' choir, encouraging the congregation by their presence and their singing of the Mass on Sunday. In their own convent the daily Mass is always a dialogue Mass in the "fourth degree."

The program of the people's participation in the liturgy which has distinguished St. Paul's grew out of this steady indoctrination. The pastor came to see how life naturally expresses itself in outward action; the people realized that participation is a logical corollary of their share in the priesthood of Christ. In this way the rapport and sympathy necessary before changing lifelong habits of piety was established.

When he went on retreat in 1948, Monsignor took along the recently published encyclical of Pope Pius XII, *Mediator Dei*. He says that it provided the last rung of the ladder he had been building. "I see," he said when he came home, "It's simple. The liturgy makes present now what Christ did then." The National Liturgical Week was held in Boston that summer, and Monsignor took an active part in it, but the program he initiated at St. Paul's derived its inspiration and development rather from the encyclical and from a half-century of prayer, reading, and experience than from that Week.

From the beginning he was fortunate to have as his assistant Fr. Joseph I. Collins, a returned Army chaplain and a convinced advocate of liturgy for the people, whose sympathy, good humor, and priestliness have given him unfailing support. Monsignor feels that he has, in fact, been greatly blessed in his assistants. "Every one of them," he says, "takes his priesthood seriously. And don't forget that two of them are silver jubilarians."

Importance of Choir Director

He was fortunate again in being able to engage as choirmaster Mr. Theodore Marier, the eminent organist, choral director, composer, and professor of music. Mr. Marier brought to his work a contagious enthusiasm for the music of the Church, an authority which only professionals can have, and a disposition for the same hard work which he asked of his singers as their share in the praise of God. The choirs of St. Paul's do not give concerts in church; they pray. And they help the people to pray.

For twelve years now the high Mass on Sundays has been a community-sung Mass. At first the people were shy and diffident, or even discontented that they could not listened passively to the "gorgeous" music from the choir-loft; they found the effort of raising their voices a strange and unpleasant one. But Mr. Marier persisted, never dominating or berating, always leading and encouraging. Now more than two-thirds of the congregation sings the ordinary of the Mass, without self-consciousness and with growing ease and pleasure.

This is the more noteworthy in view of the fact that the congregation changes so much; students take their degrees and leave, apartment-dwellers find more permanent homes elsewhere. Some of the best singers in the choir have left, too, but Mr. Marier does not regret them; they have gone into religious life and seminaries, and one of them, now Fr. Gabriel of the Trappist Monastery in Spencer, Mass., directs what many consider the outstanding monastic choir in the country.

This spring St. Paul's will install a new organ console in the transept, on the floor of the church. The new position will enable the director to lead the community's singing, not just the choir's. At Liturgical Week last summer, in the seminar for architects, Mr. Marier read a paper on the placement of the organ in the church. This paper, with illustrations, will appear in *Liturgical Arts* shortly, and will offer suggestions as to how a liturgically-minded pastor can renovate his church so as to make community singing easier and more unified.

Monsignor has a few points on which he feels very strongly. At Christmas, for instance, no one in the school mentions Santa Claus, or there is trouble. No one at any time refers to the complex of church, school, rectory, and convent as a "plant"—or at least he does not do so twice. "We

have plenty of administrators today; what we need is more priests." No one "plugs" the collection; talk of money in or out of church distresses the pastor. Once a year a formal statement is read; a collection is taken up monthly and at Christmas with the terse request, "please give as generously as your means permit." "And," says Monsignor, "there is no financial problem."

Serving the Parishioners

St. Paul's held to the old custom of a Lenten course of sermons until evening Mass was permitted. Now there is Mass at 5:30, with a fifteen-minute sermon on the meaning of Lent and Holy Week. Evening Mass is also offered on holy days, and on Lenten Fridays there are stations of the cross. There is a triduum every year in preparation for the feasts of the Immaculate Conception and of the Sacred Heart, but no novenas. Each autumn, for four weeks, there is a parish visitation, followed by a two-week "mission." Confessions are heard not only at the usual time on Saturday but also every morning during the seven o'clock Mass and on Friday evenings before the Holy Hour. Evening prayers are said during May, October, and November.

There are sixteen parish societies, not counting the ushers and the altar boys and the choirs, and they range from the Holy Name Society to the Boy Scouts and the Book Club and the Confraternity of Christian Doctrine. There is a very active St. Vincent de Paul Society to care for the many poor in the parish, and it is characteristic that Monsignor has always been its chaplain, just as he does much of the day-to-day welfare work himself.

The Harvard students who are Catholics have their own chaplain, Fr. William Porras of Opus Dei, but many come also to St. Paul's, and at eight o'clock on Saturday mornings they assist at a dialogue Mass with "fourth degree" partici-

pation. One of the students reads the epistle, another the gospel. Last year, on the feast of St. Thomas Aquinas, there was an afternoon Mass for the academic community sung by Msgr. Timothy O'Leary, archdiocesan superintendent of schools. His Eminence Cardinal Cushing presided and preached.

St. Paul's parish dates from 1875. Its traditions are not only long but deeply ingrained. Its children are few, and (aside from the transient student population) its people are mature and settled in their devotional habits. For all these reasons the pastor feels that he must initiate changes slowly and only after careful and repeated explanations.

In the years before the Instruction of September 1958, for instance, he requested permission for dialogue Mass one day a week. Gradually he asked and received permission to have it more often. He believes firmly that the people must thoroughly understand the necessity of interior participation and how this is expressed and assisted by exterior participation.

To the impatient he points out the progress already achieved, the slow but steady acceptance not only of recitation and singing but of the indispensable attitudes that will prevent exterior participation from being a novelty or a fad. By no other procedure, he feels, can he fulfill his office as good Shepherd of all his flock.

When people comment on what they see at St. Paul's, Monsignor deprecates his accomplishment. "There is nothing unusual here," he says. "We simply try to do the ordinary things ordinarily well." To which one visitor replied some years ago, "But this is extraordinary!" And it is. But so is Monsignor. And so are all those who are helping him, under God, to bring St. Paul's "mystery" to fulfillment.

Mother Theresa and John Kenneth Galbraith, former Ambassador to India, compared statures at the 1982 Harvard Commencement.

The University Community: Catholics at Harvard

"A young man in Cambridge is completely his own master and he can with effort practice his religion there happily—if he does not lose his faith!"
Bishop Cheverus of Boston, 1821.

Harvard Square is a company town, dominated in name and history by the college founded there in the seventeenth century. Although the Catholic face of the area was provided by resident families in the nineteenth and early twentieth centuries, it is now students and scholars of the university who comprise the majority of local Catholics. This chapter traces that growth and the underestimated story of the individuals who made it happen.

Early Harvard College proudly recognized herself as the first Protestant school in the New World. Two centuries later, when Phillips Brooks and Andrew Peabody conspired in 1886 to abolish mandatory daily chapel, the college garnered the nickname "Godless Harvard" from her own alumni. Whether first as Protestant or later as secular, Harvard serves well as an example of the intellectual America set apart from Catholicism and provides the longest case study of Catholic-Protestant institutional relations in this country.[1]

The story has an unhappy start, but from Revolutionary times onward Catholics and Harvard have found more contact and more collaboration with practically every decade. Nineteenth century ties are mostly the comings of Catholic gentry and the goings of Harvard converts, but they established social bonds of trust and respect which allowed a wider circle of Harvard Catholics. From the first burst of Irish at Harvard in the 1870's until the present, there has been a steady increase in the percentage of Catholics at Harvard until it now approximates the national average.

It should be said in the beginning that quotas and discrimination by Harvard are not significant issues. Harvard Catholics never encountered college limitations like those created to solve the "Jewish problem" of the 1920's, because they faced a greater limitation from another quarter, the Catholic Church.

From the time the Church first noticed Harvard, admittedly late, for every anti-Catholic comment can be found twice as many anti-Harvard ones. Thus, unlike Jewish students, Catholics have always been proportionately underrepresented at Harvard and accordingly never presented a threat or appearance of invasion.

Already, it should be obvious that this is a study of ecumenism on the social rather than theological level. True, we begin with a colonial Massachusetts so free from heterodox subjects that we learn of Catholicism at early Harvard principally through its differences from Puritanism. Equally true, the climax of our study is the extraordinary Roman Catholic-Protestant Colloquium in March, 1963. But the intervening history relates thousands of students and alumni who studied and lived together with little concern for the old Harvard as seminary. Indeed the 1963 Colloquium came about as a result of the good relations of President Pusey with Harvard Catholic alumni like Chauncey Stillman. The impetus was longstanding; the opportunity was a tardy step in tolerance and outreach by the Catholic Church—in this case the enthusiasm of Vatican Council II.

Accordingly, a recurrent theme in Harvard-Catholic relations is the comparatively greater suspicion shown by the Catholic Church and its relative slowness to acknowledge a dialogue with Protestants. The irony of the Unitarian revolution at Harvard is that as Harvard became less Trinitarian and even less Catholic doctrinally, it adopted a tolerance or perhaps indifference to religion which allowed it to disregard religious boundaries. Perhaps the asynchronism also arises from a basic metabolic difference between Harvard and the Catholic Church. Those who built the New Jerusalem along the Charles have always been susceptible to the lure of progress and their Victorian heirs were completely infected with it; the Church of Rome, however, has long pursued its race with the "slow and steady" philosophy and the archdiocese of Boston has been particularly Roman in this regard.

To be specific, Brahmins may not have cared for the Irish, and Unitarians may not have thrilled to Catholicism, but the intellectual caste discarded its prejudices more quickly than its contemporaries did. Under Eliot, merit became the order of the day, thriving in fact under the new religion of progress, which it was presumed would soon supersede previous faiths. But the Catholic view of Protestantism did not mellow so quickly. Commuters, safeguarded by parents and parish, set the first examples in number. Then, the faithful lives of Catholic alumni opened a wider breach in the charge of "Godless Harvard." William Cardinal O'Connor never acknowledged this new understanding, but by his death in 1944, Catholics composed 10% of the undergraduate population and would soon be more. By the end of the next generation, Catholics at Harvard would not be an issue.

Puritans and Papists

Although more vehement in their disagreement and the gravity of their differences, the Puritans who founded Harvard were perhaps still closer in spirit to their Catholic contemporaries than are their Unitarian descendants today. "Calvin, of course, was read; but he enjoyed no greater repute among New England divinity students than many another theologian, including St. Thomas Aquinas," says Harvard historian Samuel Eliot Morison. In the 400 volumes of John Harvard's library are found seventeen volumes of Aquinas, four of Cardinal Robert Bellarmine, and seven commentaries by another Jesuit theologian, Cornelius à Lapide. The Catalogue of 1723 "fairly bristles with commentaries on Aquinas" as well as earlier donations of works by various Jesuits and Cardinal Baronius.[2]

Awareness of Catholics, debt to Catholic scholarship, respect for Catholic universities—these considerations present some counterweight to the standard image, but it would be deceptive to imply that polite competition existed among seventeenth century sects. Even before leaving their homeland, the Puritans clearly stated that the new settlement would "raise a bulwark against the Kingdome of Anti-Christ which the Jesuits labor to rear up in all parts of the world."[3]

The Jesuit assistance to the Indians of Maine was always regarded as hostile by the expansionist colonists of Massachusetts, but the 1690's were a particularly embattled decade of warfare and frontier raids by the French and Indians. Simultaneously, Catholics supporting the Stuarts were suspect for their political ambitions in Britain. It is not surprising that in this period we see the first assaults on Roman Catholicism in the addresses of graduating Harvard students. The following *quaestiones* were defended or opposed at Commencement by candidates for the Master's degree:[4]

> 1695: *An Pontifex Romanus sit Ille Antichristus, Quem futurum Scriptura praedixit? Affirmat Respondens Caleb Cushing.* ("Whether the Pope is the Antichrist which scripture predicted?" Caleb Cushing answers affirmatively.)
> 1697: *An Jesuitae possint esse Boni Subditi? Negat Respondens Adamus Winthrop.* ("Whether Jesuits can be good Subjects?" Adam Winthrop answers negatively).
> 1698: *An Ecclesia Romana Hodierna sit vera Christi Ecclesia? Negat Respondens Simon Willard.* ("Whether the modern Church of Rome is the true Church of Christ?" Simon Willard answers negatively.)

In this decade, and perhaps in these exercises, we see the nadir of Catholic approval at Harvard. With the passing of the Mathers from Cambridge and the Puritan successes in Maine these topics lost urgency and hence frequency.

In 1757, Judge Paul Dudley bequeathed an endowment for a lecture on Anti-Popery every four years. Yet the sophisticated tenor of even these addresses shows a moderation that would have been unfashionable in earlier days. In one of the first lectures, Samuel Mather told his youthful audience to aspire to a love of God and a hatred of popery, "not indeed to a *childish* or blind or *bigotted one*; but to an understanding and rational Hatred of it."

On the eve of the Revolutionary War, this picture of anti-Catholicism was generally still accurate, and there was little suggestion of the dramatic changes soon to come. The hostile French were still consorting with the Indians and any alternative exposure to Catholicism was rare; any Catholic Scotsmen or Irishmen sold as servants in New England had quickly lost their religion in the void. As John Adams wrote in 1765, Roman Catholics are "as scarce as a comet or an earthquake."[5]

Bishop Cheverus and the Unitarians

As a consequence of the colonists' revolution, two groups of Catholics became familiar to educated Bostonians: the French and Maryland gentry. The French were no longer the insidious allies of the hostile Indians but supporters of the cause for independence; Maryland Catholics like Charles and Daniel Carroll were now patriots and moreover the priest John Carroll was even an official emissary of the colonists. Pennsylvania had also sent a Catholic, Thomas Fitzsimons, to the Continental Congress and John Adams had even attended a service at a Catholic Church in Philadelphia. The struggle for independence introduced New England not only to able and helpful French Catholics but also to a different breed of Protestants, like George Washington, who were endowed with a tolerance that would soon become contagious.

In this interval we find the first Catholic recipient of a Harvard degree, Joseph Dupas de Valmais, the first Consul of France in Boston. His honorary degree in 1779 was followed by awards to the Minister Plenipotentiary of France to the United States and the young Marquis de Lafayette (LL.D. 1784). These gentlemen were supporters of the Revolution foremost and Catholic or anything else quite secondarily. As foreigners, they were curiosities rather than threats, but on this political concord developed an intellectual respect between the leading representatives of Harvard and of the Catholic Church, the Unitarian clergy and the French priest Cheverus respectively.

Soon after 1800, the universal religious tendency to distinguish "liberals" and "orthodox" began to divide New England Christianity. Already in the preceding century, proponents of "broad-minded" Christianity (and therefore opponents to a strict Calvinist creed) had termed themselves "liberals." Their more favorable view of human nature led them to a Christian humanism which rejected the traditional doctrine of the Trinity, hence the name "Unitarians." However great the theological

Gentle and learned, Bishop Cheverus respected his many Harvard friends but feared for the Catholic students there.

differences, the Unitarian victory and its subsequent tolerance were a great benefit to the nascent Catholic Church. At Harvard, students were required to attend services but on Sunday at least could choose their own church.

Although the Unitarian takeover of Harvard permitted a new religious tolerance, a particular tolerance toward Catholics would not have blossomed without the respect and affection engendered by the amazing Jean Lefebvre de Cheverus. A famous anecdote about Cheverus is told by Josiah Quincy of the Harvard class of 1821, and conveniently for our purposes it involves his father Josiah Quincy the future Mayor of Boston and President of Harvard. It happens on a day around 1800 when the elder Quincy was driving into Boston in a terrible downpour:

"When about five miles from his destination, he overtook a forlorn foot-passenger, who, drenched and draggled, was plodding along the miry road. My father drew up his horse, and called to the stranger to get in and ride with him. 'That would scarcely be fair,' was the man's reply. 'My clothes are soaked with water and would spoil the cushions of your chaise, to say nothing of the wetting I could not avoid giving you.' These objections were made light of, and with some difficulty the wayfarer was persuaded to take the offered seat. During the ride my father learned that his companion was a priest, named Cheverus, who was walking from Hingham, whither he had been to perform some offices connected with his profession; and thus commenced the acquaintance, which afterward ripened into friendship, between men whose beliefs and ways of life were outwardly so different."

The younger Quincy ventures to conclude, "No person could have been better adapted to establish the Church of Rome in the city of the Puritans than the first bishop of Boston. The elevation of his character commanded the respect of the Protestant leaders of the place, and Channing confessed that no minister in the town would care to challenge a comparison between himself and this devoted priest."[6]

No less impressive was Cheverus' learning. He was a leading member of the Athenaeum and donated to it several dozen books (many of them explanations of Catholic teaching), more than any other single man except John Lowell.[7] There are few Harvard graduates of the period whom Cheverus had not known in some capacity or other. Nor did the bishop hide the affairs of his minority church from a possibly suspicious public. Indicative of the mutual respect which leading Catholics and Protestants shared are the circumstances of the effort of Fathers Matignon and Cheverus to raise money for a suitable Catholic Church in Boston (a chapel had previously been leased). The plans for the projected Church of the Holy Cross had been donated by Charles Bulfinch, class of 1781, architect of the State House. The subscription circulated in August 1800 was headed by a gift of $100 from John Adams, President of the United States, who thirty years before had condemned "the ridiculous fancies of sanctified effluvia from episcopal fingers." In the end, approximately one-fifth of the total came from Harvard Protestants like John Quincy Adams, John Lowell, Harrison Gray Otis, Joseph Coolidge, David Sears, Theodore Lyman and other Bostonians and local merchants. The entire town was welcomed at the Church's dedication and services for years to come.[8]

We even find a Catholic teaching at the college—an Alsatian priest no less. Fr. Francis Xavier Brosius had founded a school near Philadelphia, but in the fall of 1812 he came to Boston, perhaps as part of Cheverus' plan for a local school. He took on students and, since he was recommended by the much admired Cheverus, he was soon hired by Harvard. The Corporation records cite the desire "that those Scholars who are inclined to the study of the exact sciences may have facilities for extending their knowledge" beyond the limits of the curriculum and the time of the Hollis Professor or other instructors.[9] A month later, Cheverus wrote to Archbishop Carroll, "Mr. Brosius has been approved by the University of Cambridge as a Teacher of Mathematicks and he is going to reside near the College. He has now got 38 scholars who are to pay him 10 dollars per quarter."[10]

The status and importance of men like Cheverus and Brosius is easier to understand when one remembers how insular Boston (and her educational elite) had been. Indeed Harvard's humble state is shown by the appointment of Edward Everett, later Governor

The 1803 Cathedral of the Holy Cross, designed by Bulfinch, was the only Catholic Church in the Boston area while John Lee was at Harvard.

but then barely out of college, to the first Professorship of Greek and his subsequent decision to go abroad to educate himself appropriately. Accordingly, when Everett went abroad he received a formal Latin letter of introduction from Bishop Cheverus to faculty at the University of Paris and to the members of the Bishop's family.[11]

Mutual respect and goodwill did not mean theological unanimity. As the Unitarians moved further from orthodox Christianity, their gap with Rome widened even more. Ironically, but in circumstances hardly unique, Cheverus was closer in faith to the Congregationalists that he was to his friends the academic Unitarians. His convictions were always clear and Protestants regretted that, despite his virtues, Cheverus was not of their church. The fundamental differences between Catholicism and the faiths of Boston never eluded him. Reporting to Rome in February, 1817, he concluded sadly, "The Socinian heresy has many followers here, under the name of Unitarians, among the Protestant ministers, in the University of Cambridge, etc. A large number of the inhabitants both live and alas, die also, without baptism."[12] Into this University, amidst friendly scholars with heretical doctrines, came the first generation of Harvard Catholics.

The First Catholic Student: John Lee

When John Lee, son of the Governor of Maryland, came to Boston in 1804, there was a certain trepidation in some quarters. On the day Lee arrived, Fr. Matignon, who with Fr. Cheverus comprised the Catholic clergy of Boston, wrote back to Bishop John Carroll of Baltimore, offering every service but expressing his fears about the "influence which might be had on Lee's piety and perhaps even his religion by his residence in Cambridge and the puritanical spirit of the teachers and the philosophical spirit of the students. I implore his dear parents in all their letters to unite their efforts to my own feeble attempts to preserve him from what I see as a dangerous contagion."[13]

His family's fear that it would be difficult for him to maintain the obligations of his faith proved somewhat justified. Daily chapel at Harvard was not such a problem; he could easily afford the per diem fines he accumulated for missing prayers (an occasional lapse of most students, but John Lee's

In 1813, John Kirkland, the Unitarian President of Harvard, broke with most of his Dudleian predecessors by denying that the Pope was the biblical "Man of Sin".

$1.11 per term surpassed his classmates by far). However, arranging travel to the Catholic church must have been a problem in a college where other students were punished for unnecessary riding on the Lord's Day. A student could forego the college Sunday services only if he attended his own church instead, which was difficult for a Catholic. Accordingly, the following March the President and Fellows voted that "the request of Mr. Lee, father of Lee a member of the Junior Class, that his son who has been admitted in the Roman Catholic religion may be permitted to attend public worship at the Episcopal Church in Cambridge be granted." This has often been misinterpreted to imply that John Lee converted, when in fact it only recognizes that Christ Church (Episcopal), across the Cambridge Common, was the most convenient alternative to the Catholic Church of the Holy Cross in Boston. Since Gov. Lee had been an Anglican before his marriage, the services of that church would be familiar. There is no reason to think that Lee, much less his father, suffered a change in faith while in Cambridge.[14]

The faculty's fear was somewhat different, for he had been accruing fines for missing lectures and recitations as well. A year after his entrance it is recorded that "Lee, a member of the junior class, notwithstanding that previous measures had been adopted to reclaim him from habits of idleness and neglect of duty, had been still more negligent, than at any preceding time." He was suspended for several months, but it seems he absented himself before the sentence could take effect and it is not clear if he returned.[15] John Lee was not listed as graduating with the other members of the class of 1808, and it would appear that he only spent the one year there.

Without a Harvard degree, John Lee nevertheless managed to live a long and happy life: he married the granddaughter of Charles Carroll the signer of the Declaration of Independence, served a few terms in Congress, and was known as someone acquainted with the nation's capital from General Washington until General Grant. If there are doubts about his religion, his younger son, Msgr. Thomas Sim Lee, was secretary to the Archbishop of Baltimore and later erected St. Matthew's Church, now the Washington Cathedral.[16] His grandchildren by his older son, Thomas Sim Lee and James Parrish Lee, were both in the class of 1891, where the latter was a football hero. His sons in turn were also Harvard graduates, Charles Carroll Lee, S.B. 1923 and James Parrish Lee, A.B. 1934. So continues the oldest dynasty of Harvard Catholics.

"Children Thrown into the Furnace"

For the Maryland gentry, a few years of study in Boston could be a convenient opportunity to send sons away, and certainly more convenient than studying at the Jesuit schools in France or Belgium had been for John Carroll and his generation. As Samuel Eliot Morison describes, "They were not 'the typical Harvard men' of their period. The College was largely composed of boys from New England families of middling fortune, and the swells were outnumbered by horny-handed lads from the country districts."[17]

Although "being found deficient in the knowledge of Greek," two Carroll cousins were admitted to the Sophomore class in February 1821, with the instruction to correct that deficit at the end of the summer. As with John Lee, the Church and the Faculty were as concerned with pious conduct as with academic progress. The faculty records note they were "to be directed by the President respecting their attendance on public worship," which suggests some allowance was made for them to attend Catholic ceremonies when possible.[18] Permission to attend the Catholic Church hardly guaranteed that they would do so, as a letter of Cheverus to Archbishop Maréchal of Baltimore makes clear:[19]

I would like to write to the father of young Mitchell [another Marylander] but I don't know what to tell him. I have not seen his son since July 2, when he came to borrow $10 from me: he told me that he was expecting money from home. I am his guarantor to the University for $400, and if I have to make any advances at the moment, I shall be much embarrassed. This poor young man never comes to church, etc. I do not know if he will acquire any other knowledge, but I very much fear that he will lose, or has already lost, the knowledge of his salvation. I always received him and treated him with the greatest kindness.

Six months later, Mitchell had at least come to confession but Cheverus was continuing to act as his banker. Since the Carroll cousins were soon coming north, he recommended that their parents establish accounts with a local bank. He added a warning reminiscent of Matignon's fears fifteen years earlier: "Only a miracle can protect the faith of the dear young people in Cambridge. Assure Mr. Carroll and Mr. Harper in presenting my regards that their young people can count on my friendship and my efforts that they remain faithful to their religion. They will be the children in the furnace of dissipation and socianianism or rather deism."[20]

Although Cheverus characteristically referred to them as "children thrown into the furnace," he nevertheless was as attentive as he could be to the spiritual and general well-being of these first Catholics at Harvard: "I always receive them and will receive them with pleasure, but I can only give them the counsels of friendship. I doubt that Mr. Harper has come to church a single time. He has made two or three visits. Mr. Carroll has come three or four Sundays to church and stayed twice to

Rev. George F. Haskins '26, convert and founder of the House of the Angel Guardian, America's first 'Boys Town'.

dine with me. He was there the second Sunday of Lent." In perhaps the timeless description of Catholics at Harvard, he concludes: "A young man in Cambridge is completely his own master and he can with effort practice his religion there happily, if he does not lose his faith!"[21]

In the same period another unlikely Catholic lineage developed at Harvard: the Bonapartes. On a visit to America, Jerome Bonaparte, youngest brother of the Emperor Napoleon I, met and married Elizabeth Patterson of Baltimore despite the opposition of both families. He became King of Westphalia (1803-17), led a division at Waterloo, and by a second (non-canonical) marriage sired the imperial line of Bonapartes. But born to his American wife was a single son, Jerome Napoleon Bonaparte II, of the Harvard class of 1826, from whom the American Bonapartes descend.

Not unlike the Baltimoreans before him, Jerome Napoleon Bonaparte II was once put on special probation for "an act of irregularity," was once admonished for festive entertainment and was later suspended for the same, but eventually restored to his class.[22] This social life was probably not unrelated to his role as Deputy Marshall and Secretary of the Porcellian Club, to which most Maryland Catholics belonged. His elder son, Jerome Napoleon Bonaparte III, was once admonished for holding a cock-fight in his room and only stayed a year before transferring to West Point. The most distinguished student of the family, the much younger son Charles Joseph Bonaparte '71, became Secretary of the Navy and Attorney-General under Theodore Roosevelt.

The stories of the Maryland gentry provide a very useful paradigm. Despite great concern from the clergy, a young man ventures into the curious terrain of Cambridge, survives the snares and emerges a figure prominent in Catholic circles and a friend of non-Catholics. There is a lesson in historiography here as well. The myth of John Lee's conversion arises from a later desire to simplify nineteenth century Boston into the separate worlds of Brahmin and Irishman. The hopeful Federalist world of Bishop Cheverus and the Carrolls was dramatically altered by Catholic immigration but it did not vanish without fruit.

Rather than lapsed faith or incompatibility, from this first generation of Catholics at Harvard sprang other generations of Catholics at Harvard. Not from a vacuum came turn-of-the-century figures like Charles Joseph Bonaparte (a Catholic Overseer of Harvard University and a Harvardian trustee of Catholic University) and James Parrish Lee (a founder of the St. Paul's Catholic Club). The descendants of John Lee, Charles Carroll and Jerome Bonaparte would continue to merge Harvard and Catholicism into the twentieth century.

Official Harvard Tolerance

Although the Great Famine of 1845-47 is famous for boosting immigration, for thirty years before that debacle frustrated Irish tenants had been coming to America in substantial numbers. When the Maryland Jesuit Benedict Fenwick replaced Cheverus as Bishop of Boston in 1825, the city's composition was already changing. Fenwick inherited four thousand Bostonians to care for, but five years later that number had doubled. Neither Anglo-Saxon Boston nor its small Catholic community was

THE DUDLEIAN LECTURES

The first regular attention to the problem of Catholicism appeared at Harvard through the beneficence of Paul Dudley (1675-1751), Chief Justice of the Superior Court, whose will endowed four lectures rotating annually on a variety of topics including Anti-Popery:[23]

> The Third Lecture to be for the detecting and convicting and exposing of the idolatry of the Romish Church, their tyranny, usurpations, damnable heresies, fatal errors, abominable superstitions, and other crying wickednesses in their high places, and finally that the Church of Rome is that mystical Babylon, that Man of Sin, that apostate Church spoken of, in the New Testament.

Typically these lectures made broad assaults on the doctrines and practices of Roman Catholicism: transubstantiation, remembrance of the saints, idolatry, zealous worship of Mary, auricular confession, worship in Latin, and opposition to scripture. Rome was variously the biblical "filthy prostitute," "the mother of harlots," "the Man of Sin," "an empire of despotism more *false, sanguinary, and destructive to* [God's] creatures, than any superstition and idolatry before existing," "formidable monster," and "the substance of Paganization under the accidents of Christianity." Scripture and common sense proved all this.

In some ways, we are fortunate to have this series of often vicious addresses by distinguished scholars as a convenient bellwether of softening Harvard attitudes to Catholicism. Among the speakers were Presidents Wigglesworth, Willard, and Kirkland, and almost all were graduates of the college. Although no single speech could be said to speak for the faculty or overseers, in total they exhibit a progression of topical themes.

Colonial diatribes against the peculiarities of Catholic theology yield at the time of the Revolution. When the French are no longer seen as enemies in league with the Indians but as allies of the Independence movement, the shift in perspective leads to a more tolerant consideration of their religion. Unitarianism triumphs at Harvard in the early 1800's and ushers in an age, lasting until the present, in which Harvard is increasingly less religious and so less concerned with differences in religion. The Dudleian lecturers of the nineteenth century still think Catholicism folly but they are cooler in their criticisms, less interested in theological particulars, and more worried by the general disposition of Catholicism to the enterprise of America. The ultraconservativism and the organizational intensity of the Church of Rome were the dangerous baggage brought by ever larger numbers of immigrants.

In some sense, the Dudleian lectures always had a political angle to them. The vision of a despotic Pope epitomized might, both concentrated and abused. The institutional structures and power of European Catholicism were its most threatening features—how else would men believe such nonsense?—and the potential exercise of that power near New England was the foremost threat. At first the threat was external and French neighbors were the obvious agents, but eventually immigration allowed the danger to become internal.

From the 1850s to 1891 the entire series of lectures was omitted as the principal of the Dudleian fund was allowed to accumulate. The difference in climate when the series resumed is seen from the invitation to a Jewish rabbi to speak on natural religion in 1888 and to Bishop Keane, the president of Catholic University, to deliver the lecture on revealed religion in 1890. There was even discussion of foregoing the third lecture, and the lecturers themselves usually noted the change in times since the endowment. After 1909 the lecture on anti-popery was dropped, although after an interval the third lecture has been resumed under the description "(3) Catholicism and Protestantism." In 1984, Robert McAfee Brown spoke on "Protestant Catholicism: Our Ecumenical Legacy."

prepared for the ever increasing immigration. Occasionally, the strains showed, violence broke out, and suspicions further increased.

Conservative nativists and populists disliked not only the new immigrants but also the increasingly liberal and aristocratic Harvard. At Harvard, the Congregationalists had been defeated during Kirkland's presidency, but they had not disappeared. Since the Commonwealth still supported Harvard financially, disgruntled religious conservatives periodically mounted attacks on Harvard's self-government. The Harvard Charter created two bodies, the Corporation and the Board of Overseers. The first, a self-perpetuating group of seven officially called "The President and Fellows of Harvard College," which met frequently and took charge of finances, personnel and immediate needs, was almost strictly Unitarian. The second, a large ratifying policy board composed at different times of alumni and community representatives, represented more diverse religious sentiments.[24]

In these political controversies, we occasionally learn about Harvard religious practices, *de jure* and *de facto*. In an 1831 letter to the governor, Harvard Fellow Francis Calley Gray is at pains to defend Harvard against the charge of strict Unitarianism—a charge asserted mostly by Trinitarian Congregationalists trying to limit state support. To refute the charge that only Unitarians were being appointed to College posts, Gray made a list of the College officers who had been appointed in the preceding ten years and sent to Cambridge to obtain information about their various sects. After considering the Professors of Law and Divinity, who receive nothing from state funds, and the President, Gray surveys the permanent officers of the College: "the Librarian, the Steward, the Janitor, the Professors of Chemistry, German, and Latin, three Tutors, the Instructors in French, in Italian, and in Elocution, the Curator of the Botanical Garden, and the assistant Steward, in all fourteen. Of these, I understand, that three are Catholics, that one is of the Evangelical Lutheran Creed, one a Calvinist, one a Sandemanian, that one attends the Episcopal Church, and one belongs to a family of Quakers; eight in the whole; and I suppose these sects to be Trinitarian. The other six, I am told, are Unitarians."[25]

The numerical importance of the un-named three Catholics can be quite misleading. Gray presumably refers to François Surault (Instructor in French, 1829-38), Pietro Bachi (Instructor in Italian, Spanish and Portuguese, 1826-46), and Francis Sales (Instructor in Spanish and French, 1816-54), but their status as political émigrés teaching their native tongues was marginal to college religion. Andrew Peabody summarized the elective nature of these subjects: "French and Spanish were voluntary studies, or rather recreations; for the recitation-room of the kind-hearted septuagenarian, who had these languages in charge, was frequented more for amusement than for any thing that was taught or learned. Italian and German were studied in good earnest by a very few volunteers." These instructors were not known to have played any visible role in

Students were required to attend daily prayers at Appleton Chapel until 1886 and were fined for absences.

*Irishman Francis
McGuire was studying
for the priesthood when
the famine hit. He came
to Boston in 1846 and
graduated from
Harvard in 1853.*

*Patrick Aloysius
O'Connell of Killarney
was one of the first Irish
immigrants to attend
Harvard. He took the
A.B. in 1857 and the
M.D. in 1861.*

the Catholic community.[26]

As to the religious opportunities of students, Gray explained, "It is objected that the preachers in the College Chapel are Unitarians—But then no student is required to hear them. Every one may attend any other church, which he or his parents shall prefer." Opponents objected, however, that the Episcopal church was the only other one permitted to them. That was the rule, he replies, but the practice has always been more lenient. "It is not a great many years, since there was a Jew in Harvard College, who was expressly permitted to pass Saturday with friends of his own faith in Boston, and to abstain from all Christian exercises on the following day. Catholics have been there also, and they were allowed to attend the Catholic Church in Boston, on Sundays, and on all other holydays, obligatory according to their religion, numerous as they are, and were excused from any attendance in College on those days."

The sincerity of Harvard's policy is confirmed, however, by the treatment given a Catholic who attended the college in the fall of 1845. Acting President James Walker wrote about this gentleman to Bishop Fitzpatrick, who was delighted to look after him. He obtained a seat at the Cathedral so the student "may attend services there as often as he may be so inclined." The bishop explained that "his attendance at Church will only be requisite in the forenoon on each Sunday morning, as far as can be done without any serious inconvenience."[27]

Religious differences mattered less, anyway, because Harvard was becoming secular—and rightly so, thought Gray, who faults the union of Church and State that once prevailed in Massachusetts: "The main business of the College in that day, was to teach Theology, one particular modification of Theology. In this enlightened age, a public education embraces the whole circle of the sciences and the liberal arts, and Theology forms only a very small part of it."[28] This widening gyre was already evident in the faculty, over a third of whom had attended professional schools, and an equal number had studied in Europe. While clergymen had once dominated the faculty, President Walker observed in 1855, "now as a general rule, a professor is as much a layman as a lawyer or a physician is."[29] No

clearer statement of the Unitarian educational policy than Gray's could be wanted. The New England intellectual was becoming a humanist, still Christian in tradition, but "enlightened" in philosophy and science.

Immigration and Immigrants

While the Corporation took a defensive posture for its Unitarianism in the public sphere, opinions expressed elsewhere within the college could be more aggressive. Our primary evidence continues to be the run of anti-popery Dudleian lectures from the 1820's to their pause in 1857. While still clearly disapproving of the basic tenets of Catholicism, in general they show little disrespect—rather learning and an awareness of Catholic counterarguments. This is not the place to measure subtle theological shifts among the speakers; however, these lectures provide some useful fodder for social history—especially the considerable comment about Catholic immigration.[30]

After several placid Unitarian lecturers, in 1825 the podium was taken over by the Congregationalist William Jenks, who noted the dangers of Jesuit missionaries on the American Frontier. He also tried to reverse the then current "disposition to view the errors of Rome as unimportant and trivial," as he revived Judge Dudley's insistence that the antichrist of Revelation was indeed the Pope. Jenks' rigor was an anomaly, however, as the Unitarian lecturers of 1829 and 1833 returned to a polite condescension towards the Church of Rome. By the first, the Harvard audience was told to throw "the mantle of *forgiveness*, if not *forgetfulness*" over the corruptions of the Romish religion; the second took a tack anticipating President Eliot's attitude sixty years later, that the chief problem of Catholicism lay in its opposition to man's progress and its failure to adapt to the needs of "an enlightened age."

Several of the next lecturers noted the astounding growth of Catholics in the nation. At the height of Know-Nothingism, George Burnap in 1853 certainly knew the impact of Catholic immigration. Poor Judge Dudley could have had no idea, Burnap felt sure, "that, before a century had elapsed, a steam ferry would be established between Europe and America, and that nations should emigrate almost in a mass, and transport Europe to America unchanged." Of course, immigrants were changed, but Burnap could hardly notice with his focus on the transformation of Dudley's native city. Who would have imagined "that a convent would rise within sight of the spires of Harvard, and a Catholic College be established in the very heart of Massachusetts!"—somewhat sensationalizing the building of the College of the Holy Cross in Worcester.[31]

The morality of immigrants was not just an abstract idea at Harvard. Starting with John Colman Crowley's entry in 1848, there was usually an Irishman or Irish-American at the college at any given time. Crowley, whose family was part of an earlier migration, was born in Boston in 1832, took preparatory courses at Holy Cross, then graduated from Harvard College in 1852 and from the Law School in 1857, two years before another local Catholic, Charles Francis Donnelly. He became President of the Catholic Union and of the Union Institution for Savings in the South End. A prominent lawyer of the day said, "When Mr. Crowley began practice in this city, he and Mr. Donnelly had all the Irish practice there was. With all this practice he ought to have been successful." Unfortunately, mismanagement and competition from younger Irish-Americans led Crowley to desperation. In 1887, he went to Europe and was discovered to have stolen everything from $75,000 of trust funds under his care, mostly widows, orphans and charitable institutions.[32]

Others in that first generation of Irish at Harvard were more responsible: Patrick Aloysius O'Connell '57 of Killarney, who also graduated from the Medical School, and Patrick McGuire '53 of County Fermanagh. McGuire had studied for the priesthood in Ireland, but in 1846, to quote his own words, "when Ireland was visited by famine, when all her hopes as well as all her resources had been blasted, he resolved to come to America, to leave the old home—parents and relations—all that was dear to the heart, and seek forture in a land more blessed, where the withering blast of oppression would not blight the young hopes." After two years of printing work in Boston and tutelage in Cambridge, he entered Harvard in 1849, where he lived as a servant in a students' boarding house. With the help

"Bishop John," as Fitzpatrick was called, received an honorary degree from Harvard in 1861.

of local clergy, he continued to study theology, but the niece of a local priest turned his thoughts to medicine, which he practiced until his early death in 1861.[33]

The Dudleian Lectures did not necessarily represent the faculty viewpoints, but they demonstrated the range of Harvard responses to the new Catholic presence within college and without: some optimism, some pessimism, but general concern about the Catholic challenge. Twenty years would pass before tensions eased sufficiently to enable President Eliot to set an independent course and speed the transformation of the overgrown college into a national university.

Harvard and Bishop Fitzpatrick

During those decades prior to the Civil War, one man was principally responsible for establishing relations between Catholics and the college. John Fitzpatrick, the Boston-born son of an immigrant tailor, typified the best of mid-century relations with Protestants. A graduate of Boston Latin School, in the company of classmates with names like Abbot and Cabot, he was comfortable with Yankees. When Fitzpatrick returned from the seminary in Montreal in 1837, where he had begun teaching philosophy and theology at age twenty, his reputation was such that he was introduced with great flattery.

When Bishop Fenwick died in 1846, the coadjutor Fitzpatrick assumed control of the see. Two months later, the newly formed Thursday Evening Club invited the young bishop to become one of its first members. Here he regularly met such Harvard men as Francis Callay Gray (Fellow), Edward Everett (President), Theophilus Parsons (Dane Prof. of Law), Oliver Wendell Holmes (Dean of the Medical School), John Collins Warren (Hersey Professor of Anatomy), and George B. Emerson (former Tutor). A fascinating society given to learned entertainments and scientific demonstrations, the small Club also provided the casual intercourse which can address topics before they are public spectacles. Fitzpatrick's Catholicism seems never to have been a conspicuous issue, although he refrained from signing a testimonial commending a course of lectures given by Professor Louis Agassiz on Natural History and Theology "because of certain statements made by Agassiz concerning the origin of the human race."[34] There is no question that Fitzpatrick and the representatives of Harvard recognized each other's talents and shared a respect for reason and moderation in the common civic concerns of the next decades.

In May, 1861, the Harvard Corporation voted to confer on Fitzpatrick the honorary degree of Doctor of Divinity, the first such honor accorded any Catholic clergyman.[35] The Corporation minutes show that his name was suggested in 1860, perhaps due to whatever the bishop's influence might have been in helping the Harvard Corporation through the legislative assaults of the 1850's. By 1861, his leadership on behalf of the Union made him yet more praiseworthy. As the American Revolution had allowed colonial Catholics an opportunity to disprove the worst parodies of papism, so the Civil War gave the new Catholic immigrants their chance to fly American colors. Recognizing the significance of Harvard's first honorary degree to a "Roman Catholic Ecclesiastic," Amos A. Lawrence, the Treasurer of the Harvard Corporation explained, "this would not have been done were it not for the loyalty shown by him and by the Irish who have offered themselves freely for the army."[36] Clearly, the Harvard tribute recognized both Fitzpatrick's talents and the improving condition of his flock.

Bishop Fitzpatrick responded to the adulatory citation with reciprocal accord to the authorities at Harvard, "which undeniably represents the highest intellect and most enlightened sagacity in our community." He concludes his note with an extended personal metaphor to President Felton: "It seems to me hardly probable that whatever faint light of learning, wisdom or merit may glimmer around the Bishop of Boston in his sphere, could have been of itself discernible from the height of the moral observatory of Cambridge. It must be that President Felton, guided by some partial fondness, directed towards the spot a telescope of no small Power. But even so, I can assure you that your friendship and esteem are a possession of which I feel proud and which I shall always value in the highest degree."[37]

The next year, Fitzpatrick was elected a colleague of Longfellow and James Russell Lowell in the Literature and Fine Arts section of the American Academy of Arts and Sciences. His nominating proposal was led by former Harvard Presidents James Walker and Jared Sparks, and three other Harvard Unitarians. The Academy's records include a typically flattering biographical sketch by Robert C. Winthrop, describing the bishop as a man of "peculiar tact and sterling common-sense, of rare accomplishments, of a noble presence; without anything of presumption or ostentation, yet of striking dignity."[38]

Fitzpatrick, like Cheverus and Fenwick before him, impressed Harvard as a learned man and proved a living refutation to the lampooned stereotype of the manipulative Romish priest. On the other hand, he also set an example for his flock that Harvard was not off limits to Catholics. Nevertheless Harvard and Catholicism—and their respective constituencies Brahmin and Irishman—were understood to be polar opposites, as an uneventful episode reveals. When the legislature was debating the use of particular prayers in the public schools, one state senator attempted to resolve the whole question by having the Bishop elected to the Board of Overseers of Harvard College, thus proving the general good will towards the Catholic Church. The senate approved the bill, but Bishop Fitzpatrick had the bill withdrawn before the house did likewise.[39] In both cases, Harvard College, the city's pearl of great price, was imagined as the natural prize Boston Catholics sought. Although the bishops fostered Catholic colleges to prove this vision false, the laity would soon succumb. As the Irish assimilated and climbed into power, they inevitably measured their heights by the local hills, and Harvard was one of those.

While Harvard and the Catholic Church were building mutual policies of tolerance as institutions, official policies would have been meaningless without the actions of individuals whose lives built the bridge that thousands now travel.

The Contributions of Individuals: Harvard Converts

"Our beloved land is threatened with serious evil from the inroads of the papal church," Edwards Amasa Parks had warned Harvard students in his 1845 Dudleian lecture. He was concerned about the political dangers of the uneducated Irish, but he also had hope: "I am no alarmist. I have strong confidence in the Protestant mind. It will at last prevail over Papal discipline."[40]

While the fears of clergy like Cheverus kept Catholics away from Harvard, so voices like Parks' were supposed to protect Harvard students from Catholicism. A host of converts and the 2500 Catholic students at Harvard today prove that in the end neither succeeded. In fact, these barriers were very soon breached. In the early 1800's when, as we have seen, occasional Catholics were already risking their souls by heading to Cambridge, so likewise did occasional Harvard students and alumni make the dangerous spiritual journey to Rome.

The first Harvard convert of sorts was **Dr. Stephen Cleveland Blyth**, who entered the college in the class of 1790 but did not finish the degree program. Like most students in that restrictive environment, even in his brief stay he was disciplined for absence from recitations and prayers.[41] He converted in 1809 and later published a narrative of his spiritual journey to Rome.

Another of the first Harvard conversions came about through little more than auditory exposure to the good bishop. After returning to Maine from Harvard Medical

Rev. Joseph Coolidge Shaw, '40, preached the sermon at the cornerstone laying of St. Peter's, the first Catholic church in Old Cambridge.

School in 1819, **Dr. Henry Bowen Clarke Greene** wrote to a Boston priest about the Catholic faith: "Educated a Protestant I can have no prejudices in its favor from education but (as part of my education was acquired in Boston) I have listened with admiration to the eloquence of Bishop Cheverus, I have loved the benevolence of his character, and have concluded that the religion can not be corrupt in its principles whose professors are so exemplary."[42]

Bishop Fenwick recognized Greene as a valuable asset—an educated Catholic lay leader—and encouraged him to move to Boston. Greene lived up to every expectation. In addition to his medical work, his Harvard education and contacts made him a respected and popular lecturer among Catholics and non-Catholics. In the fall of 1840 he became the first Catholic elected to the Massachusetts General Court. He served four consecutive terms until his death in 1848. Each year he gathered the support of leading non-Catholics to compensate the Ursuline Nuns for the destruction of their Charlestown convent. His son of the same name followed Dr. Greene's

Brahmin convert Rev. E. Holker Welch, S.J., class of 1840, received so many other converts into the Church that he was called "receiver-general".

steps and received the M.D. in 1851 but also died young in 1862.

From the beginning of his ministry, **George Foxcroft Haskins** was devoted to homeless boys caught stealing food and plotting worse. That ministry was in the Episcopal Church from the time Haskins graduated from Harvard in 1826 (in the class of Bonaparte) until through his ministry to the poor, he met determined Catholic laity and a Roman priest. Ordained at St. Sulpice in Paris, he returned to Boston and served for thirty years in a number of Boston parishes. As a substitute he was also temporarily pastor of St. Peter's Parish in Cambridge, which then included Harvard College.

As a proper Bostonian and a wealthy one, Haskins was able to use his own resources to help the struggling Church. As a Catholic priest in 1858, he used his own money to buy three houses in North Square in Boston and started the House of the Angel Guardian, later moved to a large building in Jamaica Plain. In a time where little sympathy was had for the derelict children of Irish immigrants, Haskins'

personal standing no doubt also considerably aided the home for convicted boys. Highly successful, the school avoided corporal punishment and relied on regimented life rather than the rattan. The House of the Angel Guardian, which has been called America's first "Boys' Town," became a nationally known Catholic institution, partly through its publication, *The Orphan's Friend.* By the end of the century, the House had "sheltered, cared for and instructed 10,883 boys."[43]

Perhaps the major mid-century tension between Protestants and the new Catholics was public education, which throughout America used Protestant hymns, prayers and catechisms, as well as textbooks larded with derogatory references. Eventually public opinion shifted enough that in 1859 Fr. George Haskins was elected a member of the Boston School Committee.[44] It was extraordinary for Catholic clergy to run for office and Fr. Haskins may have been put forward because, as a Harvard Catholic, he had credentials from both sides. While a Harvard Brahmin could not *per se* achieve miracles—his Catholic orphanage was not approved originally—he was in a stronger political position than his confreres. The school debates continued, but this election was an important shift.

It should be less surprising than it often is that the most important benefactions to Boston College in the nineteenth century were by Harvard men—two of them Jesuits of the class of 1840. After graduating both a member of Phi Beta Kappa and the most popular man in his class, **Joseph Coolidge Shaw** studied and travelled in Europe. In Italy, the Boston Brahmin met the distinguished Fr. Frederick W. Faber, then still an Anglican but already enthusiastic about the "Holy Roman Church." Introduced by Faber to an English Jesuit in Rome, Shaw soon converted. His ordination in 1847 was attended by a full church of Protestants and brought great attention to him and Bishop Fitzpatrick. Fr. Shaw preached the sermon at the dedication of St. Peter's, the first Catholic church in Old Cambridge. A very gentle man, he was eulogized by many Protestants after his early death in 1850. He had just become a Jesuit and his legacy of 1,800 books (many of them collected in Germany and Rome) and $4,000 in cash for "establishing a school or college of the Society in Boston" was the benefaction on which Boston College was founded.[45]

Edward Holker Welch, travelling with his classmate Shaw, also came under Faber's influence, and eventually followed the same steps to Catholicism, Harvard Law School, and the Jesuits. His fifty years of ministry were mostly divided between the Church of the Immaculate Conception in Boston and Georgetown College. At the former, Welch was famous as a confessor and drew overflow crowds as a preacher—he also won the sobriquet "receiver-general" from the large number of conversions he witnessed. A model of Catholic eloquence, he offered a prayer at the inauguration of Hugh O'Brien as Mayor of Boston on January 4, 1886 and represented Boston College and the Archdiocese at Harvard's 250th anniversary in 1886.[46] His spiritual writings and unpublished sermons have recently been rediscovered, and many reprinted, for their "synthesis between the Ignatian and American cultures that eluded most of his contemporaries."[47] Welch died in 1905, leaving his share of his father's estate ($100,000) to Boston College, the largest legacy in its history at the time.

The 1840's not only saw the combined labors of Greene, Haskins, Shaw and Welch in Boston but also the full flourish of the Know-Nothing party. As natives with impeccable Yankee ancestries and Harvard friends, their very presence in the Catholic Church was a voice against the equation of Catholicism and the faults attributed to immigration.

A member of the class of 1857, **George Mary Searle** launched into a career in astronomy. He discovered the asteroid Pandora and, after converting to Catholicism in 1862, taught mathematics at the Naval Academy. He left his position at the Harvard Observatory in 1868 to join the Paulists. At Catholic University he established an observatory, was associated with the Smithsonian Astrophysical Observatory and in 1898 became Director of the Vatican Observatory. He served as superior of the Paulists from 1904 to 1909 and was then appointed Newman Club chaplain at the University of California, Berkeley. His religious pamphlets and book *Plain Facts for Plain Minds* (1895) were often reprinted.[48]

A Bostonian who would later travel

George Searle '57 left the Harvard Observatory to become a Paulist.

widely as a Passionist superior, **James Kent Stone** took his first trip to Europe after his freshman year at Harvard and was eventually recorded with the class of 1861. After service in the Union army, Stone took Episcopal orders, taught Latin and became President of Kenyon College in Ohio. Like Newman before him, Stone slowly slid into a more Anglo-Catholic theology. A sermon by him on the Incarnation aroused the suspicion of his bishop and he felt obliged to resign, whereupon he was invited to the presidency of Hobart College in upstate New York. During his first and only year there he realized he was a Catholic and again resigned. The following year, this accomplished young man (he was not yet thirty) explained his conversion in *The Invitation Heeded*, a book compared with Newman's *Apologia Pro Vita Sua*. The death of his wife freed Stone to become a Paulist and eventually a Passionist priest in 1876. Over the next forty-five years, under the name Fr. Fidelis, he served that order in Latin America, Rome and the United States, as "the most outstanding figure that his congregation has produced in

*After his wife died, James Kent Stone '61 became
Passionist Fr. Fidelis. Hundreds were turned away
when he preached at Harvard in 1897.*

this country."[49]

In measuring contributions to the
Catholic Church in Boston, it can be seen that
five priests had graduated from Harvard before Boston College's first class even finished.
In fact, the 1858 Latin School of the Sodality
of the Immaculate Conception (what one Jesuit
historian "considered as a forerunner of Boston College") had only one teacher, Michael
Norton, a student in his senior year at
Harvard.[50]

In the winter of 1854, while a student at
Boston Latin School, **Nathaniel Bradstreet
Shurtleff** '59 attended a series of anti-Catholic
lectures, which merely served to incite his interest in the other viewpoint. He continued his
reading on Catholicism (again through anti-
Catholic literature) and during a visit in Maine,
he was baptized by Rev. John Bapst, S.J.

Although he was a successful debater
and writer in school, Shurtleff's religious interests led him increasingly away from the
mainstream of Harvard life. Some classmates
considered him aloof, as he devoted himself to
reading, discussion and work with the Catho-

lic youth in the city.[51] After graduation,
Shurtleff entered the Jesuit Novitiate in
Frederick, Md., and various letters to his
mother attest to his happiness there. However,
the long work without customary comforts put
his health at risk and on the advice of his
spiritual counselors, he temporarily laid aside
his vocation and returned to Boston. He began
the study of law, but was no less active in religious matters: he lent oratorical skills to the
cause, delivering public lectures on the education of Catholic children and on the history of
the Society of Jesus. Shurtleff also worked with
the poor and especially supported St. Mary's
Catholic School in Boston.

Having been quite involved in the
political issues of 1860, Shurtleff was one of the
first to organize units for the Union army and
was elected Captain of the "Latin School
Guard."[52] In August, 1862 he was shot near
the heart at the Battle of Cedar Mountain. The
intensity of his conversion emerges from the
report of Lt. J. Otis Williams, a cousin in the
same company, "He only exclaimed, 'I am
shot! Mary, pardon!'"

By his own request, he was buried
from the Jesuit Church of the Immaculate
Conception and was interred with military
honors at Mount Auburn Cemetery. Thousands are said to have followed his coffin from
the station to the church; Father Haskins noted
the change in the city that had not so many
months before applauded the policeman who
locked Shurtleff up "simply because he insisted on his right to search in a Protestant
school of notorious proselytizing character for
some of his Catholic boys."[53] Several obituaries of this popular young man, inscribed as a
patriot in Harvard's Memorial Hall, gave notice of his Catholic sentiments. As the son of
a prominent family—his father, a schoolmate
of Bishop Fitzpatrick at Boston Latin School,
was later Mayor of Boston—Shurtleff's short
life was a favorable mark for the general regard for Catholics.[54]

Dr. Thomas Dwight, a childhood
convert to Catholicism, graduated from
Harvard in the class of 1866 and embarked on
a distinguished career in medicine. He succeeded Oliver Wendell Holmes as Parkman
Professor of Anatomy and taught at the
Harvard Medical School for almost thirty
years. He received an honorary degree from

Georgetown in 1889 and was a Fellow of the American Academy and several international societies. For many years, he was also President of the Boston St. Vincent de Paul Society.

In a later generation, **William Merrill '88** provides an example of the impact of the treacherous Harvard education on a young man's spiritual development. He entered Harvard unsure of his religion (a rationalist preferring the Episcopal service) and left unsure. But in that time, the seeds were sown for his later conversion. The broad philosophical and psychological program taught by James, Royce and Palmer had trained him to view problems on their own merits and to use his "own powers of mind in solving them." Ironically, this sceptic Harvard department, which was particularly suspect to Catholic critics, freed Merrill to consider the merits of Catholicism independently. "Whatever may be the educational value of such a mode of teaching philosophy, in my own case it rendered me more ready than I think I should otherwise have been to give a fair hearing to the claims of the Catholic Church."

A sense of the Catholics then in the college can be gathered from Merrill's description of the admittedly unusual Peter J. O'Callaghan, '88. "Among my classmates at the University," Merrill wrote, "was a young man of quiet, refined manner, a Catholic with whom I often talked on questions of philosophy and religion. When points were raised by me or by other classmates against the Catholic Church, as would sometimes happen when we were gathered about the dining table, he would good-humoredly but effectively hold his own in defence of his faith; but he never tried to make a Catholic of me or even suggested that I should look into the claims of the Catholic Church."

O'Callaghan, one of six brothers who attended Harvard, may have adopted a low-key approach in college, but not later. When Merrill wrote him after graduation and mentioned that he was still "wandering about like a lost sheep in search of a fold," O'Callaghan replied "You will never find rest for your reason except in the Catholic Church." Upon reflection, Merrill realized that he knew nothing about Catholicism and began a correspondence with O'Callaghan that culminated two years later in his reception into the Church.

Thomas Dwight '66 succeeded Oliver Wendell Holmes as Parkman Professor of Anatomy. A convert as a boy, Prof. Dwight was a prominent Catholic leader in Boston and President of the St. Vincent de Paul Society.

Obviously a natural guide for converts, O'Callaghan joined the Paulist order of which he was later Superior.[55]

The National University: Catholics at the College

Under President Charles William Eliot (1869-1909), Harvard College multiplied the count of its students, faculty, endowment and its prestige. Part of that growth was in the graduate schools, as Harvard became one of the first real universities offering graduate work in almost every professional and academic subject, but the college also grew dramatically. The college was now more secular, overtly more attuned to wealth and progress than to religion. As the impulse of Unitarianism faded, various new movements, and especially the impact of Phillips Brooks' Episcopalianism, would in-

Charles Carroll '87, dressed as Esmeralda for a D.K.E production, was the third generation of his family at Harvard.

stead be the agents of religious revival. Eliot's "new religion" was progress, and it had little interest in the variations among Christian sects. Meanwhile, Catholics interested in education recognized the opportunity the institution provided.

In the thirty years before 1893, when the Harvard Catholic Club was formed, 84 Catholics graduated from the college. All in all, one would estimate the percentage of Catholics graduates from the college in 1893 at about 3% (higher for non-graduates) and double that a decade later. In gross numbers, however, Harvard's output of Catholic graduates was not insubstantial. In 1877,

Harvard graduated four Catholics with the bachelor's degree, not many fewer than Holy Cross (13), Boston College (12), Georgetown (7) or Fordham (5), and more than St. Louis, Xavier, and Loyola of Baltimore. In addition to the new wave of Irish-Americans, Harvard educated another generation of Maryland gentry: Charles J. Bonaparte, '71, the yacht builder Royal Phelps Carroll, '85, Charles Carroll '86, and James P. Lee, '91. All were descendants of Harvard alumni, and the two Carrolls (sons of a Governor of Maryland) were the third-generation of their family to study in Cambridge.

It should be remembered that many students in that day never stayed to finish degrees and Irish Catholics in particular, since they sometimes lacked the required preparation, were recorded at Harvard as special students. What Harvard had that the Jesuit colleges did not, however, was large graduate programs. In the 1890's the Harvard Catholic Club regularly claimed the University had 250 or more Catholics—a number which would make Harvard one of the largest Catholic universities in the country.

Although 1894 was the first year in which more than ten Catholics graduated from the undergraduate program, from the small group of earlier graduates a number distinguished themselves in academics, politics or religion. James Sullivan O'Callaghan, the first of the O'Callaghan brothers to attend Harvard, graduated third in his class of 1875, *summa cum laude* in Philosophy, before entering the law. James Byrne '77, the first Catholic member of the Harvard Corporation, was a prominent New York lawyer and member of the Executive Committee of the Catholic War Council; Charles F. Aiken, who was second in the class of 1884, entered the seminary and spent much of his career as Dean of the Faculty of Theology at Catholic University; Hugh Brogan, A.B. 1885, was the first holder of the Tyndall Fellowship at Harvard and went on to earn a Ph.D. in Strasbourg. Daniel W. Shea, A.B. 1886, served in the New Hampshire House of Representatives for two years before receiving a professorship of Physics at the University of Illinois.

Just as Fr. Robert Lord, a Harvard convert, was the major historian of the archdiocese in the twentieth century, so in the

The female servants of the college, mostly Irish-Catholic after 1850, were called "goodies." With sophomoric wit, the leading scrublady was dubbed Regina Bonarum, "Queen of the Goodies".

nineteenth century it was Harvard graduates who pioneered in Boston Catholic history. William A. Leahy, of the class of 1888 and Literary Editor of the *Boston Traveller*, wrote the 350-page chapter on Boston for the *History of the Catholic Church in the New England States* (1899); and James Sullivan (M.D. 1894) edited the encyclopedic *One Hundred Years of Progress. A Graphic, Historical and Pictorial Account of the Catholic Church of New England, Archdiocese of Boston* (1894).

As a lifelong Bostonian, Archbishop Williams (prelate from 1866 to 1907) was welcomed throughout local society but he could not be drawn into it. The Archdiocesan history recounts that "when Phillips Brooks and a few others attempted to induce him to join their favorite club, he replied, 'No, my place is among my people.' Twice, it is said, Harvard offered him an honorary degree, and twice he begged to be excused from accepting such a distinction."[56] A taciturn man of the well-known Yankee type, who wished to avoid the appearance of a domineering, political Roman hierarchy, he rarely spoke out to defend the Church against frequent anti-Catholic attacks. Likewise, he avoided public attention as he avoided the pulpit, although by all accounts his laconic phrasing made him

a forceful preacher. Accordingly, the good relations with Protestants which he encouraged had to be carried out by people other than himself—and Harvard educated Catholics were obvious intermediaries.

In describing Archbishop Williams' intimates, the archdiocesan history names three bishops, two priests and four laymen. Of the laymen—Dr. Thomas Dwight, Dr. John G. Blake, Charles F. Donnelly, and John Boyle O'Reilly—the first three were Harvard educated. Dr. Thomas Dwight was mentioned above. John G. Blake (M.D. 1861), a member of Williams' inner circle, had no difficulty in sending his sons to Harvard rather than Boston College or some other Catholic college. His two sons followed him into medicine: Dr. John Bapst Blake (A.B. '87; M.D. '91), who taught at the Harvard Medical School from 1903 to 1923, and Dr. Gerald Blake (A.B. '01; M.D. '05) who taught at H.M.S. from 1921 to 1929. For forty years, Charles Francis Donnelly (LL.B. 1859) was legal counsel to Archbishop Williams, as well as scholar, poet and font of generosity.[57] Two members of the "Four of Us Club"—the very heart of Boston Catholic intellectualism—were also Harvard alumni. John F. McEvoy graduated in 1854 (one of the first local Irishmen to attend the college) and as a law-

Patrick A. Collins, LL.B. 1871, the first Catholic Congressman from Massachusetts.

yer and friend worked especially hard in supporting the Sisters of Charity. Patrick Collins received a law school degree in 1871, then served as a congressman from 1883 to 1889, Chairman of the Democratic National Convention in 1888, American Consul-General in London from 1893 to 1897, and twice as Mayor of Boston. Any measure of nineteenth century Boston Irish politics is incomplete that leaves out the number of lawyers with Harvard Law School backgrounds.[58]

The National University: Catholics at the Graduate Schools

Harvard Law School attracted quite a number of Catholics during the early nineteenth century. Granting its first degrees in 1820, the Law School was as large as the college by the 1840's. As a professional school it posed no religious threat to Catholic students who had attended a Catholic college for the formative baccalaureate. As one of the few large law schools, Harvard held a national appeal through the mid-Atlantic, Midwest and Louisiana where most American Catholics lived. Before the war, the Harvard Law school records as students fifteen alumni of Georgetown (not all Catholic) and several from Mt. St. Mary's, St. Joseph's (Ky.), and various colleges called St. Mary's. The first of these was Thomas Charles Evans, son of the Hon. Josiah J. Evans of South Carolina. An 1833 graduate of Mt. St. Mary's, he spent some of the two following years in Cambridge but did not take a degree.[59]

Perhaps the most distinguished early Catholic alumnus of the Law School was Thomas Jenkins Semmes, top of his class at Georgetown in 1840. After taking the LL.B. at Harvard in 1845, he settled in Louisiana, where he became active in Democratic politics and was elected to the Louisiana lower house in 1855. An outspoken critic of the Know-Nothing movement, Semmes defended the Roman Catholic Church and on this account dissolved his law partnership with Harvard classmate Matthew Edwards, a supporter of the movement.

Semmes came from a family of Whigs, but ironically his exposure at Harvard to several prominent constitutional jurists converted him to a states' rights Democrat. His role as a Confederate Senator was pardoned by President Johnson and after the war he returned to law practice in New Orleans. He later taught civil and common law at the University of Louisiana (now Tulane) and was elected president of the American Bar Association in 1886.[60] He campaigned for the presidential election of his Harvard Law classmate Rutherford B. Hayes and in general worked to heal the rift between North and South. He was almost named an associate justice of the U. S. Supreme Court by Grover Cleveland. From his days at Georgetown, Semmes maintained intimacy with the Jesuits and put his legal expertise at their service in New Orleans. Similarly, he was a friend of several archbishops in that city and contributed to many Catholic charities there. He also spoke out against the Bismarck government's oppressive laws against Catholics in Germany.

By 1880, approximately fifty Catholics from other colleges had graduated from Harvard Law School, and many more who had done partial studies there. By the end of the century, a number of the Catholics graduating from Harvard College continued at the Law School. Many of these became the most active members of the early Harvard Catholic Club, due to their extended time in Cambridge. Among those graduating from both the college and the law school was William Schofield, A.B. 1879, A.M. 1880, who clerked for Justice Gray of the Supreme Court before returning to teach Torts from 1886 to 1890 at the Law School.

The Medical School has never been as large as the Law School but drew a similar proportion of Catholics. A check of the Medical School Catalogue of 1885-86 reveals 9 alumni of Holy Cross, 6 of Boston College, 2 of St. Joseph's, Ky., and one alumnus each from Georgetown, Fordham, and Mt. St. Mary's. Including the several Irish-Americans, a number from South Boston, it is likely that at least 30 students out of 264 were Catholic, that is to say, over 10%.

Neither Holy Cross nor Boston College offered medical training, so it was inevitable that Boston Catholics interested in professional education would attend Harvard or Tufts. For example, soon after Michael Gavin came to America in 1857 he read privately in medicine and entered the Harvard Medical School in 1861, the same year his friend John Blake was finishing. With a recommendation from Oliver Wendell Holmes, Gavin served as a Navy surgeon while in school. He was a major figure in the early history of Boston City Hospital, starting in 1864 as one of the two house surgeons when the institution opened. Other doctors from Harvard played important roles in local Catholic life. William Dunn (M.D. 1875) was Professor of Chemistry at Boston College and president of that college's alumni association. John F. Fitzgerald, "Honey Fitz," congressman, mayor of Boston and grandfather of John Fitzgerald Kennedy, attended Harvard Medical School for a year but was forced to drop out to help support his family. Dr. Thomas Dwight was not the only Catholic on the Medical faculty—Dr. Hasket Derby, an ophthalmologist, was also a convert.

Canadians make up the largest number of Harvard foreign students. Of the Catholic ones, an early graduate was Laurence Power, Speaker of the Canadian Senate, who took the LL.B. in 1866. Born in Halifax, he also studied at St. Mary's College there, Holy Cross in Worcester, and the Catholic University of Dublin. A reformer, he was appointed to the Canadian Senate in 1877 and served there forty-four years.

Charles Joseph Bonaparte

At a time when Catholics at Harvard were few, one like Charles Joseph Bonaparte '71 counted for many. After private tutelage in Baltimore, Bonaparte entered Harvard in the fall of 1869 with junior standing. With a firm faith, he wrote to his mother soon after his arrival at Harvard: "I have several times been to prayers but, as I sit near the door, I cannot hear what Dr. Peabody says at all. As he is a heretic, however, it is of no moment."[61] For the next five years he lived in Cambridge, attaining the A.B degree in 1871 and the LL.B. in 1874.

Cosmopolitan but devout, the grandson of the King of Westphalia but a friend of the poor, Bonaparte did much to show both Harvard and the Catholic Church that neither had to fear the other. Although a Harvard legacy—his father was class of 1826, his brother class of 1849—his faith was not in jeopardy; although a Catholic, his powers of argument were undiminished. His loyalty to neither faded; he held the unusual honor of having been both an Overseer of Harvard College and a Trustee of Catholic University.

That the Church had nothing to fear from articulate Catholics attending Harvard can be seen from another letter home, in which Bonaparte explains his role as *defensor fidei*:[62]

Speaking of Holy Week reminds me to ask you to send on a copy of the Archbishop's pastoral letter in regard to the Infallibility dogma. I have numerous combats—oratorical ones—with the heretics at our table, who, although differing widely among themselves, and mutually accusing each other of bigotry and unchristian tenets, all unite to assail the doctrines of the true church, valiantly defended by poor little me. The dogma of the Infallibility is the most tempting ground of assault, and I should like to refresh my memory in regard to some of the old Councils the Archbishop quotes in such numbers.

I do not think the Catholics, although Heaven knows they are ignorant enough of the tenets of their foes, can be charged with

Both as an exemplary student and a political reformer, Charles J. Bonaparte improved the impression of Catholics as moral and dutiful citizens.

case was principally caused by the manipulation by a set of intriguers of the H.H. and Hasty Pudding Societies, the principal open societies in the College. I was so disgusted at the way in which these societies were run for the benefit of wire pullers and toadies that I went quite eagerly into a project to establish a society free from the influence of personal ambition and also from that of the secret fraternities that to a great extent control our class 'politics'. Out of this idea grew the Signet. It is a secret society, of course, but has the full support of the President and faculty, and if it become what we hope it will become, it will certainly be a force for good introduced into our College life."[63] He carried these reform sentiments into his political career.

For Bostonians to whom Catholic and Irish were sometimes synonyms, Bonaparte introduced an international perspective. With a pedigree no Brahmin could match, he recognized that the source of human dignity was not of one's classmates concoction. "My conduct in not having any connection with the affairs of the class has excited much astonishment among those of the Aristocracy who have heard of it," wrote the heir to numerous Napoleonic titles, "and, when it is generally known, I think the amazement of the descendants of the Puritans will know no bounds. The average mind of a Bostonian cannot conceive of any less fortunate mortal's avoiding an occasion to be honored by their presence."[64] Although he avoided the competitions for class offices and speeches, he was entrusted by the faculty with the Latin Salutatory Address at the Commencement.

At the end of Bonaparte's college career, Andrew Peabody, the Professor of Christian Morals whom he had labeled a "heretic" at his arrival, wrote of the Marylander: "There is not a member of College who has precedence of him in character, and in claims on the highest respect and honor, as there is certainly no one who excels him in substantial ability and valuable acquisitions."[65]

Physically, Bonaparte resembled Napoleon I and was the legitimate heir of that line, although European politics and unsanctioned marriages had prevailed. In spite of or an account of this, Charles Joseph Bonaparte spoke often on the glorious themes of America, political integrity, and the

an unusual amount of ignorance on the subject. It certainly is extraordinary that young men who can go to College should devoutly believe convents to be houses of prostitution, and mendacity a virtue in our creed; but there are such persons to be found here in great numbers. At our table we have one high church Episcopalian, one low church ditto, one Presbyterian, one Baptist, one Lutheran, one Unitarian, one who has never been baptised, and one infidel, besides myself; you see, we form a very happy family.

That he was an asset to the College appears not only from his academic excellence but from his role in the founding of the Signet, Harvard's student-faculty society for the arts. A letter in December, 1870 explains the organization's origin among fifteen of Bonaparte's friends: "I think I mentioned to you that the class election was conducted in a very discreditable manner. That such was the duties of Catholic citizens. A popular speaker on campuses, he not only addressed the Harvard Catholic Club but lectured at the Tremont Theatre on "Civil and Religious Liberty" in 1898 to raise money for the Holy Ghost Hospital for Incurables on Cambridge Street. His Phi Beta Kappa address at Harvard in 1899 started from Washington's aphorism "virtue or morality is a necessary spring of popular government."[66]

Active in Republican reform politics, Bonaparte was an ally of a younger Harvard man, Theodore Roosevelt, and served as Secretary of the Navy 1905-06 and Attorney General 1906-09. In that office he reformed the civil service, brought numerous suits against trusts and was largely responsible for the end of the American Tobacco Company. Other titles he accrued in his lifetime were Indian Commissioner, Founder and President of the National Municipal League, President of the Enoch Pratt Free Library, and Supervisor of Elections for Baltimore City. Bonaparte's "independent proclivities" sometimes brought denunciations on him from fellow Republicans—as a Harvard Overseer he had voted against giving an honorary degree to President McKinley. When later pressed by Henry Cabot Lodge and others, he refused to budge: "I further believe President McKinley has not deserved it....During the twelve years I was overseer of Harvard I voted on every question brought before the board as I thought right."[67]

Bonaparte was a trustee of the Catholic Cathedral of Baltimore and a good friend of Cardinal Gibbons, but when he was elected a Harvard Overseer in 1891, President Eliot claimed that no mention was made of his religion.

Founding of the Catholic Club

Under President Eliot the last vestige of the Puritan seminary disappeared. "A remnant of ancient encroachments upon civil liberty and therefore tyrannical and unjust" was the charge of undergraduates against the compulsory daily chapel attendance. But in 1886, when Phillips Brooks declined the post of university preacher and no one else was considered suitable, the nature of the position changed. At the suggestion of Brooks and Francis Peabody, a Staff of Preachers was appointed in 1886 to direct an expanded series of voluntary prayers. These pastors were to preach for four Sunday evenings during the college year and for the intervening five weeks of daily Prayers. A full choir was added, a new hymn book was prepared, and special services attracted large numbers of listeners. From this point on, the college required no religious observance from its students, a position far more open than the public schools with their Protestant prayers—hence "Godless Harvard." Furthermore, Harvard continued its policy of supporting preferences by paying for one "College pew" in St. Paul Church for the use of Catholic undergraduates. Other than historically, Harvard was no longer a Protestant college.[68]

In 1890, in a conspicuous sign of Harvard's openness, Bishop John J. Keane of the new Catholic University of America was invited to give the Dudleian Lecture on revealed religion. Eliot had defended the founding of the Catholic institution in 1889 and now Keane, the first Rector and a prominent liberal, showed the reasonableness of Eliot's confidence by a diplomatic argument for the truth of revelation. A Unitarian newspaper commented, "He was not disputatious or controversial in his treatment of his subject."[69] The occasion gave Catholic students an occasion to gather publicly, and the 1891 selection of Charles Bonaparte as Overseer gave them an obvious patron.

It is not surprising that the occasional suggestions of a Catholic club should now take a further step. Some students discussed the idea with President Eliot and found him supportive. According to a contemporary account, the Catholic club began early in 1893:[70]

> In the winter of 1892-93 a self appointed committee of Catholic students from the various departments of the University met and unanimously agreed that some sort of union among the Catholics of Harvard was desirable. Accordingly in May, 1893, the Harvard Catholic Club was organized. The membership is open to all Catholics in Harvard University and to-day numbers one hundred and seventy-five.

While this statement claims 175 students as members, on other occasions the club suggested there were over 300 Catholics (not all members) in the university. Of these, probably less than half were undergraduates. On aver-

NOTABLE 19TH CENTURY HARVARD CATHOLICS

Catholics who came to Harvard and Harvard converts to Catholicism were generally talented people who sailed against the prevailing winds of their day. It is not surprising to find that they made their mark on the world or the Church.

John Lee, class of 1808—first Catholic student at Harvard, member of Congress from Maryland.

Rev. Francis X. Brosius—first Catholic faculty member, an Alsatian priest hired as a tutor in Mathematics in 1814.

Dr. Henry Bowen Clark Greene, M.D. 1819—first Catholic elected to the Massachusetts General Court.

Richard B. G. Mitchell, A.B. 1822—first Catholic to graduate from Harvard.

Jerome Napoleon Bonaparte, A.B. 1826—nephew of the Emperor.

Rev. George F. Haskins, A.B. 1826—founder of the first Catholic reform school in New England.

Rev. Edward Holker Welch, S.J., A.B. 1840—Jesuit spiritual writer called "receiver-general" from the many conversions he sponsored.

Rev. Joseph Coolidge Shaw, S.J., A.B. 1840—died young in 1851, but left his library and money to establish Boston College.

Thomas Jenkins Semmes, LL.B. 1844—opponent of Know-Nothing Party, Member of the Confederate Congress, President of the A.B.A.

Rev. George Mary Searle, C.S.P., A.B. 1857, A.M. 1860—discoverer of the asteroid Pandora, Superior of the Paulists from 1904-9.

Rev. James Kent Stone, C.P., A.B. 1861—known as Father Fidelis, President of Kenyon and Hobart Colleges before he converted, "the most outstanding figure that the Passionists have produced in this country."

Dr. Thomas Dwight, A.B. 1866—Parkman Prof. of Anatomy at Harvard for thirty years, President of the Boston St. Vincent de Paul Society.

Laurence Power, LL.B. 1866—Speaker of the Canadian Senate.

Charles J. Bonaparte, A.B. 1871, LL.B. 1874—first Catholic Overseer, Attorney General and Secretary of the Navy under Theodore Roosevelt.

Patrick Collins, LL.B. 1871—first Catholic congressman from Massachusetts.

Rev. Henry Leonard Sargent, A.B. 1879—converted in 1909, a founder of Portsmouth Priory.

Rev. Peter J. O'Callaghan, C.S.P., A.B. 1888—Superior of the Paulists, one of five brothers who attended Harvard.

Most Rev. James A. Walsh, M.M. '89 (special student)—Founder of Maryknoll.

Jeremiah Denis Matthias Ford, A.B. 1894, Ph.D. 1897—Smith Prof. of French and Spanish, President of the A.A.A.S and the Amer. Cath. Hist. Soc., a founder of the Harvard Catholic Club.

Pierre La Rose, A.B. 1895—designer of the coats of arms for many American dioceses as well as for the Harvard Houses.

A grandson of Harvard's first Catholic, James Parrish Lee '91 was one of the founders of the Harvard Catholic Club—and a football star.

age, the number of Catholic seniors was about fifteen or twenty in that decade, an increase from the average of three for the preceding thirty years, whereas the Harvard Law School was the largest in the nation and attracted many graduates of Catholic colleges.

Among the nine gentlemen who first circulated a notice for a Catholic Club, it is interesting to note the diversity, well exemplified by the recent graduates James Parrish Lee '91 and George F. McKelleget '92. Lee, a football hero and the grandson of John Lee (Harvard's first Catholic), illustrates the continuity of the Catholic gentry at Harvard; McKelleget, a Cambridge native elected Phi Beta Kappa, illustrates the now predominantly Irish composition of Catholics at Harvard. He graduated from Harvard Law School and was a prominent member of St. Paul's Parish. Also active, not only in the first years but for many to

come, was J. D. M. Ford, A.B. 1894, Ph.D. 1897, later Smith Professor of the French and Spanish Languages and for thirty years chairman of the Romance Languages and Literature Department at Harvard. A steady friend of both the Harvard and Radcliffe Catholic clubs, he was President of the American Catholic Historical Association in 1935 and received the Laetare Medal from Notre Dame in 1937. He married the sister of another Harvard Catholic, Rev. John Charles Fearns.

If at times the stories of Harvard Catholics in the nineteenth century seems somewhat isolated, in the 1890's the lives of these talented and dedicated people come together. They had lived and worked, some for many years, both in Harvard circles and in Catholic circles. Suddenly, with the founding of a new institution, these circles could be seen visibly to overlap. The creation of the Harvard Catholic Club brought about a communal power that only institutions can achieve. These gentlemen were no longer fellow travelers but part of a distinctly named tribe. A year after the founding of the Harvard Catholic Club, the monthly *Donahoe's Magazine* devoted thirteen pages to this new group in an article aptly labeled "Catholic Sons of Harvard." As does every tribe, this one cared for its young and was conjoined in that effort.

The Club formulaically announced addresses by a "lecturer who is deeply interested in the advancement of Catholic interests at Harvard." In its initial year, one of these was a clever young priest whose talk in March, 1894 so delighted the audience that on the spot the Harvard Catholic Club elected him its first honorary member.[71] It was an inspired moment. Rev. William H. O'Connell, who was always grateful to those who were grateful to him, would be Archbishop of Boston a dozen years later.

The euphoric five year interval that began with Bishop Keane's lecture in 1890 reached its high point on April 1, 1894 when Fr. Peter J. O'Callaghan filled Appleton Chapel on Easter Sunday. The newly ordained priest argued for the rationalism of faith in a sermon which the *Boston Globe* called "a very scholarly, logical production, delivered with the greatest earnestness, but yet simply and with no attempts at oratorical devices." O'Callaghan

Paulist Fr. Peter O'Callaghan '88 was the first Catholic clergyman to lead prayers at Harvard, on Easter Sunday 1894.

was the first priest to lead devotions at Harvard, since a previous invitation to a Catholic priest had been declined. Some Protestants were disturbed by the event and more so by Rev. Peabody's enunciation of the now well-known Harvard policy of diversity. "The occasion," Peabody said, "while it is very interesting, is not so surprising as will generally be supposed. We have always intended to have Catholics represented, as well as other religious faiths.... If the people are looking for any significance in the action, it is simply that Harvard wishes to show that her services are purely unsectarian, and that any earnest disciple of any faith is welcome in Appleton Chapel."[72]

While Peabody was defending Harvard from Protestant critics, O'Callaghan was defending the college from Catholic critics. A year after his sermon, he wrote an article called "Catholics at Harvard" for the *Catholic Family Annual*, in which he praised the "Oxford of America" as seeking only truth. A true Paulist, he saw the opportunity for Catholics in Cambridge: "Harvard is the most splendid and richest field for missionary effort that can be found in the United States. It is a field wide open and inviting us to enter."[73]

The intention of having occasional Catholic preachers was confirmed by the invitation to Fr. Fidelis (James Kent Stone '61) in 1896. When he declined, the college merely reinvited him the next year. A newspaper account of his captivating hour-long sermon noted that hundreds of people were turned away from Appleton Chapel and that people were even seated along the platform of the pulpit—O'Callaghan was certainly right about the potential Harvard interest in Catholicism. The report emphasized Fr. Fidelis' simplicity and emotional earnestness:[74]

> The sermon was different from those of most of the preachers who come to Harvard. It was not a deep argument, drawn from experience of the present time; rather it was a splendid exposition of the goodness of the Creator, founded on the Bible, and on the experiences and teachings of the Saints.

Eliot Insults the Jesuits

One episode, however, brought into question much of the goodwill which President Eliot had built with Catholic leaders. In 1893 Harvard published a list of about eighty colleges from which a graduate would be accepted into the law school. On the first list, only one Catholic college, Georgetown, appeared. An appeal was made for Holy Cross and Boston College, which had the same curriculum and Jesuit superiors. But when other Catholic colleges appealed, the list was reduced again to Georgetown. The *Pilot* editorial adverting to discrimination in Harvard's law school policy—and Eliot's response—appeared in the summer of 1893. It was a curious situation: the Catholic Club had just been founded with Eliot's participation and Bishop Keane had just received an honorary degree.

President Eliot's unhappy affair with the Jesuits confirmed a visible need for the Harvard Catholic Club. Although the opening charter of the Catholic Club is silent on questions of admission, its statement two years later hints at the topic (emphasis added):

> The purpose of the Catholic Club generally stated is two-fold: First, to promote the religious interests of the Catholic students of Harvard, *to assist in every way possible Catholic young men who purpose coming to Harvard,* and to receive them upon their

PRESIDENT ELIOT'S INSTINCTS

"I hate Catholicism as I do poison, and all the pomp and power of the Church is depressing and mortifying to me," seethed Charles William Eliot four years before he became President of Harvard. Writing to his mother from Rome on April 17, 1865, he commented mostly on Lincoln's assassination, but he described the city no more cheerfully:[75]

Under Charles W. Eliot's forty-year tenure as president, Harvard became non-denominational.

> I can't bear to see even the poor degraded peasants going on their knees up the Scala Sancta, and kissing Jupiter's toe (or St. Peter's). The beastly Friars are an abomination to me and even the good which one recognizes in the mass of superstition and corruption is distressing, because it will lengthen the life and prolong the influence of the Mother of abominations. Nasty smells are not cheerful, and all Rome *stinks*."

Thirty years later, in the university's greatest insult to Catholic education, Eliot maligned the quality of Jesuit colleges and supported scrutiny of their applicants to Harvard Law School. It is not surprising that at the end of Eliot's tenure Catholic officialdom viewed Harvard with suspicion.

Yet, this same hostile Eliot worked with Catholic politicians on tax issues, appointed a Catholic to the Board of Overseers, gave an honorary degree to a bishop, and supported the founding of the Harvard Catholic Club. During Eliot's forty-year reign over Harvard, from 1869 to1909, Catholics became established and almost commonplace at Harvard.

The paradox between Eliot's attitude and actions arises from his "religion of progress." Several steps down the trail opened by the Unitarians, it left little room for traditional Christianity. Unlike the early Unitarians, who had shared friendships and great respect with Bishop Cheverus at the beginning of the century, President Eliot was an intimate of no Catholic cleric and apparently had no taste for them, in Rome or elsewhere. But Eliot's opposition was only to the erroneous ideas of Rome, not to the victims who held them—he had great confidence that Roman Catholics would be enlightened by the civilizing influence of American culture. In fact, a certain union of purpose between Eliot and the Roman Catholic community was based on common cause against the evangelical orthodoxy intolerant of immigrants. Although he preferred that parochial schools not exist ("the breach between the Catholic population and the Protestant population is one that should be closed and not widened"), he opposed the attempt at legislative interference in private schools in 1888 on the grounds that such legislation would divide the community.[76]

In principle the epitome of tolerance, in practice Eliot found institutional Catholicism destructive and never really overcame his early bias against it.

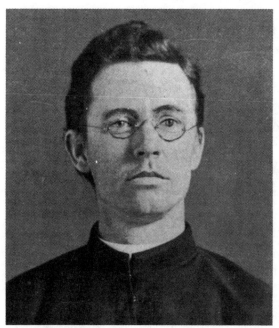

Rev. Timothy Brosnahan, S.J., successfully disputed Eliot's claims that Jesuit colleges "have remained almost unchanged for four hundred years."

admission. Secondly, to quicken the spirit of Christianity among the students. The Club meets once a month, when it is addressed by prominent men, both lay and clergy. Twice during the year public lectures are give in Sanders Theatre.[77]

By 1900 a bitter dispute (often in the press) had arisen from this problem. President Eliot wrote to the President of Boston College that "in the judgement of Harvard University, the Jesuit Colleges in the United States do not stand and have never stood" on a level with Dartmouth, Amherst, Oberlin, Rutgers, et al. Despite repeated requests, Eliot never gave satisfactory evidence for his view.[78]

Slightly before, in an article in the *Atlantic Monthly* on the desirability of a largely elective system in high schools, Eliot had criticized Jesuit Colleges, which have "remained almost unchanged for four hundred years, disregarding some trifling concessions to natural sciences." Lumping this with Koranic practice in Moslem countries, he charged that "nothing but an unhesitating belief in the divine wisdom of such prescriptions can justify them." Fr. Timothy Brosnahan, S.J., former President of Boston College, was unable to obtain a reply in the same journal, so he published a separate pamphlet, which was well received as a masterful defense of the Jesuit College system. A Columbia professor commented that throughout the country professional educators "are immensely amused at the cleverness with which [Eliot's] alleged facts and his iridescent theories have been turned into a joke." The Rector of Trinity Church, Boston, remarked "Fr. Brosnahan, throughout this dispute, made no pretense of being a gentleman, but showed himself a thorough one. Dr. Eliot made all pretense to be a gentleman but failed evidently to be one at all." Of course, Eliot was an extremist in his views on the elective system and they were countered locally through the actions of his successor and the direct language of Harvard's 1945 faculty report on the need for general education.

Although the President of Boston College, Rev. Read Mullan, S.J., accused Harvard of seeking "to discredit all Catholic education in order to full its halls more surely with Catholic students," Eliot's remarks brought suspicion on Catholics at Harvard. Eliot's particular views assailing revealed religion and scoffing at ceremonial rites can hardly have reassured moderate Church leaders at a time when charges were mounting against modernist heresies in Europe and the anti-Christian views of social science in America. In addition, it is unfortunate that some of the Catholic personalities in Cambridge and Boston were inherently less than symphathetic to Harvard. After a slight dip from 1901 to 1905, Catholics enrollment at the university continued to increase, but it kept a lower profile.[79]

Club Meetings

When Phillips Brooks House was opened in 1900 as a religious and philanthropic center, the Catholic Club, the four then-existing Protestant organizations, and the Social Service Committee shared office space, endowments and other facilities. Each was given a room; the Catholics seem to have had the "Worcester Room," which they outfitted with almost $500 worth of rugs, curtains, sofas, and bookcases. John LaFarge, '01 (of whom more later) was given $200 to furnish the room with suitable reading material, but "after I'd put them on the shelves I noticed that nobody ever used them. It was discouraging."[80] In 1904, the six groups formed the Phillips Brooks House Association while maintaining their individual identities.

For the first decades after the Catholic Club's founding in 1893 we have very good records of their activities. Like most student groups they invited popular faculty for lectures, hearing from Prof. Charles Eliot Norton and other Protestants on topics in the humanities and sciences. They also invited national Catholic figures like George Parsons Lathrop who talked about St. Francis of Assisi. In 1897, the Club heard a talk on "Emerson from a Catholic Point of View" by Dr. James Field Spalding, who had converted while Rector of Christ Church, Cambridge. One February, a hundred students turned out for a lecture by the Oxford Catholic Chaplain, the Rev. Arthur Stapylton Barnes of Oxford.

But as a group devoted to encouraging Catholics at Harvard, they turned most often to their own kind. Within their first two years (1894 and 1895) they had invited: Harvard Overseer Charles J. Bonaparte, Prof. Thomas Dwight of the Harvard Medical School, Rev. George M. Searle, C.S.P. the astronomer, and Rev. P. J. O'Callaghan, C.S.P.—all Catholic alumni of Harvard. Within a few years, other alumni speakers included Dr. Hasket Derby, Prof. J.D.M. Ford, Dr. W.H. Ruddick, and Rev. Charles Aiken. More recent Catholic alumni often gave casual "smoke talks" in various halls or the Union. Once the club had a room of its own at PBH, they held meetings and the "smokers" there—when a debate arose two years later, the informal consensus of the Catholic club favored smoking in their room. The Club was quite aware of its own history and the last smoke talk of 1903 even advertised "Thomas F. Mullen, Esq of Boston, who was the first president of the Harvard Catholic Club." Twenty years later, Fr. Ryan always gave a brief history at the opening meeting and Prof. Ford was living evidence.

Apparently for its first few seven years, the Club operated strictly as a Harvard student group without any formal connection to the local Church. At first alumni and graduate students provided mature guides, and initial enthusiasm provided the rest. By all accounts the club was thriving. The spiritual advisor for a while was Fr. Thomas I. Gasson, S.J., a convert from Anglicanism, then professor of philosophy and economics at Boston College. Through the course of the year 1898-99, he gave a series of doctrinal

Prof. J.D.M. Ford '94, one of the founders of the Harvard Catholic Club, received the Laetare Medal from Notre Dame for his writings on Spanish literature.

conferences that had a great impact on John LaFarge, '01.

But in 1901, some forty members expressed their interest "to come under the spiritual care of Father Orr," the pastor of St. Paul's, and Rev. John Farrell then became the first appointed chaplain for Harvard students. On Monday, May 6 of that year, under the new administration, Father Farrell gave a sermon at St. Paul's, followed by Benediction of the Blessed Sacrament. That fall, devotional exercises were held regularly on the third Friday of each month at St. Paul's church and doctrinal conferences on the first Friday of each month at Phillips Brooks House. Apparently clerical control was occasionally a struggle. In 1905, for instance, the Catholic club used up much of its energy " in a discussion as to the power of the Spiritual Director over the undergraduate activities of the Society."[81] A decade later, plans had to be scrapped for residential use of the clubhouse, because Fr. Ryan had misunderstood them when he approved them.

81

LaFarge, O'Connell and Ryan

The most detailed Catholic view of this period comes from the notes of John LaFarge, '01. The son of the distinguished painter of the same name who had done stained windows at Memorial Hall and Trinity Church, he was well-connected. Cabots, Masons, and Perrys were relatives; Miss Agnes Irwin, Dean of Radcliffe, was a cousin; in fact he had come to Harvard at the advice of family friend Theodore Roosevelt. His perspective on Catholicism at Harvard betrays both his social background and his pre-college intention to become a priest. Later, as a Jesuit and editor of *America*, he was a nationally known leader in interracial causes.

LaFarge found no formal opposition to Catholicism at Harvard, just indifference. "Expectedly, some Catholic students gave up the practice of their religion; others simply fell back upon their household faith and passed through Harvard anonymously, while a third group attempted to establish some kind of presence and recognition for their co-religionists."[82]

He resented the homeliness of the old St. Paul's Church, but "the personal attention accorded students was even less satisfactory." Fr. William Orr, zealous pastor at St. Paul's from 1875 to 1907, was acknowledged to be "most painfully out of harmony and sympathy with the student life"; indeed he was "often a cause of mortification to many who attended his sermons or heard him discussed by non-Catholic fellows." LaFarge recalled, "On an alternate Sunday we heard the rather depressing discourses of the famous Father William Orr concerning the state of his own health or the sins of his parishioners, including the well-known campus character, ancient John the Orange Man with his diminutive donkey cart. Father Orr frequently denounced the vices of Harvard youth in general."[83]

The attitude of Fr. John J. Ryan (at St. Paul's from 1889 to 1925) toward the university was no better, LaFarge felt, and he "never attempted to conceal his opposition and unfriendly attitude toward" Harvard. Catholic students in his congregation had to be "prepared to hear a great deal of strong language regarding themselves and the institution."

The sermons of Fr. Farrell (at St. Paul's from 1899 to 1907) were "homespun" but

A colorful Irish-Catholic, "John the Orangeman" was the official Harvard mascot of the 1880's and '90's. Named John Lovett, he lived on the present site of Mather House.

helpful, and he was sympathetic to the students. Soon after he arrived in Cambridge, he was assigned to work among the students and the results were successful. When he "feared that his efforts might draw Catholics from Catholic colleges," Archbishop Williams "encouraged him to work in as open and as expansive a way as possible and not to worry about such possible effects."

After returning in 1904 from Austria, where he had entered the Jesuits, LaFarge went up to Maine to ask Bishop William O'Connell of Portland (later Cardinal O'Connell), "if he wouldn't do something to provide spiritual help for the Harvard Students if and when the Pope made him Archbishop of Boston." LaFarge recounts that O'Connell listened attentively, before saying that "if by the grace of the good Lord such an event would happen, he would take proper measures and see that the Harvard students were looked after spiritually. Then he put me at ease by inviting me in swimming."[84]

When Rev. John LaFarge, S.J., gave a Dudleian lecture in 1947, he was joined by three other graduates of 1901: Class President James Lawrence, Joseph A. O'Gorman, and Class Secretary Wm. T. Reid.

1907 was a year of two eventful transitions. First, the aged Archbishop Williams died and was succeeded by O'Connell, who fulfilled his pledge by generously giving the students the double house at 32 and 34 Mt. Auburn, later the site of the St. Paul's rectory. The back was the caretaker's residence and the students had the street side of "Newman House"—on the ground floor was a living room, library and cardroom; on the second floor was a poolroom and an officers' room; bedrooms on the third floor catered to visiting guests. Since many Catholics lived at home and were not members of other social clubs, a place for study or recreation between lectures was much valued. Although the Catholics gave up their room at PBH, they still belonged to the Association. Officially exempt from contributions to the PBH budget, they nevertheless asked to be able to contribute five dollars annually towards expenses. Over the years all five religious student groups withdrew from the Association, leaving only the Social Service Committee and its offspring philanthropic committees now there. In 1929 the Catholic Club withdrew from PBH on friendly terms, and at no time does there seem to have been anything but goodwill between the Catholic and Protestant student groups.

Secondly, the death of the equally old Fr. Orr left the Rectorship of St. Paul's vacant. Harvard Square and the number of Catholic students there had changed dramatically since 1875 when he had become first pastor of the parish. This appointment was an opportunity for new visions and approaches to the student chaplaincy. At the time Harvard had the largest number of Catholic students of any non-Catholic university in the country, public or private—Harvard (400), Columbia (350), Michigan (250), Minnesota (250), Berkeley (250+), Wisconsin (200), and Yale (190).[85] As part-time Harvard chaplain, Farrell had become a national figure in the rise of Newman Clubs. He had set up clubs at M.I.T and Boston University, was organizing the first association of Catholic chaplains in state universities, and was invited to speak on the topic at the Catholic Educational Association's annual convention. The Harvard parish was an opening for a model chaplaincy with national implications.

One possibility was the execution of a lengthy plan LaFarge had developed a few years before. He made the following points:[86]

a) The nearly 400 Catholic students at Harvard suffered no discrimination, but the "all-pervading indifferentism" and "erroneous teaching in history and philosophy" were still dangers to their faith.

VITA DEDO
DUL SPES

Insignia Universitatis
Nostrae Dominae a Lacu

The Coat of Arms of the University of Notre Dame, like those of many dioceses, were designed by a Harvard man, Pierre La Rose '95. After teaching English at Harvard for a few years, he devoted himself to architecture and heraldry.

b) The Church was doing little for the Catholics at Harvard. Leaving the deplorable pastoral situation aside, the Catholic club had trouble finding suitable persons for theological lectures. He noted, however, that Fr. Farrell hoped to become full-time chaplain and to found a Harvard Catholic Alumni Association.

c) Only a religious order could meet the student needs. The corporate apostolate of a religious order would offset the zealous individualism or the lack of interest in college chaplaincies from talented diocesan priests. Finally, he thought only a religious order could make the parish and the proposed student chapel function in harmony. The Jesuits, he thought, would tend less to proselytizing than the Paulists and less to elitism.

d) The danger that such a center would encourage Catholics to attend non-Catholic colleges was beside the point.

When suggested in 1904, this proposal for a religious order to address the spiritual needs of the Harvard students met with interest from the Jesuits, who might give up St. Mary's in the North End, if given St. Paul's parish. Pope Pius X's encyclical on education the following year

had also supported "schools of religion" for students attending secular academies; and in 1906, the nation's first full-time Catholic chaplaincy at a public university (U. of Wisconsin, Madison) was established. The "Newman Movement" was just beginning and as the foremost Catholic educators, the Jesuits were the natural workforce.

Another possibility closer to home was to name the chaplain Fr. Farrell pastor. In the same week, the Archbishop received letters from Emma Cary Forbes (the patron of Radcliffe Catholics), Prof. J.D.M. Ford (the only Catholic on the college faculty), and even President Eliot—variously asking for a "sympathetic and trained priest" (preferably scholarly) or recommending Farrell by name.

Neither of these possibilities happened. The result was not disaster. Ryan was named pastor and Farrell was replaced as chaplain by the learned Fr. Charles A. Finn, D.D., later director of St. John's Seminary. This pious and Roman educated man was the scholar-priest whom the Harvardians had sought. But when Finn left in 1913, Ryan took on the title of chaplain as well. Although by comparison Fr. Ryan may not have been the first choice of the students, the reports of club presidents suggest he was a helpful organizer—as the building of the present monumental church also testifies. It is quite possible that the Fr. Ryan who dealt with a large group of more diverse students during the period from 1913-1925 may have reacted differently than the Fr. Ryan whom LaFarge disliked at the turn of the century.

But his clerical orientation comes out clearly in a 1915 article for the *Harvard Alumni Bulletin* as part of a series on the various religious organizations. Although entitled "The St. Paul's Catholic Club," the piece mentions no students except in a list of talks to be given that year; and although appearing in the *HAB*, Fr. Ryan's audience is clearly the Archbishop to whom he submitted the article for approval. Focusing on the controversy of "education vs. religion," he asks, "Is it a matter of surprise that the local clergy received letters from many homes asking that the faith of their sons be safeguarded?" Cardinal O'Connell is applauded for determining that "the St. Paul's Club must lose some of its society form and become in very truth a real Catholic family in life and action," i.e., become more closely tied

Fr. John J. Ryan, pastor and chaplain, offered lectures on doctrinal questions, but the architecture of St. Paul Church was his most enduring educational statement.

to the St. Paul's parish (this is probably related to the authority problems of 1905 and other years). The club received communion as a body four times a year and "practical Catholicity" was emphasized apparently to good effect. Lectures on doctrinal questions, followed by quizzes, were balanced by student-led discussions on "The Church and Private Property" and "Socialism and Religion."

The Clubhouse Era (1907-1925)

Like a fraternity, or more approximately a proper Harvard club, the members thought the clubhouse itself was not unimportant and the club was often raising money for some renovation or improvement in it—repapering rooms, installing a new lighting system, adding furniture. This often necessitated fundraising from alumni. Quite lucrative turned out to be the plays the Harvard students put on with the Cecilian Guild of Boston. "The Commuters" at the Plymouth Theater starred John Rock, later a birth control leader; in 1914 "The Fortune Hunter" at Jordan Hall netted $1500, of which the club received half.

The Harvard Catholic Club year always began with a large general meeting in October, in which President Eliot or Lowell, a Catholic faculty member, and the Chaplain made introductions to a crowd of 150 to 300. At other meetings, held in two or three week intervals, a variety of political, academic or religious speakers addressed the group, which often numbered over a hundred. Catholic mayors, judges, congressmen and ex-governors jostled on the schedule with Professors Perry, Copeland, and Norton. A later generation, under the influence of Catholic defensiveness, would try to create a barrier around Harvard students, but in the beginning every major Catholic politician seemed to wander into the Harvard Newman house sometime, while the St. John's Seminary faculty gave talks on their summer travels in Greece, and school superintendents or newspapermen gave students a taste of what awaited them in professional life. Topics might include political issues, German poetry, Christian economics, the Inquisition, or Daniel Webster. The schedule for 1919 gives a cross-section of the guests. Abbe Ernest Dimnet, a Parisian professor and Lowell lecturer at Harvard, first addressed the club on conditions in post-war Lille. Later that year speakers were Mayor Quinn of Cambridge, Mr. James Barrett, Pres. of the Cambridge City Council, Mr. McLaughlin, Chairman of the Boston Chapter Knights of Columbus, James T. Sullivan, City Editor of the *Boston Globe*, Senator Walsh, and Col. Edward Logan, a past president of the club.

Since most Catholic students were local and might spend Sundays at their home parish, holy days were the major liturgical occasions on which Catholic students gathered. On All Saints Day, the Feast of the Immaculate Conception, Ascension Day and other dates they would attend St. Paul's Church in a body, an event they called a "corporate communion," sometimes followed by a breakfast at the Harvard Union. Attendance varied between thirty and a hundred. In various years, doctrinal conferences or lectures on religious topics were also arranged.

Besides talks on religious and secular topics, the most obvious activity of the Catholic club was its annual ball, before or after Lent. There were smaller dances after football games but the annual ball at the Copley Plaza or Hotel Somerset was both a social and fundraising highpoint—drawing up to a thousand couples. Since many Catholics commuted and few be-

In 1907, Harvard Catholics acquired their first student center, Newman House given by Cardinal O'Connell. This clubhouse on Mt. Auburn Street was demolished to build the rectory in 1925, and the club moved to 10 De Wolfe St.

longed to Harvard's elite clubs, it is inevitable that the Catholic club would fill a highly social role, especially in a cultural atmosphere that encouraged them to find a Catholic spouse. Few events were more sacred than teas after football games, and in 1920 the Club even voted to have a dance floor laid in one of the club rooms and to run dances in this room in the fall after the weekly football games.

The records of Phillips Brooks House show that Catholics signed up for social work at the same rates as other religious affiliates at Harvard, but they also patronized Catholic charities on their own, like the Home for Destitute Catholic Children. In 1912, more than a quarter of Catholic students at Harvard were involved in some sort of philanthropic work, either with local boys clubs, the Prospect Union, or Boston's Italian immigrant communities. A 1925 letter to P.B.H. from Elliot Norton, later drama critic but then President of the Catholic Club, gives an example: "Regarding Pendergast, the blind chap, whose case you referred to me, I have obtained eleven members of the St. Paul's Catholic Club who have volunteered to divide his open time among them.... Always glad to help in any matter of this sort."[87]

In 1917, Fr. Ryan began an apostolate to the Spanish-speaking, starting with several Harvard students from Mexico, Cuba and Puerto Rico. At his invitation, Rev. Louis Rodez, a Spanish Jesuit studying at the Observatory took over this ministry—although "like all organizations," Ryan explained, "they soon started up in factions, one favoring a liberal policy, the other insisting on being Catholic." Finally they organized the Catholic Spanish association with about forty members from around Cambridge. When the Passionist Fr. Fidelis (James Kent Stone, A.B.1861) first arrived in Cuba in 1915, he found several acquaintances among the Cuban teachers for whom he had acted as chaplain at the Harvard Summer School.

Apart from a few large social events, the Catholic Club had only marginal impact on the college at large. Charles A. Tierney '22 attributed this low profile to dormancy during his years:[88]

I think very few non-Catholics knew of the Club—and many Catholics either did not know of it or were indifferent. It was not a force in the University and no great effort was made to interest Catholics to join. Harvard University and the student body treated me with the utmost respect and gave me every opportunity to make something of myself at the university. There is no question in my mind that the Catholic Club should have had a more active interest in affairs at the university. It lacked the spark to set it off. It was dormant. I blame myself along with others for not creating more interest in it. However I was busy with football, Lacrosse, and a member (honorary) of the Institute and Dichey Club and Hasty Pudding Club and an elected member of the Pierian Sodality Orchestra and the D.U. Club. I lived during the week in an attic room at the Catholic Club, going home on weekends.

However, the limitations on the energy of the Catholic club were more than a one-year problem. Some commuters found the clubhouse convenient; other pious Catholics had little time for additional activities. For example, William Doherty '27 lived in Cambridge and was active in his home parish (Sacred Heart, Mt. Auburn), so he did not even learn of the Catholic Club until the middle of freshman year when a classmate told him about it. Further, he felt sure "non-Catholics generally were hardly aware it existed." Much of the feeling of lukewarm interest is based on the hope that all Catholics should be actively involved, a type of assumption that few other college clubs make. So one can understand the assessment of J. Barron Fitzpatrick '37:

> Outside of a hard core of interested members—around 50—sometimes more, sometimes less, who attended the monthly meetings, and a larger number who came to the dances, the club did not have widespread influence or impact. I recall each year we received a list of the Catholics at Harvard and only a comparative few responded to the invitation to participate. It left little impression one way or another on non-Catholics.

But in his own case, he wrote, "I think the St. Paul's Catholic Club was a big help to me as a homesick lad from the West Coast."

Few Signs of Discrimination

The status of Catholics in the university during Abbott Lawrence Lowell's presidency (from 1909 to 1933) was unexceptional and rarely noted, certainly not comparable to the difficulties encountered by Jewish students.

The relative advantage of Catholics can be seen in the election of James Byrne as a Fellow of the Harvard Corporation in 1920 to replace Henry Lee Higginson. James Byrne (A.B. 1877, LL.B. 1882) had donated the Byrne Professorship of Administrative Law to his alma mater and been chosen President of the Harvard Alumni Association in 1919. His selection as a member of the Harvard Corporation was unusual not only in the choice of a Catholic but also of a New Yorker, rather than a resident Bostonian.

When he was offered the position, Byrne declined it both because his health was poor and because he feared his religion would be a hindrance to his classmate President Lowell. Lowell wrote back, "The fact that you are a Catholic by religion seems to me a very distinct advantage; for something like half the population of Massachusetts is now of that religion, and it is eminently proper that we should have a broad-minded Catholic like yourself on the Corporation." Obviously, the word got out that Lowell wanted to broaden the composition of the Corporation, since before the Corporation's decision had been announced, Overseer J. P. Morgan wrote to the President, "I think I ought to say that I believe

---

JAMES BRENDAN CONNOLLY: THE FIRST OLYMPIC VICTOR

A distinguished athlete from South Boston, but somewhat low in his academic standing, was James Brendan Connolly. Never finishing high school, Connolly had to work five years on dredgers and with the U.S. Engineers while studying nights to get to Harvard in 1895. "I was a freshman at Harvard," Connolly recalled, "when I saw in the papers that the Olympics were to be revived. Right away, I wanted to go. I was National A.A.U. hop, step, and jump champion and I asked Harvard if I could represent them at the Games. They said if I left I'd have to resign and might not get back in school when I returned. So I quit."[89] While several other Harvard students went as members of the elite Boston Athletic Association, the red-haired Irish-American wore the colors of the old Suffolk Athletic Club of South Boston. In Athens, after some sprinting heats, the first contest of the games was the hop, step, and jump (the modern "triple jump"). After dramatically throwing his cap ahead of the best performance, Connolly reached another three feet and became the first Olympic victor in over 1500 years. Shouts of "nike, nike" (victory, victory) accompanied the first raising of the American flag. He also placed second in the high jump and third in the long jump, as three of the other Harvardians also took gold medals.

Connolly never retired from adventure. He fought in the Spanish-American War, reported for *Collier's* and the Navy during WWI, and served as Commissioner of the American Committee for the Relief of Ireland during the Black and Tan terror of 1921, with escapades in each endeavor. Most of his life, however, was spent working or writing on the sea. Starting as a reporter on English cattle-boats, oil tankers and Russian immigration, Jim Connolly is best known for 25 volumes of sea stories. Admired by Booth Tarkington and Teddy Roosevelt, Connolly's skills elicited a preface from T.S. Eliot for the British edition of *The Book of the Gloucester Fishermen*.

Connolly never went back to earn a college degree, settling for honorary degrees instead. He turned down an honorary degree from Harvard, but he did accept his "H" for track at his fiftieth reunion in 1949. A long-time member of the Knights of Columbus, he died in his native Boston in 1957, aged 88.

At the turn of the century, Catholics were stereotypically seen as better athletes than scholars, comparable to the image of black students in recent generations. Some of the same reasons applied. On the one hand, some Catholics were indeed distinguished athletes, and on the other hand most Catholic students at Harvard lacked the prep school scholastic training of their peers.

An additional reason was provided by Fr. Ryan, who wrote that the increasing numbers of Catholics at Harvard were "supplied by our high schools, brought hither by the wide field of opportunity for athletics, and by the scholarships for ambitious but needy students."[90] A subsequent report on the St. Paul's Catholic Club mentioned its seven Phi Beta Kappa members and then noted "among the prominent athletes who belong to the club are Thomas J. Campbell, '12, Joseph P. Kennedy, '12, J. B. Cummings, '13, F. J. O' Brien, '14, H. McGuire, '14, Charles E. Brickley, '15, Malcolm J. Logan, '15. and Albert J. Weatherhead, '15." Most were football letter-winners, but Kennedy won his "H" for baseball and Cummings was captain of the track team.[91]

Talented athletes usually supply the pool of good coaches and the Catholic presence on the field soon became one in the office as well. After Cambridge Latin School, Charles F. Crowley spent three years at Harvard (1907-1910) before transferring to Notre Dame Law School (LL.B. 1913). His first love, however, was football and he coached for several powerhouses, including Harvard in 1921-2 and Columbia from 1924 to the 1940s.[92] He was a Cambridge native and maintained his residence on Huron Avenue while coaching in New York. Likewise, Edward Casey '19 started coaching football a year after his graduation. Returning to Harvard in 1926 as freshman coach, he later became head coach before taking over the Boston professional franchise in 1935. By this time, Catholics were too well established at Harvard and college football had become too professional for religious differences to be significant.

The club minutes for Nov. 18, 1913 noted that: "Athletic Night was observed in honor of the five Catholics on the Varsity Football Team. Mr. Alfred G. Shrubb, coach of the cross-country team, told of his experiences in the running game. Dr. Daniel Hurley, former captain of the football team, and Mr. James Clarke, both ex-presidents of our club, made remarks."[93] Hurley and Clarke had degrees from Harvard Medical and Law Schools respectively, so one must not underestimate the academic status of athletes.

Charles E. Brickley (holding the football) was captain of the 1914 team. He scored all the Harvard points in the previous year's 15-5 victory over Yale, and the majority of the points in the 1914 match.

Athlete Joseph P. Kennedy, Sr. '12 was on the governing board of the Catholic Club. Joseph P. Kennedy, Jr. '36 was secretary of the club.

eloquent against discrimination in his response to Morgan, "Can a university be great which does not purport to welcome all classes of people to the benefits of its instruction, and can it do this if it takes the ground that the members of a great religious communion are unfit to be entrusted with a share of its management?"[95] Although Eliot was more open than Lowell in his attitude towards Jewish admissions, the comparison must be reversed for Catholics.

The university had also been supportive in 1915, when Professor Maurice De Wulf from the Catholic University in Louvain, Belgium, gave a course on Scholastic Philosophy, a subject which was previously "treated only in the most cursory way at the University." Prof. James Woods, head of the Philosophy Department, even tried to raise several thousand dollars from Catholics to help create a regular chair on the topic.[96] De Wulf continued as a occasional visitor until 1921 when he was made Professor of Philosophy. Another visiting lecturer during the war years was Leon Dupriez, a Professor of Law at Louvain. In 1919, Harvard, like Yale and Columbia, awarded an honorary degree to the Belgian Primate, Desire Cardinal Mercier, a hero for his staying at his post during the German occupation. Cardinal O'Connell was, belatedly, invited to the event, but was not awarded an honorary degree himself until 1937—after President Lowell's retirement. The lack of formal contact between the archdiocese and the university should not, however, be taken as the only measure of the Cardinal's relationship with Harvardians. He maintained independent friendships with the Coolidges and various Catholic alumni.[97]

The most active Catholic faculty in the beginning and middle of the century have been in the Romance Languages, a culturally Catholic field. Prof. Ford, a founder of the Harvard Catholic Club, taught Spanish; Prof. Louis J. A. Mercier taught French from 1911 to 1946, lectured around the country on teaching innovations and the philosophy of education, and served as President of the American Association of Teachers of French from 1933 to 1935; Prof. Francis Rogers, who was elected a Junior Fellow after his doctorate at Harvard, taught Portuguese from 1945 to 1981, serving as Dean of the Graduate School of Arts and

there is a strong feeling among the Overseers that the nominee should by no means be a Jew or a Roman Catholic, although, naturally, the feeling in regard to the latter is less than in regard to the former . . . the Jew is always a Jew first and American second, and the Roman Catholic, I fear too often a Papist first and an American second." In his response that Byrne had been chosen, Lowell again pointed out the large percentages of Catholics in the state and the university. He added, "Unless we are to furnish aid to Cardinal O'Connell in attempting to prevent Roman Catholics from entering Harvard, we surely cannot take the ground that a Roman Catholic is, in the nature of things, unfit to be a member of the Corporation." In the end only John Jay Chapman attacked the Corporation for the religion of its candidate.[94]

Lowell favored diversity—but within what he felt was the university's capacity to absorb it, whence his concern for a proportion of Jewish students over 25%. In contrast, only about 7% of Harvard students were Catholics and not a problem for Lowell's careful social chemistry. On their behalf, he could even be

Former President Lowell and Cardinal O'Connell at the 1937 commencement, where the latter received an honorary degree.

Sciences in the early fifties. In their times, these three gentlemen were the faculty sponsors of the Harvard Catholic Club.

More unusual was the path of History Professor Robert Howard Lord, a convert who had received three degrees from Harvard and studied in Vienna, Moscow and Berlin. As a specialist in Slavic history, he was also attached to the Peace Commissions in Paris and Poland after World War I. Prof. Lord was a member of the Harvard faculty from 1910 until 1926, when he left to train for the priesthood at St. John's Seminary. He was the principal author of the three-volume *History of the Archdiocese of Boston,* President of the American Catholic Historical Association and often spoke to meetings of the Harvard and Radcliffe Catholic Clubs.

Among students or alumni there are few reports of discrimination. The impression of William Doherty '27 is typical:

> As far as I was aware, no one heeded the fact that I was a Catholic, and the Catholics I knew did not tend to draw

together but mixed freely with everyone else. We had some fine Catholic classmates (e.g. Leo Daley, president of the Freshman Class and now Class Marshall). As a freshman taking History 1 with 800 others in New Lecture Hall, I was pleased to find the emphasis on the role of the Church as expressed by Prof. R.B. Merriman. It was something to make the sprinkling of Catholics among us feel that we had something. At mid-term (February, 1924) we had Prof. Robert Lord (a convert) on French Revolutionary history and someone told me his interest in the Church had been initiated by a challenging question from a Radcliffe girl. A few years later, when he had become a priest, he celebrated his first Solemn High Mass at St. Paul's and I was told that the faculty turned out in great numbers.

Summer School

Under President Lowell, Harvard became a pioneer in evening and summer courses. These programs soon brought a wider population into contact with the University, as those of limited means or time availed themselves of these extra opportunities. Catholics attended in large numbers, since short term or part-time courses were unlikely to damage anyone's religious fiber.

In response to World War I, Harvard opened special military programs which brought large numbers of Americans to Harvard Square for short periods. Fr. Ryan pleaded with the Cardinal for extra staffing: "there are 5000 Radio men here at Harvard; 350 or more in the Ensign School; also R.O.T.C. men. We have been obliged to give extra Masses on Sunday to accommodate those men who are Catholic; also special work among them and all hours for Confession."[98] These visitors were hardly anonymous, for as with regular students the Phillips Brooks House collected information on the religious background of those at the Radio School and passed that information on to the relevant chaplains.[99]

The war was a special case, but not for long. By 1921, so many Catholics were spending their June through August along the banks of the Charles that Fr. Ryan had to ask for an extra priest during those months: "Each summer there is a large attendance at the Harvard Summer School (2500) and of these there are sure to be several hundred Catholics, mostly teachers and professional people. Their presence in the Parish means no suspension of our church activities till after August 15."[100]

The requests for summer help continued for several years, but a new solution arose. Not only were Catholic students coming to the Harvard Summer School, but also Catholic clergy. Between 1927 and 1930, the new pastor Fr. Hickey received permission for the following summer visitors to say Mass and preach: Rev. Fulton J. Sheen, Ph.D., and Rev. D.A. MacLean of Catholic University, Rev. George Abel of the Archdiocese of Quebec, and Rev. Jean Louis Chartrand of the Diocese of Montreal. The presence of figures from Catholic University gives a measure of the wide approbation accorded the Harvard Summer School in Catholic circles.

The Cautious Thirties

Fr. Ryan's successor, Rev. Augustine Hickey, was a serious man who seemed to think the Catholic students somewhat frivolous. He took over in 1925 just as the Rectory was being built on the site of the Newman House, which had already moved to 10 DeWolfe Street. While dutifully attentive to his responsibilities to students, he focused his energy and his resources on the parish.

Catholic student affairs were quiet through the late twenties and thirties. The only full list of members of the St. Paul's Catholic Club we have for that period is from 1926-27. It gives the names of 95 members (including 6 Murphys and 6 Sullivans): 24 were graduate students, 20 seniors, 14 juniors, 12 sophomores and 23 freshmen. This is merely a listing of the gentlemen who had paid their dues—a system that prevailed for all college clubs until the sixties—and only represents a quarter of the total Catholic population of the college.

In April 1930, Cardinal O'Connell asked Fr. Hickey to make a survey of the effect of a Harvard education on Catholic students, especially in philosophy and history, and to state what practically becomes of Catholic graduates of Harvard regarding Church attendance and allegiance. Hickey submitted the following reports: [101]

Certain teachers do say things occasionally which are detrimental to the Catholic Church. These statements simply reflect their outlook on life. Harvard is utterly indifferent to religion and maintains an attitude by which religious faith and religious principles are utterly ignored.

It seems to me that the effect of Harvard on the Catholic student depends entirely on the individual himself. Harvard does nothing to strengthen Christian faith and Christian principles. The tendencies are all in the opposite direction. The Catholic student seems to me to be always on the defensive. When the student is strong in faith with good Catholic training in early years he survives his Harvard experience without loss of faith. On the other hand I am of the opinion that students born of mixed marriages who come here with little Catholic instruction are confirmed in their indifference and laxity by the life here.

It is a difficult matter for us to keep in close touch with the Catholic students at Harvard. More than half of them do not live in this immediate neighborhood. Those who do are not easy to find in their dormitories. Catholic Clubs at these non-Catholic colleges are mainly social organizations. It is truly a matter to cause concern.

While granting Hickey's point that the effect of Harvard depends on the individual, the students themselves were less pessimistic about the opportunity for faith. J. Barron Fitzpatrick '37 thought the students who "lost" their faith had done so beforehand:

The closeness of St. Paul's Church, the interest of the priests and the activities of the Club made it comfortable to be a Catholic at Harvard as far as it was concerned. There were a few teachers who showed some anti-Catholic bias. Cardinal O'Connell frowned on Catholics attending Harvard and gave no moral support or interest to the St. Paul's Catholic Club which was pretty much a parish project. While several Catholics I knew at college went through some struggles and doubts about their faith they were a minority. The ones who fell away from practice were already having home difficulties when they came and a Harvard education rather than driving them away from the faith merely helped their rationalization to sound more intellectual.

Fr. Hickey complained "Catholic Clubs at these non-Catholic colleges are mainly social organizations. It is truly a matter to cause concern."

In fact, Harvard indifference to religion left the door open for non-Catholics to pursue another tradition, just as they had in the preceding century. Gardiner Howland Shaw '15, the great-nephew of the convert Joseph Coolidge Shaw, S.J., was received into the Roman Catholic church just after he finished his master's degree in 1917. A career diplomat, he served as assistant Secretary of State under Roosevelt, but his greatest contributions were in his private work for penal reform and solutions to juvenile delinquency. The rehabilitation expert made his home in Georgetown a halfway house for ex-prisoners and thought that he had been able "to help about 30% of the men who have come to me." He was twice president of the National Conference of Catholic Charities.[102]

In the mid-twentieth century, conversions led to priestly vocations as frequently as in the nineteenth. In addition to Rev. Avery Dulles, S.J. '40, whose tells his own story at the end of these pages, one might mention his contemporaries Msgr. Christopher Hunting-

ton, '32, Rev. Henry Sims '36, Rev. Albert Smith, S.J. '42, and Rev. William Macomber, S.J. '42. Of course, not a few students who entered Harvard as Catholics have also pursued Holy Orders. While leading the Catholic Club in his senior year, Henry Vincent Fox '18 began coursework at the Harvard Business School but ended up as a Trappist monk. His managerial skills, however, did not go not unexploited. Fr. Fox eventually directed the large abbey at Gethsemani, Kentucky, which included Thomas Merton, and, it is said, guided the successful marketing of their preserves.

At the beginning of the school year of 1933-34, the parish converted the club house on DeWolfe Street into a parish house, with the justification that it was not serving the majority of students. One factor may have been the opening of the Harvard Houses in 1930, which provided a new social complex for students of all backgrounds and brought into residence many students who had formerly commuted. In transferring the club meetings

Dom James (Henry Fox '18) was Thomas Merton's concerned Abbot from 1948 to 1968.

to the Harvard Houses, Hickey and the chaplain Fr. Greene were doing their best to adapt the student ministry to the changing times, but the absence of a specific center for students would later prove a mistake.

An example of somewhat curious pastoral relations is found in a 1938 report by Fr. Golden to the Chancellor about a talk given by a visiting Benedictine prior. The evening at Leverett House was arranged by a Fr. Duffy, O.S.B. and a graduate student who lived in a group apart from the Catholic Club at Harvard, says Golden. He continues:

> This group appears to be concerned about esoteric subjects a little beyond the grasp of the ordinary student. The Prior took as his subject, 'The Difference between Amor and Caritas'. Before entering upon his talk, he stated that he would not answer any questions relating to conditions in Germany or Spain. After the lecture a few questions were asked on the subject of his talk. Father Duffy was at his side. Both priests had told us at the rectory they were fearful of Nazi spies in the audience. No priest from St. Paul's attended. We had sensed the whole thing was too hot. About fifty students attended the lecture. Included among this group were two or three instructors.

Without much effort by St. Paul's, various in-

dependent initiatives in campus ministry arose like this, the most famous of which was the St. Benedict Center.

The St. Benedict Center and Fr. Feeney

Across the street from St. Paul Church, a new home for Catholic intellectual ferment and evangelization was founded in 1941. Important in the establishment of the St. Benedict Center were Avery Dulles '40, Christopher Huntington '32, (then an assistant dean of freshmen at Harvard), and John Julian Ryan, (a Professor of English at Holy Cross). The ongoing organizational strength of the Center was Mrs. Catherine Clarke, one of the operators of the St. Thomas More Bookstore. "We knew there should be an excellent Catholic library," she later wrote, "indeed, the need of a Catholic library for the use of Catholic students at Harvard was one of the reasons for having a center at all."[103]

In 1942 she appealed to the Jesuits for Fr. Leonard Feeney, S.J., well-known author, wit, and captivating lecturer. Like G.K. Chesterton, whom he called "a tank of paradoxygen," he could talk long and well on practically anything. "As soon as you walked into the Center," wrote one of his admirers, "you would be aware of Father. A compact, dark-eyed, endlessly mobile figure, loosely contained in a Jesuit cassock (I look like a

Convert Gardiner H. Shaw, '15, receiving Notre Dame's Laetare Medal in 1945 for his work with prison reform and help for the delinquent.

character in a Saroyan play, was his description of himself), he seemed the very proto-type of the 'dynamic personality.' You might find him at the blackboard, furiously covering it with diagrams and symbols to facilitate an instruction on the meaning of person and nature in the hypostatic union; or slumped down in his huge red leather chair, reading aloud and expounding on the poetry of Gerard Manley Hopkins; or entertaining a newcomer with one of his convulsively-funny impersonations (the trick was to put a likely subject on an unlikely topic—FDR on the state of the Church; Al Smith on Descartes; Fulton Sheen on Coca-Cola)."[104]

The combination of Leonard Feeney's intellectual vigor and Catherine Clarke's hospitable organization attracted hundreds of students, professors, priests, and literary notables. The Harvard Catholic Club had numerous meetings there and the St. Benedict Center enjoyed favor from the Jesuits and the diocese until about 1947. "In its healthy years it was almost a perfect answer to the Catholic student problem," was the later comment of Harvard Chaplain Fr. Francis Greene, whose very term "Catholic student problem" illustrates the parish staff's view of campus ministry then.

Many of Feeney's listeners at the St.

Benedict Center converted to Catholicism, but a somewhat personal and overzealous atmosphere arose in which students were encouraged to leave non-Catholic universities. He was silenced in 1949 and excommunicated in 1953 for his disobedience and strict interpretation of *extra ecclesiam nulla salus* ("Outside the Church there is no salvation"). Feeney did not set out to lead a movement: he was not an organizer, nor really even a theologian, but rather an irrepressible priest with a love of the institutional church and unswerving fidelity to its tradition. In what became known as the "Boston Heresy Case," Feeney and his followers held rallies and pamphlet campaigns on Boston Common critical of any interfaith efforts. Ironically, the reaction to this Catholic isolationism fostered the ecumenical experience of Archbishop Cushing and other church leaders in anticipation of Vatican II. Meanwhile, an unhappy relationship existed between St. Benedict's and St. Paul's until the center moved out to the town of Harvard, Massachusetts in 1958. Finally, in the early 1970's, Fr. Feeney and most of his community were reconciled to the Church. (For more on the St. Benedict Center, see the reminiscences of Fr. Dulles and Fr. Greene at the end of this volume.)

REV. ROBERT FRANÇOIS TURNER

*Fr. Turner, who attended Harvard from 1934 to 1936, lives
in France, where he wrote this reminiscence in 1990.*

I must first explain that I am a convert: I was received into the Catholic Church in 1933 at the age of 18, in Paris, France. I wanted to go and study in the United States before deciding whether I would answer the call to the priesthood I had received in Spring 1934. As I have told my friends, I fled West on a ship bound for Tarshish instead of going to Nineveh to preach there like Jonas. Curiously, my first mission as a Dominican priest was at Mosul, Iraq, which is fifteen minutes walk from the ruins of Nineveh.

As a Catholic at Harvard College, the only Catholic layman with whom I had conversations was Bob O. Carleton, also a convert. I remember him telling me he was brought to the faith through his studies, at Harvard, of

Paul Claudel whom I also admired as the greatest French poet of our century, and a great Catholic. He was a congenial friend, an unassuming man. I owe him much, perhaps my perseverance in the faith. The only priest I talked to was Father Greene, my confessor.

My feelings as a Catholic at Harvard were that I belonged to a minority and I even thought, although perhaps wrongly that the Jews were more numerous. I had acquaintances among them, and even struck up something like a friendship with one of them, I.B. Cohen, who later taught at the University. How brilliant he was! As a Catholic, I did not suffer from anything. I did not experience any form of anti-Catholic

bias, neither among the students or among the professors.

Do I remember any noteworthy guest speaker? Yes, Hilaire Belloc. I was greatly interested and even remember part of what he said. Yes, I do think those years had an influence on my subsequent religious life. They strengthened my love of studies and may have played a part in my decision to enter the novitiate of the Dominican Order into which I was received during the occupation of France by the German army, and where I was privileged to have excellent professors of philosophy and theology. At Harvard College, I majored in physics. On the other hand, I felt a freedom of studies, research and thinking which I kept alive since, up to this day.

The Harvard and Radcliffe Clubs joined together for a communion breakfast annually. The 1954 event was held at the Hotel Continental.

New Vitality in the Fifties

After the Feeney episode, the Harvard and Radcliffe Catholic clubs adopted a relatively lower profile. For a number of years after the war, the Harvard chaplain was part-time and frequently changed. As had many before them, students noted that the chaplain "must be eminently qualified to handle the intellectual problems of students on the university level." About this last point, neither Fr. Hickey nor the Archbishop was in disagreement, but such priests were rare and as chaplains tended to be busy with other assignments (Rev. Laurence Riley was also secretary to the Archbishop, Fr. Vincent McQuade was President of Merrimack College). A lack of attention, however, did not mean a lack of faith or spiritual activity. Bernard F. Law, '53, recalls "I think we had a very effective campus ministry (we didn't call it that in those days), which was practically all student generated. We had no center, we had no full-time priest, we had no staff. We did it mostly ourselves, out of conviction, and sharing the faith with people that we were with."[105] From the class of 1953 came at least five priests, a reminder that Harvard vocations have often flourished without institutional support.

Annual events were registration mixers, a Spring Ball at a downtown hotel, the communion breakfast, and something new in the 1950's—a graduation tea for students and parents which Archbishop Cushing and President Pusey regularly attended. A somewhat sporadic string of publications appeared, *Sursum Corda* from 1948-50, then the *Harvard Catholic Club Newsletter* before the *Current* began mid-decade. Within a few years the *Current* had moved from mimeograph to typesetting, publishing or reprinting articles by distinguished Catholic scholars throughout the world.

As Catholic culture flourished in that decade, many suitable speakers were invited, sometimes repeatedly, by the officers of different years. Perhaps the ones most memorable now were Catherine de Hueck Doherty, John Julian Ryan, Rev. John LaFarge, S.J., Rev. Martin D'Arcy, S.J., and Dorothy Day—the last for a joint Harvard and Radcliffe meeting. The Radcliffe students also heard John Cort, while Bishop John J. Wright and other important figures spoke at the annual Harvard Communion Breakfasts at the Hotel Continental.

There were occasionally series of lectures on philosophy, often drawing many non-Catholics, and a group of graduates (Daniel and Sidney Callahan, Michael Novak, John Noonan among others) organized events that showed there was in fact Catholic intellectual life in America—it was just in a Protestant university. From that network arose books about the American Catholic Renaissance like Novak's *A New Generation: American and Catholic* and Callahan's *Generation of the Third Eye*. In 1959, students reported, "A new de-

In the fall of 1951, Rev. Lawrence J. Riley, S.T.L., was the Harvard Chaplain and Bernard F. Law '53 was a junior. Forty years later the two return as bishops to dedicate the new Catholic student center.

velopment has been possible thanks to the help of the Jesuit Fathers who are studying at Harvard. This consists in our so-called "House Meetings" organized by the students living in each house. The meeting is held in a private dining room during dinner with one of the Jesuits leading a discussion on some point of common interest."

For a century, since Harvard became "godless" rather than "Puritan," every generation has faced the challenge of being Catholic in a secular university. However, the chaplains and students of the fifties were less defensive—greater numbers alone made Catholics more confident in this setting—and more intent on establishing the spiritual and material means to nourish and fortify Catholic students at Harvard. In answering an inquiry about "the dangers of a non-Catholic college for Catholic students," Fr. Porras suggested that Harvard was only a danger for Catholics who come with little formation: "they are influenced by the environment instead of being an influence on it....Any Catholic is apt to lose his faith if he lacks spirituality and lives in a non-Catholic environment, whether it be a college, an office or digging ditches."[106]

Although various dioceses and Catholic schools around the country contin-ued to present barriers for high school seniors applying to Harvard, the reputed dangers of the college were less credible to local Catholics. Hockey coach Bill Cleary, '56, whose father grew up in Kerry Corner, was an altar boy at St. Paul's and went to St. Paul's parish school, says, "It was a big thrill for him to see my brother and myself go to Harvard."

The Catholic Student Center

The disappearance of the Newman House soon after Hickey's arrival had left a serious gap. The St. Benedict Center had filled this vacuum for a while—and proven the vigor a flourishing Catholic center could have—but with its censure the issue of a physical home for Catholic student activities arose again. The correspondence of the following years proves a continuing effort for a permanent facility by the undergraduate officers (with hopes of graduate support), although they are willing to settle for renting a temporary location. After 1955 the shared room in Phillips Brooks House was a convenience, but hardly the answer to student prayers.

In May 1957, James Manahan and Patricia Meo, presidents of the Harvard and Radcliffe Catholic Clubs, submitted a five-page proposal for a Catholic Center at Harvard.

James Manahan and Pat Meo, Presidents of the respective Catholic Clubs, host Cardinal Cushing, Harvard President Pusey and Radcliffe Dean Lacey at the April, 1957 tea at Phillips Brooks House.

"The Harvard Catholic Club has at present a room which it shares with all other campus religious groups, and which must be used for executive meetings, mimeograph work, and chaplain's office hours, when not in use by the other groups." Archbishop Cushing sympathized but said it would be "very, very expensive." That year, Manahan, who was also writing for Catholic monthlies, was runner-up as the Most Outstanding Catholic Youth of America.

Interest in a center by students, alumni and even the archbishop had been steady, but what was needed was the support of the St. Paul's clergy, who had seen the fate of the St. Benedict Center. The critical step came in 1960, when the student chaplaincies were merged under the care of Rev. Joseph I. Collins, Radcliffe chaplain and assistant at St. Paul's since 1946. Collins knew that diminishing numbers had left the school annex at 20 Arrow Street vacant, and he immediately asked the pastor if a center could be equipped there. Together, they were able to garner the Cardinal's funding of the renovation, carried out by Josep Lluis Sert, dean of the School of Design. Sert transformed the four-room addition into a functional student center, to which he personally contributed large photographs of *The Last Supper* and an oil painting of the head of Christ. At the time the new Harvard-Radcliffe Catholic Student Center

opened, its mailing list included over 500 undergraduates and another 500 graduate and professional students.

The Stillman Professorship

President Pusey's arrival at Harvard in 1953 gave a new boost to the Harvard Divinity School and to the the spiritual dimension of the university in general. Harvard had had no hesitation in awarding honorary degrees to individuals with a distinctly Catholic association, but during the tenure of President Pusey most commencements included a religious leader of some denomination among the honorands. Of the Catholic degree recipients, Rev. John Courtney Murray, S.J. was honored in 1954, Cardinal Cushing in 1959, and Augustin Cardinal Bea in 1964.

"Never before in the history of the United States has there been anything resembling this professorship—a chair of Roman Catholic Studies in a university divinity school Protestant in tradition and Protestant in outlook." So wrote Dean Horton in offering British historian Christopher Dawson Harvard's new Charles Chauncey Stillman Professorship in February, 1958.[107] Chauncey Stillman '29 donated the $400,000 for the chair in memory of his father, but a number of midwives are also to be credited: timely suggestions by the Harvard Catholic Club, the enthusiasm of President Pusey, and the support of Archbishop Cushing.

97

The exterior of the old school annex remodeled by Sert in 1961 as the Catholic Student Center.

The 1981 Chaplains at the door: Fr. Thomas Powers, Sr. Evelyn Ronan, S.N.D., Fr. John MacInnis, and Fr. John Boles.

Dawson's classes did much to bring the broad, historical scope of Catholic Christianity to the Harvard Divinity School, and the value of the Stillman chair was soon obvious. The only difficulty was Dawson's rather quiet English manner, and since Dawson had no experience of seminars, an assistant, Daniel Callahan, was appointed as a type of interpreter.[108] Before he could finish his five-year term, however, Dawson suffered a stroke, regretfully resigned the professorship and returned to England in 1962. There he kept above his fireplace a picture of Harvard Yard in the snow, a farewell gift from the Catholic community at Harvard and Radcliffe.

Dawson's departure coincided with the exciting first year of the Second Vatican Council. So, with the chair vacant, the Stillman income was used to sponsor the unprecedented Roman Catholic-Protestant Colloquium at Harvard. One hundred and sixty invited scholars and specialists met for three days of discussion and three Stillman Lectures by Augustin Cardinal Bea, President of the Vatican Secretariat for Promoting Christian Unity. An all-star cast of theologians and church historians—Catholics like Baum, Brown, Weigel, and Willebrands meeting Protestants like Richardson, Robinson, Stendahl, Wilder and Williams to name a few—contributed to this new burst of Roman Catholic ecumenism. It was an amazingly large and diverse gathering enjoying the first fruits of Vatican II, including the young scholars Curran, Drinan and Greeley, more well-known a generation later. The important book which resulted from the colloquium helped publicize the new connection between Harvard and Catholicism.

Successors as Stillman professors have included Rev. Joseph Fichter, S.J., a sociologist, Rev. George MacRae, S.J. a biblical scholar, and Francis Schüssler Fiorenza, a systematic theologian. The success of this chair has led to similar professorships of Roman Catholic Studies at Yale (Riggs) and Chicago (Greeley).

The Council and its Consequences

An almost indescribable fervor energized Harvard-Radcliffe Catholics in the early sixties. John F. Kennedy, one of their own, had been elected President of the United States; an ecumenical council suddenly affirmed their presence as Catholics coexisting with Protestants; Rev. Thomas Buckley '49 had come back as their first alumnus-chaplain and visible proof of Harvard vocations; and a new home, a genuine center with library, kitchen and a game room, gave them a staging ground for wondrous ideas.

A look at a single semester will suffice to show what is possible when the chemistry is right in campus ministry. The distributed activities program for the fall term of 1964 lists ten pages of lectures and events including: Prof. William Alfred, selected readings; Prof. Oscar Handlin, "Historical and Sociological Aspects of the Church in the City"; Sydney Callahan, "New Freedom for Women in the Church"; Msgr. Francis J. Lally (editor of the *Pilot*) "The Church and Urban Renewal"; Prof. Frank Moore Cross, "The Messianic Expectation"; Profs. Krister Stendahl, John Mansfield, Henry Aiken, "The Place of Religion in the University"; Rev. Charles Curran, "Birth Control and the Church"; and Dr. John Rock, "Birth Control and the Pill." These are only selections from the busy schedule comprising four talks on "The City and the Church," eight on "Reform and Renewal," a five-part series on Christianity in Asia, liturgy and comparative religions workshops, three parties, two mixers, a concert by Parisian organist Paul Langlais, and the annual communion breakfast. Center dinners offered different populations of Catholics a chance to gather and that fall permission was given for Masses in the Harvard Houses.

Meanwhile, Michael Novak and talented undergraduates were still publishing the *Current*, and a group of sixteen students established Harvard-Iberoamericano Catholic Action (HIACA). While six women taught health classes and networked with local families, ten

---

CONTRIBUTIONS OF HARVARD COLLEGE CATHOLICS IN THE 20TH CENTURY

Rev. John LaFarge, S.J. '01—editor of *America*, preeminent Catholic spokesman on the race issue.

Rev. Howard Bishop, class of '10—founder of Glenmary Home Missioners.

Rev. Robert H. Lord, '06—Professor of History at Harvard, major author of the *History of the Archdiocese of Boston*

Joseph P. Kennedy, '12—Ambassador to the Court of St. James, member of the Governing Board of the Catholic Club.

Gardiner H. Shaw, '15—Assistant Secretary of State under Roosevelt, twice president of the National Conference of Catholic Charities.

Rev. Henry V. Fox, '18—Abbot of Gethsemane Monastery, President of the Harvard Catholic Club.

Elliot Norton, '26—drama critic, President of the Harvard Catholic Club.

Chauncey Stillman, '29—donor of the Stillman Professorship of Roman Catholic Studies.

Paul C. Reardon, '32—Judge of the Massachusetts Supreme Court.

Rev. Avery Dulles, S.J., '40—theologian and author.

John F. Kennedy, '40—first Catholic President of the United States.

Donald Regan, '40—Secretary of the Treasury, Vice-President of the Harvard Catholic Club.

Albert V. Casey, '42—Postmaster General of the United States.

Bernard Cardinal Law, '53—Archbishop of Boston, Vice-President of the Harvard Catholic Club.

Fr. Thomas Powers welcoming Jesuit theologian Karl Rahner to St. Paul Church. Rahner was in Cambridge to receive an honorary degree from the Weston School of Theology.

men built a medical dispensary in a small village on the outskirts of Mexico City.

The Vietnam War and student political action forced adjustments to all sectors of university life, and campus ministry was not excluded. Rev. Richard Griffin, S.J., a member of the Harvard Class of 1951, returned to his alma mater in 1968 and engaged students in social action. As an undergraduate he had been publicity chairman for the Catholic Club and he knew how to attract attention: Cesar Chavez of the United Farm Workers and Archbishop Dom Helder Camara of Brazil spoke at Harvard at the Center's invitation. Fr. Griffin's co-workers were Sr. Ann Kelly, O.P. and Caroline Bohn. However, a combination of awkward times, splintering in the Catholic community and lack of funds made many facets of student ministry difficult. In 1974, an explosion in the boiler room of the Student Center caused one death and closed the building for a year.

Like other Catholics, as early as the thirties clergy had started to attend Harvard for graduate work or special studies. These visitors, like the summer school priests, have been a regular source of substitute preachers for St. Paul's ever since. The pull of the university and the Episcopal Divinity School even attracted the Jesuits' Weston School of Theology to Harvard Square in the 1970's, and now the academic sector of town houses more priests than the parish.

A new era at the Catholic Student Center began in 1975 when a new team of chaplains, Rev. Thomas Powers and Sr. Evelyn Ronan, S.N.D., joined pastor-chaplain Rev. John P. Boles. They transformed the lower church into a specifically student chapel, reorienting the space from a "shoebox" design to an open semicircle. The student folk Mass at five o'clock Sunday, which began with a few hundred in attendance, doubled then tripled its size in the following decade. From a core of spaghetti dinners radiating out to a system of house Masses, the Center has emphasized a balance of spiritual growth, social action, and hospitality. In the 1980's, Rev. John MacInnis and Sr. Mary Karen Powers, a Sister of Mercy, were appointed chap-

The wide pastoral mission of Bernard Cardinal Law '53 includes fielding questions at Harvard's Kennedy School.

lains, and in 1990 Rev. Richard Malone.

Perhaps no university in the world attracts dignitaries as frequently as Harvard. Consequently, the Catholic Student Center has hosted intriguing guests like Hans Küng in 1977, and the St. Paul's Rectory had lodged simple priests like Karol Wojtyla, the Archbishop of Krakow and later Pope John Paul II, who lectured in the Summer School in 1976. For Mother Teresa of Calcutta, speaker at Class Day in 1982, the students and parish raised over five thousand dollars to support her religious order. While Harvard may attract the famous, more im-portant is what she sends forth. In this re-gard, the life of John Leary '81, peace activ-ist and companion of the poor, stands as a model, recognized by an annual social ser-vice fellowship established in his enduring memory (see the Reminiscences).

It is not clear whether the bigoted Judge Dudley or the concerned Bishop Cheverus would have been more surprised to learn of the strangest event of 1984. In that year, Bernard Francis Law, A.B. 1953, found himself the Archbishop of Boston—premier Papist, as it were—and a Harvard graduate with his Catholic faith quite intact.

Mother Theresa told her Class Day audience in 1982: "You have many poor people here. Find them, love them, put your love for them in living action." She is pictured here at the Cardinal's residence with Fr. Boles and the Catholic Club officers.

HONORARY DEGREES AWARDED BY HARVARD TO CATHOLIC LEADERS

Starting with Joseph Dupas de Valmais, LL.D 1779, first Consul of France in Boston, numerous Catholics have received honorary degrees from Harvard. The following list includes those conspicuous for their work within the Catholic community.

John Bernard Fitzpatrick, LL.D. 1861—Bishop of Boston from 1846 to 1866.

John Keane, LL.D. 1893— the Rector of Catholic University, Dudleian lecturer, later Archbishop of Dubuque.

Desiré Cardinal Mercier, LL.D. 1919—Primate of Belgium, hero of World War I.

Etienne Gilson, Litt. D. 1936—Thomist Philosopher, Harvard Goddard Lecturer.

William Cardinal O'Connell, LL.D. 1937—Archbishop of Boston, donor of the Newman House in 1907, first center for Catholics at Harvard.

William D. Cleary, LL.D. 1946—Priest and Brigadier General, Director of the Harvard Chaplain's School during World War II.

Charles D. Maginnis, Dr. Art. 1949—Ecclesiastical architect of the firm Maginnis & Walsh, President of the A.I.A.

John Courtney Murray, S.J., Litt. D. 1954—Theologian of religious liberty.

Richard Cardinal Cushing, LL.D. 1959—Archbishop of Boston, funded the Harvard-Radcliffe Catholic Student Center in 1961.

Augustin Cardinal Bea, LL.D. 1964—President of the Vatican Secretariat for Christian Unity, Stillman Lecturer in 1963.

Leon Joseph Cardinal Suenens, LL.D. 1970—Moderator of Vatican II, Belgian prelate later active in the charismatic movement.

Theodore Hesburgh , C.S.C., LL.D. 1973—President of the University of Notre Dame.

Helder Pessoa Camara, LL.D. 1974—Bishop of Recife (Brazil), social activist.

Mother Teresa of Calcutta, LL.D. 1982—Founder of the Missionaries of Charity.

J. Donald Monan, S.J., LL.D. 1982—President of Boston College.

The University Community: Catholics at Radcliffe

Would you choose Radcliffe again? "Yes, if conditions were the same as then, for I had hoped for a Harvard degree and there were no sectarian limitations."

Mary Josephine Foley, class of 1888

The Early Years

Although Harvard lectures were experimentally opened to women from 1863 to 1872, it was not until 1878 that several Cambridge residents, concerned for their college-age daughters, had persuaded President Eliot to have the Harvard faculty give separate but equal instruction to women. In 1879, the "Harvard Annex" began to operate, and three years later the plan was formalized and incorporated as the Society for the Collegiate Instruction for Women.[1]

The first Annex students were mostly the daughters of Unitarian ministers, but almost immediately local Catholics joined them. The two Foley sisters, Mary Josephine '88 and Rosana '89, were followed by Henrietta McIntyre '90, and Theresa Frances Donovan '92. Natives of Roxbury, Cambridge and Lynn respectively, they were typical of many Radcliffe commuters. An unusual early Catholic was Henrietta Channing Dana, the daughter of the High Episcopalian Richard Henry Dana, author of *Two Years Before the Mast*. After a convent education in Europe, against her family's wishes, she converted to Catholicism when she reached her majority in 1878. She studied under the Harvard faculty in 1886-7 and later wrote a number of Catholic novels and non-fiction. She married Henry Whipple Skinner (Harvard LL.B. 1891).

The Class of 1899 had two Catholics out of forty; most others were Unitarian (13), Congregational (8), or Episcopal (6). From 1900-1910, there are about three to five Catholics in every class, almost all Irish with a few French names. They came from the general Boston area, including South Boston, Roxbury, Dorchester, Arlington, Newton Upper Falls, Lawrence, and Dedham. The Class of 1917 had at least fifteen Catholics among its 104 members.

Even when Radcliffe built dormitories, commuting was not only a practical matter of cost, but a matter of social environment. Like Harvard contemporaries, a Radcliffe Catholic who lived at home and attended her family parish was less open to the danger of losing her faith. In any case, the Harvard Annex had no chapel or religious meetings of any sort and student religious groups sprang up on their own. Opportunities in women's education were still limited in the 1890's, and Catholic options were just beginning—there was no local Catholic college for women until Emmanuel in 1919. Catholics at Radcliffe, therefore, met with less resistance than those at Harvard and were accordingly represented in a higher percentage.

Still, the typical Irish Catholic student was in an unusual position and may have adjusted to the Radcliffe experience with some sense of isolation. Looking back on college days, Susanna Teresa O'Connor '99 of Lawrence wrote:

> My four years at Radcliffe mean much to me in teaching me self-reliance. I felt then and still feel that a girl entering college as I did, the only one from her city or her school, has a very hard time learning college routine. Her college life is nearly over before she finds out what there is to strive for in the way of honors, what part of the social life of the college she could fit into, or with whom she might form permanent friendships.

However, the largest number of Radcliffe students were Cambridge residents and graduates of Cambridge High and Latin School. Catholics were no exception:

> Agnes Loretta Tracy (1892-94)
> Henrietta Elizabeth McIntire '90
> Mary Teresa O'Donnell '98
>   17 Grant St.
> Elizabeth McGlinchey (Pelletier) '99
>   9 Athens St.
> Mary Agnes Teresa Ford (Doran) '01
> Clara Flanigan '01
>   51 Brookline St.

Apparently, all of the early Catholics at Radcliffe were graduates of public schools and, unless they married, followed a career

Teas at Emma Forbes Cary's home on Brattle Street gave rise to the Radcliffe Catholic Club.

THE FIRST RADCLIFFE CATHOLIC: MARY JOSEPHINE FOLEY '88

The first Catholic to attend Radcliffe was Mary Josephine Foley—a founder of the college's Phi Beta Kappa chapter. Born in Roxbury in 1864, she inherited from her father Mathew Foley a love of books and his desire for the educational advantages he had lacked. Her early excellence at the Lewis Grammar School in Roxbury led to her promotion to a higher grade and in 1883 she completed one year early the course at the new Girls' Latin School in Boston and started at Radcliffe. Her parents had not attended college but some relatives had been at the Harvard Medical School. Her sister Rosana followed her to Radcliffe one year later.

When asked years later whether she would go to Radcliffe if she could choose again, Mary Foley answered, "Yes, if conditions were the same as then, for I had hoped for a Harvard Degree and there were no sectarian limitations." For unknown reasons, she took off the year after her sophomore studies, but she was an excellent student, especially in mathematics, and a foundation member of the Iota Chapter of Phi Beta Kappa. In 1888, she received the Harvard Annex Certificate which was converted into the A.B. in 1895 when Racliffe College was formally established.

After graduating from Radcliffe, Miss Foley was appointed teacher of Latin in the Girls' Latin School and remained there as a popular instructor for forty years. At her death June 21, 1928 from a heart lesion, the school characterized her as "an efficient, faithful, and devoted teacher, greatly beloved by the many hundreds of girls who appreciated her kindly spirit and tireless efforts on their behalf." Over the years she refreshed herself through various courses without credit at Harvard and M.I.T.

She was a member of the College Club of Boston and of the Classical Club, of St. Cecilia's Church, St. Cecilia's Guild, and numerous other Roman Catholic societies. Her alumnae survey responses reveal her as a regularly voting Democrat, with a schoolteacher's exactness and doubts that a woman could successfully carry on a career and a marriage.[2]

teaching in public schools. Teresa F. Donovan '92 taught at Newhill school in her native Lynn and then in the Chicago public schools for 35 years; Elizabeth Tracy '97, educated in the Dedham public schools, taught English for 41 years at South Boston High School; Helen Keefe '05 was one of the organizers of St. Peter's High School in Dorchester, taught at Cambridge High and Dorchester High School for Girls, and led a long but unsuccessful campaign to secure equal pay for equal work for the women teachers of Boston. The alternatives were not easy. After Radcliffe, Agnes Tracy opened a private school for boys known as Cheverus Hall and conducted it for seven years. But in 1904, she took a stint as assistant principal in the Agassiz School before returning to Cambridge High and Latin, of which she was a graduate, to teach French, Latin and Mathematics.

Similarly, after graduation, Susanna O'Connor '99 returned to her hometown and taught English at Lawrence High School for over 40 years. She was active in the League of Catholic Women and through professional and volunteer routes she found the opportunity to help young people, especially during the depression:

> It seems to me tragic to see these bright, ambitious, hopeful young people find no opportunity to use their talents. They want so much to do something, to earn money that they may have the things which youth craves. And they are so grateful for any help in finding even temporary work that it is really pathetic. I have no official authority in this search for work. I simply watch for openings anywhere and occasionally I can help to bring the worker and work together.

She lived with her two single sisters in a large house next to her married sister. Summering in Kennebunkport, Maine or Rockport, Mass., they were hardly constrained to a Catholic ghetto. Likewise, her three nephews all went to Dartmouth.

Some went on for a mastger's degree. Henrietta Elizabeth McIntire '90, the daughter of a Scotch-French father and an Irish mother, was a student at Cambridge Latin School before she entered the Harvard Annex. On graduation she returned to Cambridge High and Latin School, where she taught Romance languages, in which she obtained a Master's degree in 1902.

Gertrude Myles '06 at the Catholic Student Center for a tea honoring Radcliffe's centennial in 1979.

An avid traveller, she was privileged to have audiences with three Popes and often recalled the contrast of "the startling spirituality that shone from the alabaster face of Leo XIII—the keen mentality of Pius X—the inherent fatherliness of Pius XI." [3]

Sister and later collaborator of Harvard Prof. J.D.M. Ford, Mary Agnes Theresa Ford '01 graduated with high honors in modern languages, but was initially denied permission to register for her A.M. on the topic of education (then called pedagogy) on the grounds that such a subject was too vocational for an academic degree. Professor Hanus intervened, however, and she went on to a distinguished teaching career in Danbury, Conn. where she married Charles Doran in 1911.

As opportunities for women increased on college faculties, so did the number pursuing graduate work. By the time of World War I, a number of graduates chose to pursue doctoral study. Religious orders in particular offered the opportunity for advanced study. For example, Sr. Margaret Mary Fox, S.N.D. '11, Sr. Catherine Dorothea Fox '13, Sr. Mary Rosa Doyle, C.S.J. '17, obtained doctorates from Catholic University or Boston College.

For educated Catholic women, who had already set themselves slightly apart from their peers, the religious life was not a surprising way to pursue the common careers of teaching or nursing. The first student to enter the religious

(continued on p. 108)

EMMA FORBES CARY (1833-1918)

Like other Brahmin women of the nineteenth century, Emma Forbes Cary's search for something beyond Cambridge progressivism had led her to Catholicism. When her sister Elizabeth Cary Agassiz became Radcliffe's first president, Emma was the obvious patroness for Catholic women at the new college. Living a few blocks down Brattle Street, she naturally sought to host Catholic students when they became numerous enough, although she was over seventy when the Radcliffe Catholic Club was founded in 1906.[4]

Late in life, Emma Forbes Cary recalled the Unitarianism household in which she was raised as "full of spiritual feeling and high ideals" but not necessarily belonging to Protestantism. When her governess read to her the medieval *Imitation of Christ*, she recognized the home for these lofty ideals. "As if I had found a precious bit of Mosaic and sought for the work of art from which it had been severed, I hid these maxims in my heart and pondered on them."

The account of her conversion attests to the vigor of Catholic social ministry and the personal powers of a young Bostonian, Harriet Ryan. Emma was tall and fine looking and when she was about twenty-one, her mother, dissatisfied with her daughter's hairdressing, had sent for a girl to arrange it. "I knew nothing of Harriet Ryan and cared little for my coiffure, but I never disputed my mother's decisions. So, one morning there appeared in my room a lovely young woman who looked like a Fra Angelico angel. I can see her now, her rippling hair, her shining eyes and peach bloom complexion. Her mouth was beautiful, whether it expressed joy or grief or enthusiasm, or gave that enchanting laugh which only belongs to those of Celtic blood."

"I don't remember much about the hair-dressing, but I soon found out that Harriet Ryan was a Catholic, and possessed of faith such as I had never seen. We became intimate friends and she took me with her to visit her sick poor, to whose desolate homes she brought cheer and sunshine. . . . But not only did she show me how to love and serve the poor, but she advised me to go to see Bishop Fitzpatrick (Bishop John, every one called him) to consult him about a charitable scheme of mine. I remember well the November day that I went to see him in the shabby old house opposite the Cathedral. I remember the grand looking man in a faded purple garment who came into the room where I had waited an unconscionable time. I remember that he 'spoke as one having authority and not as the scribes and Pharisees.'"

After this visit, she began a course of instruction in the faith. Later she claimed that what induced her conversion most was the unsavory books on the other side which attacked Catholics rather than explained dogmas. But from the time of her conversion in 1855, she wrote, "I have never met with anything but affectionate courtesy from non-Catholics, and many of my relatives and friends came to see me received." By the mid-nineteenth century, Cambridge intellectual circles showed a tolerance toward Catholics in general, and they regarded the several converts from their own midst as still primarily members of their families and society.

A few years after their meeting, Harriet Ryan opened a home for destitute and dying women which was later endowed and incor-

Emma Forbes Cary (left) and her sister Elizabeth Cary Agassiz, Radcliffe's first president, around 1900. In a description suitable to each, an alumna recalls Miss Cary: "Her perfect profile of marble whiteness impressed the onlooker by its majesty of outline. A rare piece of lace in mantilla form was draped over her white hair, giving her a similarity to Queen Victoria in old age."

porated with the assistance of the Cary family. She married John Albee, a Unitarian with a degree from Harvard Divinity School, but maintained her strong devotion to the Roman Catholic Church. In 1987, the Harriet Ryan Albee Professorship was established at the Harvard Medical School to honor her pioneering work.[5]

Continuing the work with the poor to which Harriet Ryan had introduced her, Miss Cary was a member of the Prison Committee of Massachusetts for twenty-five years. She was also involved in the reformatory work of the Houses of the Good Shepherd, the building up of Trinity College in Washington, and other Catholic charities.[6] She wrote articles for the *Catholic World* as well as a book of meditations, *The Day-Spring from on High*. She even taught Sunday school classes, as Rev. Daniel Hudson, C.S.C., longtime editor of the *Ave Maria* wrote, "I yet remember—I hope she has forgotten—all the trouble she had in getting me to pronounce 'Epiphany' and 'Transubstantiation' correctly."

After her death in 1918, President Briggs of Radcliffe wrote to Mrs. C. C. Felton, "I wonder whether it is not partly through her influence that the tradition of thoughtful courtesy in the Radcliffe Catholic Club is stronger than in any other club of students that I have known."[7]

life was Sr. Anna Louise Goodrow, C.S.J., who attended Radcliffe in the academic year 1894-95. She was later Superior of Regis College. Two other nuns from the last century were Sr. Helen Laurine Houston (student in 1898-99) and Sr. Ellen Juliana Somerby, C.S.J.B, '01.

It is said that more religious vocations came from Radcliffe in the first half of this century than from Emmanuel or Regis, and whatever the comparison it is clear that alumnae of the first few decades did enter religious life in substantial numbers, among them: Sr. Catherine Louise Powers '12, Sr. Mary Bernard (Ruth) Vanderwater '15, Sr. Agnes (Eunice) Coyle '18, Sr. Angela M. Murphy '18, Mother Agnes Hoye, O.S.U. '19, Sr. Catherine Mary Sears '22, Sr. Mary Yolanda Herlihy '24, Mother Columba (Elizabeth) Hart, O.S.B. '26 of Regina Laudis, Sr. Dorothy Boland '30, Sr. Angela G. Robinson '32, Sr. Aimee Bourneuf '32 (who headed the Charitable Board in her time at Radcliffe), Sr. Clara R. Mahoney '35, and Sr. Elizabeth Corbin '37.

In the sixties it also became common to see women of religious orders pursuing graduate work at Harvard, especially in the School of Education. A further integration occurred in the eighties when Sr. Mary Hennessey '51 joined the staff of the Harvard Divinity School.

The Radcliffe Catholic Club

The Radcliffe Catholic Club, founded in 1906, was shepherded through its first decade under the patronage of Emma Forbes Cary, the sister of Radcliffe President Elizabeth Cary Agassiz. Her Brattle Street home was not only a convenient center of hospitality for Catholics but provided an emblem of distinction for a group otherwise lacking in status. Gertrude E. Myles, '06 recalls:

As I remember the first steps to form a Catholic club at Radcliffe took place in the early spring of 1903. Fr. Farrell, a curate at St. Paul's, was assigned the task. At that time I was a freshman at Radcliffe and a parishioner of St. Paul's. Therefore he asked me to speak to the Catholics I knew and sound out their feelings on the matter and also to speak to the Dean to see if there would be any objection to the plan.

A little later Miss Emma Cary gave a tea for the Catholic girls at Radcliffe. Some attended out of courtesy to Miss Cary, some did not. It was a delightful occasion, a lavish tea with Miss Cary as hostess and Fr. Farrell as a guest. After that Miss Cary gave several teas in her attempt to bring the club into existence.

In 1906 when I was in Paris, I received a letter from a classmate, saying that the club had been founded and the first meeting had taken place at Miss Cary's house and under her auspices. It was understood that

Dorothy Barry '27 reading reminiscences of Marie Scollard Degnan '17 at the centennial tea.

The 1928 Radcliffe Catholic Club on the steps of Agassiz. Eighty members and former members attended the Communion breakfast that year.

the club would not meet at the college. So I believe in the early years of its existence it met at Miss Cary's house. She provided the place, the refreshments, and a very warm welcome. Later the Club was accepted at Radcliffe and the meetings took place there.

Marie Scollard Degnan '17, Vice-President of the Catholic Club, remembered those teas vividly:

> Sitting by the fireplace, her beautiful black taffeta skirts spread wide about her, an exquisite lace scarf on her white hair, our hostess, Miss Cary, would have inspired any artist. Professor Jeremiah Dennis Mathias Ford, head of the Department of Romance Languages at Harvard and a loyal friend of Radcliffe, was a frequent guest as was President Briggs and Monsignor Petersen. Between fifteen and twenty came to the teas.
>
> The table, set with lovely linen, silver, china and glass, awaited our arrival. Later with the assistance of pretty little maids in dainty uniforms, Miss Cary served tea and cakes. The cakes we'll just mention in passing, thus giving a most false impression of their importance to us at the time. Most of us had had a light luncheon, and would have a long road to travel before reaching home and dinner in the suburbs. The subway had not yet been built, and the Harvard Square

trolleys were cold, inhospitable vehicles, I assure you. *Those cakes*, some had white frosting and chocolate frosting decorations, were most tempting.

At Miss Cary's death in 1918, Lucile A. Harrington, President of the Catholic Club, wrote to President Briggs that despite their sorrow they were "looking forward to a closer union with the College, which the meetings—henceforward to be held at Agassiz House—will bring." She invited Briggs to come to their first meeting, where Prof. Ford was to speak on Christine of Pisan. Briggs must have been unable to attend, for the next month the Club asked him to address their second meeting, at which he spoke on the English Catholic poet Richard Crashaw. Some sense of Briggs' support for the group can be perceived from the fact that President Briggs and his wife were also invited to the third monthly meeting, where the Director of Diocesan Charities spoke on "Vocational Opportunities."[8]

Talks on "Mixed Marriages" and "The Psychology of Public Worship" combined with readings from Hiawatha and holiday parties for the poor over the course of a typical Radcliffe Catholic Club calendar. In its first thirty years, the Club usually gathered for three or four meetings a term, excluding an occasional series at Lent or other times.

109

Prof. J.D.M. Ford, at one time the sole Catholic on the faculty, avidly supported Radcliffe, where his sister and daughters were educated, and for over a generation was a regular speaker at the Radcliffe Catholic Club. Guest speakers tended to be clerics or those engaged in education. The Very Rev. John B. Peterson, D.D., Rector of St. John's Seminary, a friend of Emma Forbes Cary, variously talked on "A Phase of Spanish Life," gave an illustrated lecture on the passion play, and delivered a talk prepared by Dr. David Supple on "Rise of the Mediaeval University."

Several lecturers chose to address the interest of a group of educated Catholic women. Early in the club's history, Miss Katherine Conway talked on "Woman and a Career" and Prof. Ford on "Leading Catholic Women." Also invited was Mrs. Slattery, President of the League of Catholic Women. At the 1932 Communion Breakfast, the Rev. R.J. Cushing (future Archbishop) spoke on Saint Catherine of Siena. Mrs. Charles Maginnis '04 spoke that year on Radcliffe as it was in her day.

DISTINGUISHED SCHOLAR: HELEN WHITE

Sixty years after graduation, a classmate remembered a remarkable contemporary at Radcliffe:[9]

> At that time the most superior scholar in the college was one of our group, Helen Constance White, a Catholic, who graduated in three years Phi Beta Kappa, summa cum laude. She was a novelist, essayist, poet. The President of the United States appointed her to many committees and, after World War II, chose her to go to France to organize care for the orphans. She was a faithful friend, a gracious lady. May she rest in peace.

After leaving Radcliffe with the A.M., Helen Constance White taught English at Smith for two years and then began a lifelong association with the University of Wisconsin. She took the Ph.D. there in 1924 and was a full professor by 1936. "A big-throated, strongly-built woman, dressed simply and in good taste, informal and gracious in manner, she lectures from card notes in a clear, audible, richly inflected voice," wrote one reporter. Popular, literate, and known for an ability to separate the important from the trivial, she quickly became a linchpin of her university, as the first female president of the University Club and as president of the state university's teachers' union.

Soon a leading figure in American academics, Professor White served as President of the American Association of University Women from 1941 to 1947 and was the first (and before 1970 the only) woman elected President of the American Association of University Professors. She was also Vice-President of the Modern Language Association, a Senator of Phi Beta Kappa, and a Director of the National Council of Teachers of English and the American Council on Education. In addition to numerous awards, she received twenty-three honorary degrees.

A profoundly religious person, White's scholarly interests in mysticism and devotional literature emerged from her faith and led to publications like *The Mysticism of William Blake* (1929), *The Metaphysical Poets: A Study in Religious Experience* (1936), and *The Tudor Book of Private Devotion* (1951). In recognition of her national contribution to Catholic causes, the University of Notre Dame presented her with its Laetare Medal in 1942. In an essay on "Religion in

Since many graduates went into schoolteaching, appropriate speakers were found among the mostly Catholic officialdom of the Boston school system. Mr. A.L. Rafter, assistant superintendent of Boston Public schools, gave a lecture on "Cardinal Newman" in 1909. In later years, speakers from the system included Miss Mary Mellyn, supervisor of substitutes, and Mr. Jeremiah Burke, assistant superintendent (speaking on Thomas More). Fr. Lyons, superintendent of the Boston parochial schools, regaled the Radcliffe ladies with "Scenes and Memories of Student Days" accompanied by stereopticon views and music.

The arts were not unimportant for a society of learned women. Periodically, members or guests presented music or readings for the meetings, especially at holiday times. The last meeting of the academic year 1914-15 was such an occasion, and Fr. Ryan invited the Archbishop to attend: "This meeting is to be of a musical and literary character by the members themselves and intended as a complimentary manifestation of grateful appreciation for all

State University Education," she painted a perceptive portrait of the experience of religion:

> Yet religion is a good deal more than humanity, a branch of study. Religion is something to be experienced. It engages not only the reason but the will and the imagination and the emotions. It involves not only the flash of insight, the decision, the conclusion, but also discipline and habit with its building of contexts. For religious life is dependent not only upon the individual insight but upon group support, not only upon the electric flash of momentary discovery and reaction but upon all the sustaining rhythms of the dear and the familiar. In short, religion is not only a matter of knowing but of living. Obviously, knowledge about religion is not enough.

Her "discipline and habit" was Catholic, but she could phrase her thought so persuasively because she understood something of the habits of others. She served on the Board of Directors of the National Conference of Christians and Jews, and internationally she was connected with UNESCO.

In her historical novels, Helen White stripped the romantic illusions from the Catholic past and presented "the true mixture of high ideals and sinful performance" in a genre notoriously sentimental. Offering suggestions to the aspiring Catholic writer, she advised the pursuit of excellence: "It is blasphemous to call an essentially feeble thing *Catholic*. One needs no other picture of Catholicism in Norway than the virile *Kristin Lavransdatter* by Sigrid Undset, and no thin little job of apologetics can substitute for the grim realism of David Matthews' *History of Catholicism in England*. Truthfulness is the first essential of success for the Catholic novelist." Her typical clarity and lack of bias may have reflected the balanced result of "the good intentions to do the right and progressive thing" characteristic of the debating society at Girl's High School in Boston and "that cynicism which a Radcliffe girl like myself, at least in her freshman year, suspected was typical of Harvard professors."[10]

Born in New Haven but reared in Boston, she died in 1967 while visiting her family in Jamaica Plain.

Miss Cary has done for the Club. It has been suggested that possibly, Your Eminence might see your way to drop in as a sort of Visitory to Miss Cary's House and thereby meet the Club at the same time."[11] Sadly, Ryan's letter implies that visiting the Brahmin patroness would be more appealing to the Cardinal than meeting the Radcliffe students. O'Connell was apparently not able to appear, so that fall Miss Cary herself invited O'Connell to a meeting. The chancery expressed the Cardinal's blessing for her work with the students and his hopes to attend one of the meetings of the Radcliffe Catholic Club, but his focus still seemed on the influential older woman: "At any rate His Eminence says that he would like to see you sometime before Christmas."[12]

In addition to the usual officers, the Radcliffe Catholic Club had a Chairman of the Charity Board through the 1940's and a Chairman of Forum in its early years. There were many in need in Cambridge and the Club typically supplied Christmas dinners to a few poor families or answered the volunteer invitations of speakers like Miss Eleanor Colleton, president of the Boston Italian Immigrant Society. A common Yearbook notation was: "The charitable work is under the direction of the Charity Board, which arranges for weekly visits to the Holy Ghost Hospital and holds each year a large whist party, the proceeds of which are given to Catholic Charities." Eventually whist yielded to bridge, but the charity games continued.

The major religious service was the annual Communion Breakfast held on the Feast of the Immaculate Conception in St. Paul's Convent, but other gatherings had theological content. Different series of weekly meetings on Christian Doctrine were arranged and by all accounts the special topic for the year 1919-20, "Higher Criticism of the Bible," proved extremely interesting. The "eminent scholastic philosopher" and relative of a Radcliffe student, Father Fulton J. Sheen spoke at the banquet three times.

But Catholics at Radcliffe spent most of their college years in the company of non-Catholic classmates. "Except for the pleasure derived from the Catholic Club meetings, and the resulting friendships—some of which I am enjoying now, sixty-five years later—I can remember nothing to distinguish a Catholic student from all the others" recalls Marie Scollard Degnan '17. "We all studied under our appletree, read in our library (now the Schlesinger), swam in our pool in the gym, wielded rapiers in fencing classes,

Helen White was only one of fifteen Catholics in the class of 1917. At the fiftieth class reunion, Sr. Mary Rosa Doyle, C.S.J., stands out.

played basketball with our neighbors (Sargent School) and once in a while we won a game. We all cheered our famous jumping center Florence Feeley, marched in suffrage parades, and danced at proms."

Edith Gartland '13 (born in Cambridge, lived in Dorchester) was not only President of the Catholic Club but also President of her Class. Likewise, Mary Cecilia Smith '12 was Vice-President of each, and Beatrice Cashman was Secretary of the Catholic Club and Vice-President of the Class of 1909. In these pre-war years, it would appear that leadership in the Catholic Club garnered the respect that won class offices rather than opprobrium. In fact, it is difficult at any time to find evidence of any discrimination against Catholics at Radcliffe, since in its early years it attracted many commuters and was considered less elite than Smith or Vassar.[13]

In May, 1913 the Cecilian Guild and the St. Paul Catholic Club jointly presented "The Commuters" at the Plymouth Theatre. The Cecilian Guild was an organization of Catholic young women who met weekly downtown to make clothing for children and provide help for mothers. The elaborate program attests to the generosity of over 100 patronesses, mostly Irish but also including Mrs. Oliver Ames, Mrs. LeBaron R. Briggs, Miss Emma Forbes Cary, Mrs. A. Lawrence Lowell, Mrs. C. Bruen Perkins, Mrs. R. M. Saltonstall, and Mrs. Paul Thorndike. Whether these women, Brahmins by birth or marriage, supported the cause for the sake of charity, duty, or friendship, it is clear that educated Catholic youth were able to meet and attract a broad range of society.

FLORENCE HUNTER RUSSELL

Mrs. Russell, Radcliffe '32, was for many years a teacher in Cambridge. She wrote this reminiscence in 1989.

The Catholic Club in my time was a small group made up mostly of commuters. I don't recall any special schedule of meetings. We usually had a Communion Breakfast, a final dinner, a series of Lenten talks, and now and then a meeting in one of the attic rooms of Agassiz. The club came under Fr. Hickey at St. Paul's, and Fr. Wm. Gunn was our spiritual leader and usually gave the Lenten talks.

I do think the encouragement and support of prominent Harvard professors, Jeremiah Ford and Louis Mercier, contributed to our stability, and recognition by the college. Prof. Ford had sisters and daughters who went to Radcliffe; Elizabeth Ford was in '32; and Prof. Mercier's daughter, Marie-Zoe was in '33. Through Mary Carr Baker ('29 or '30) we had the good fortune of having her uncle, Fr. Fulton Sheen, as speaker a couple of years, and that gave us a certain prominence. Also, Fr. Lord, who had been Professor in the History Department, resigned, joined the Church, and spoke to us. And Alice Maginnis's father, Charles D. Maginnis, a prominent Church architect, favored us with his presence.

I would certainly say Catholics were in the minority at the time. A few years before, Emmanuel College had been launched, and some of my classmates had felt some pressure to go there. And, of course, too, there was the idea that if you went to Radcliffe, you were going to lose your faith and go straight to Hell!!! Fortunately for me, such ideas didn't affect my parents' actions or thoughts at all.

As for contact with Harvard, there was none! In our day professors gave a course at 9 at Harvard and crossed the Square to repeat it at 10 for us (undergrads)! We couldn't (or they??) be contaminated! Only grad students could sign up for a course in Harvard, and then, of course, these were the days too, when we "ladies" wore our hats and gloves to the Square. Some of my classmates hardly saw the inside of the Harvard Yard during the four years!

Radcliffe showed Harvard the way at the 1948 Archdiocesan parade. Ruth Kennedy '50 and Anita Palmer Fenessey '49 carry the banner. Further right are Jean O'Brien Erickson '51 and Shirley Johnson McCarthy '51.

From the Thirties

By the 1930s, there were occasional open meeting with students from men's colleges. Charles Maginnis, the noted ecclesiastical architect of Maginnis and Walsh, was husband and father of Radcliffe women and an occasional speaker to Radcliffe Catholics. At an open meeting he spoke on "Modern Tendencies in Architecture," a talk illustrated by lantern slides. Prof. Copithorne of M.I.T. was invited to speak on "Certain Modern Catholic Poets" at a gathering in 1931 with Harvard and M.I.T. The then famous, and later infamous, Jesuit Fr. Leonard Feeney also read from his poetry at an open meeting in 1933. The connections of the Harvard and Radcliffe Catholic Clubs was tenuous at most in these days, rarely intersecting other than for communion breakfasts and occasional talks. Obviously, individual students from the two college did not need their pastors in order to meet each other, but the establishment of the St. Benedict Center in the forties gave male and female Catholics a place to see each other more frequently.

A 1937 survey, conducted by the college for comparison with other women's colleges, found Catholics the "best balanced" of the different religious groups. The class of 162 students was 57% Protestant, 22% Jewish, 21% Catholic. Of the 34 Catholics in the class, 80% were from Massachusetts—a higher ratio than

for the other groups—but it was from these local students that the "outstanding girls of the class in extra-curricular activities" came. A number of them held the highest class offices and achieved high honors, but they were not the exception. We learn that 91% of Catholics joined at least three clubs, a much higher percentage than for Protestants (58%) or Jews (44%). With such small class sizes, this year may not have been representative, but like their predecessors, the 34 Catholics came from a mix of family situations: 15 were from a "cultured background," 19 from an "average simple background," and 5 from a "very simple background."[14]

In response to a lapse in activity by the club in the late thirties, the Emma Forbes Cary Guild of Radcliffe alumnae was formed. An organizational meeting was held at Marie Mullen's house on Commonwealth Avenue in December 1941 or early 1942. The hostess was elected president; a fellow teacher from Cambridge Latin, Mary E. Murray, became vice-president; Connie Dowd, a lawyer, was elected treasurer, wrote the bylaws and incorporated the organization.[15] Genevieve McGlinchey Mathison '32, secretary from 1942 to 1946 recalls the next step:

We needed a chaplain and the girls wanted Msgr. Robert Lord. I went over to Cardinal O'Connell's office to make the request (my uncle Father Joseph McGlinchey made the appointment to meet with the Cardinal). Although he would have preferred Father Wright, we got Father Lord, because we felt he had been close to students at Harvard and Radcliffe. We met at St. Benedict's Center from 1942 to 1945, a basement room located across the street from the front door of St. Paul's Church.

Twenty years later the guild had almost a hundred members. This alumnae group meets about five times a year at various Catholic institutions for social, charitable, and spiritual activities.

Although the location of Radcliffe College put the Catholic Club under the jurisdiction of St. Paul's, many students from the Radcliffe Quad naturally found Mass at St. Peter's on Concord Avenue more convenient. Particularly sympathetic was Fr. Francis V. Murphy, D.D., the pastor of St. Peter's from 1933 to 1958 and a Harvard graduate, who had been an occasional speaker to the Radcliffe

Catholic Club in the twenties. Prof. Ford used to joke that Murphy had gone from being his pupil to being his pastor.

In September, 1946, Miss Clare McDonough received a note from the archdiocese stating that the Radcliffe Catholic Club had a new chaplain in Rev. Joseph I. Collins, recently returned from service as an army chaplain. It was in the person of Fr. Collins that the ministry of Harvard and Radcliffe Catholics was united in 1960 and more visibly in the form of the Harvard-Radcliffe Catholic Student Center in 1961.

For the first twenty years after the merger of the Harvard and Radcliffe Catholic clubs, the student leadership reflected the greater proportion of men in the combined student bodies. However, since the decision to open the joint college admissions on a gender-blind basis in 1976, the men and women among the Catholic Student Association officers have been almost balanced.

The 1957 Catholic Club sponsored a charity fashion show. Nancy Megley, Jill Fraser, Alice Walsh and Eleanor Coyne volunteered here.

PART II
In Their Own Words

The Catholics of Harvard Square speak for themselves here in reminiscences which have been left fresh with only minimal editing. In introducing this section, Avery Dulles, S.J., recalls the many sides of Harvard Square which influenced him fifty years ago: the scholars, the parish liturgies, and the centers for Catholic conversation. Reminiscences by others of the university, parish or choir school proceed in a roughly chronological order from the beginning of the century until the present. Some were collected by questionnaires in 1964 by Mary Ann Reardon, some by recent requests and interviews with Marie Daly or Jeffrey Wills. In addition to the following excerpts, relevant memoirs can be found in print by John LaFarge, S.J., Christopher Huntington, John Cort, Michael Novak, and various members of the St. Benedict Center.[1]

Avery Dulles, S.J., '40, receiving congratulations on his ordination from his father John Foster Dulles, while his mother and Archbishop Spellman look on.

Harvard as an Invitation to Catholicism

*a reminiscence describing the influence of Harvard and St. Paul's
on the religious life of one man*

Avery Dulles, S.J.

"Oxford made us Catholics," wrote John Henry Newman. Conscious of the paradox involved, I could echo that statement and assert, "Harvard made us Catholics."

Harvard in the 1930's was not a uniformly Catholicizing influence. One could move all sorts of directions as a student there, but at least it offered a strong possibility of immersing oneself in the Catholic heritage of medieval and modern Europe, and that is what occurred in my own case.

I have written about my intellectual groping toward faith in a small book, *A Testimonial to Grace*, composed in 1944, and published in 1946. But the account is deliberately abstract, short on facts and long on theory. In this brief essay I would like to reverse the emphasis.

I entered college in 1936, Harvard's three hundredth year. At the tercentenary celebration one of the main speakers was the French Thomistic philosopher, Etienne Gilson. I subsequently read and applauded his address on "Medieval Universalism at Its Present Value," an eloquent protest against the fragmentation of Europe into hostile nation states, replacing the cosmopolitanism of the past. Gilson had taught at Harvard before I arrived, and had left a great reputation behind him. He returned to Harvard in the spring of 1941 to deliver his lectures on *God and Philosophy*. By the time I heard him give these lectures I was a student at the Law school and a Catholic.

My progress toward the Church was closely linked to my studies in history and philosophy. Before I arrived in September 1936 I had begun to read the work of another great French philosopher, Jaques Maritain. As a prep school senior I was deeply impressed by his *Art and Scholasticism*, which propounded a theory of art and beauty that harmonized with the last chapter of James Joyce's *Portrait of the Artist as a Young Man*, another of my favorite books in those days. Thus I was oriented toward Thomism even before my freshman year.

My religious development was accelerated by some courses I took as a freshman. History 1, a survey of European history since the fall of the Roman Empire, acquainted me with the Middle Ages. Among the readings for that course, I was struck by Emile Mâle's analysis of thought-world reflected in the cathedrals of medieval Europe. Professor Roger B. Merriman lectured eloquently on the papacy, the Holy Roman Empire, and the Spanish monarchy. He described with relish how the Emperor Henry IV stood in the snow doing penance before Pope Gregory VII. In a survey course on French literature under Professor Louis Allard, I discovered the vibrant prose of Pascal's *Pensées* and Chateaubriand's *Mémoires d'outre-tombe*. I was troubled by the rationalism of Descartes until I found a critical commentary on the *Discourse on Method* by Etienne Gilson, who seemed to put his finger exactly on the weakness of Descartes' argument. I determined to read more of Gilson when the opportunity arose.

In my sophomore year my thinking developed more decisively along the same lines. Under the guidance of Raphael Demos, who

119

taught the survey course, Philosophy 1, I became a devotee of Plato and Aristotle. While the assigned readings skipped from Lucretius to Descartes, some medieval philosophy was offered as an option for the Christmas reading period, and I selected, with keen interest, Gilson's *The Philosophy of St. Thomas Aquinas*. About the same time I deepened my medieval studies, by taking Charles H. Taylor on the intellectual history of the Middle Ages. I also delved into Renaissance Art under the guidance of Professors Wilhelm Koehler and Charles R. Post at the Fogg Museum. To this day I can vividly recall Professor Post pointing to a slide of Tintoretto's Crucifixion and declaring it the greatest painting ever made of the greatest event in the history of the world.

It was my good fortune to have as my tutor in my sophomore year a brilliant historian of France, Paul Doolin, who was at the time a recent and enthusistic convert to Catholicism. His combination of Platonic philosophy and Catholic faith challenged and delighted me. I have written a few pages about Doolin in my *Testimonial to Grace*.

In my last two years as a student at Harvard I specialized in the Italian Renaissance, including its art, music, literature, philosophy, and religion. Concurrently I studied the reformation and the Counter Reformation, comparing the doctrines of Luther, Calvin, and the Council of Trent. I read extensively in Ludwig Pastor's *History of the Popes*, and came to sympathize with the problems of the papacy in an unruly age. At every point I found myself more at home with the Catholic tradition than with its Protestant counterparts. I read with fascination the autobiography of St. Ignatius, and admired the work of Jesuit theologians, Diego Laynez and Alonso Salmeron, at the Council of Trent.

Another major influence during these years was that of Charles Howard McIlwain, an authority on the history of political theory. In his book, *The Growth of Political Thought in the West*, he communicated a deep appreciation of the seeds of modern constitutional thought in the Christian humanism of the Middle Ages.

I wrote a senior thesis on the 15th-century Italian philosopher, Giovanni Pico della Mirandola. He had been hailed by Jakob Burckhardt and many European idealists as the very prototype of Renaissance humanism liberating itself from the shackles of medieval scholasticism. With the brashness of youth I adopted the opposite position, maintaining that, while Pico did reach out to include various forms of Platonism in his synthesis, he remained essentially a medieval scholastic. To my delight I was informed, at the time of graduation, that my thesis had been selected for the Phi Beta Kappa prize, and would be published the following winter by the Harvard University Press. I spent part of the summer of 1940 revising it for publication with the help of Dana B. Durand, who was by that time my tutor, since Paul Doolin had left to teach at Georgetown. Durand was an authority on medieval Nominalism then doing research on the physical and astronomical ideas of Nicole Oresme. He taught me to distrust the myth that empirical science began only with the Renaissance.

What I have just narrated about my academic formation is central to the process of my conversion, but it is not the whole story. As I studied history and philosophy I could not help becoming aware that the faith of the Middle Ages was a living heritage for many of my neighbors—not so much professors and students of Harvard or the Protestant establishment as the great masses of townspeople. Cambridge, Massachusetts was in those days a predominantly Catholic environment, and its Catholic churches were thriving centers of devotion.

During my undergraduate days I sampled nearly all the churches in the area, including the university church, several Anglican churches, and two Catholic churches, St. Peter's and St. Paul's. I would often go to a Catholic Mass in the morning and then go to an evening service at Christ Church, which was Episcopalian. Francis B. Sayre, Jr., a young associate at Christ Church, impressed me as the best preacher in the area, but I could not get over the feeling that Anglicanism was an uneasy compromise between Protestantism and Catholicism. The rector, C. Leslie Glenn, in a sermon at Christ Church, remarked that there are some individuals who have a vocation to go over to Rome, and I felt that he was speaking to me.

In my last two years of college I found a favorite bookstore, named for St. Thomas More, then located on Church Street. The manager was a charming, dynamic, well-read woman named Catherine Goddard Clarke, and she was ably assisted by Madeleine Mercier, a daughter of Professor Louis J. A. Mercier of Harvard's French department. At the store I equipped myself with a large Gasparri catechism, a Latin-English missal, and a number of other basic religious books. Since the bookstore served also as a lending library, I found it possible to borrow a few books each week for leisurely reading in my room at Lowell House. In this way I was able to keep up on the latest publications of Gilson and Maritain and to familiarize myself with other Catholic authors, including Karl Adam, Otto Karrer, E. I. Watkin, C. C. Martindale, Cuthbert Butler, Martin D'Arcy, Ross Hoffman, and Paul Hanly Furfey. Many of them, I found, were converts who had followed intellectual paths similar to my own.

As a result of this reading I became convinced that the faith that I so admired in patristic and medieval authors such as Augustine, Aquinas, and Dante was not simply a thing of the past. It was very much alive in the hearts of living intellectuals. It was also alive in the simpler faith of the crowds who pressed into the Catholic churches of Boston and Cambridge.

At St. Paul's the Sunday Masses were always crowded. There were numerous altar boys who rattled off the Latin responses with perfect ease and looked like angels. The singing and ceremonies for Holy Week were magnificent. During the annual parish missions for men and women (in separate groups) the lower church would be filled before daylight by the vast range of humanity, most of them from the blue collar working class. I was amazed to hear the people singing the hymns of St. Thomas Aquinas in Latin at

Sunday Benediction. Where else could a budding medievalist feel so much at home?

Although I was rather certain as an undergraduate that I would end up as a Catholic, I did not take the step until later. During the summer of 1940, after working on the revision of my thesis, I read a lot more Catholic literature, including the *Confessions* of St. Augustine. When I returned to Cambridge in the Fall, I went to the St. Thomas More bookstore and asked Mrs. Clarke how one might proceed if one wanted to become a Catholic. She offered to put me in contact with a priest who would help me. With her unerring instinct for what would work, she selected a Jesuit graduate student in classics, Father Edwin A. Quain, who met with me about once a week for about six weeks, until he was satisfied that I knew what I was doing. For my reception I chose the feast day of St. John of Berchmans, November 26, 1940.

A few weeks before that date I wrote to my parents, telling them what I was about to do. I did not think that it would be a surprise to them, but it seems that they had no inkling of the way my mind was moving. They asked me to come to New York and discuss the matter, which I duly did. My father, being a tolerant man, agreed that it was correct for me to follow my conscience, and that he should not oppose my decision since I was an adult. So I went ahead.

I was received into the Church in a private ceremony, with conditional baptism in the basement of St. Paul's Church. Father Quain presided and received my profession of faith—along with a renunciation of heresy, which I said with particular relish. For my Godfather I had Christopher Huntington, then an assistant dean of freshman at Harvard, and now a retired monsignor living in Norwich, Vermont. My godmother was Catherine Clarke. After the ceremony, I had a small dinner at the Commander Hotel for the group, including a few friends. One of them was Albert Smith, a junior at Harvard, who was a recent convert. He died in 1979 as a Jesuit of the California Province.

For a little more than a year after becoming a Catholic I remained a student at Harvard Law School. During that time I regularly attended meetings of the St. Clement Society, a Catholic group that met on Commonwealth Avenue at the home of a zealous convert, Mrs. Francis Gray. Among the members of that society were prominent intellectual converts, such as Daniel Sargent and Hugh Whitney.

Mrs. Gray also allowed her home to be used for meetings of a Catholic student group known as the St. Andrew Society. It consisted of Catholic students from a number of colleges—including Harvard, M.I.T., Radcliffe, Cambridge Junior College, and Emmanuel—who wished to explore their faith more deeply and live it more intensely. Under Mrs. Clarke's leadership this club grew in numbers and enthusiasm, so that by the spring of 1941 we felt the need of a facility of our own, somewhat larger and more accessible than Mrs. Gray's livingroom. One day we noticed that a furniture dealer was moving out of a store at the corner of Bow and Arrow Streets, just opposite the main entrance to St. Paul's Church. We signed the lease and several of us agreed to take care of the rent for the next few months.

During the summer of 1941, Mrs. Clarke and several friends, including Christopher Huntington, an English teacher at Holy Cross named John Julian Ryan, and a young woman named Margaret Knapp who was waiting to be admitted as a Religious of the Sacred Heart, made plans to establish a student center at our newly leased premises.

Sydney Callahan, Avery Dulles, S.J., Jana Kiely and John Noonan prepare for a 1991 panel at St. Paul's on "Catholicism and American Culture."

I wanted the center to be named for St. Robert Bellarmine, but others thought that his name and reputation would not appeal to Protestants. At John Ryan's suggestion we settled on the title, St. Benedict Center.

In the fall of 1941 the center opened with the full approval of the pastor of St. Paul's, Monsignor Augustine Hickey, and Father Francis Greene, an associate pastor who also ran the Harvard Catholic Club. St. Benedict Center was an independent organization not officially connected with Harvard or any other institution. It was under lay control, but we obtained, whenever we could, the services of a chaplain. The priest who most frequently assisted us was Father Richard Rooney, a Jesuit associated with a national organization of Sodalities known as the Queen's Work.

During the war years from December 1941 to the Spring of 1946 I was away from the Center, but I did keep in close touch with the Center through correspondence with some of its members, including especially Catherine Clarke, who wrote frequent letters reporting in great detail everything that was going on. I also made a brief visit around Christmas of 1943.

When I returned in the Spring of 1946, at the end of the war, the Center was flourishing. It had obtained the services of Father Leonard Feeney, S.J., as its full time director. Father Feeney was a brilliant poet, orator, humorist, and mimic, very knowledgeable in theology and ardent in his apostolic zeal. The Center opened about noon every day except Sunday. Mrs. Clarke presided at afternoon tea. Each evening of the week was regularly set aside for a different kind of event. On Monday evenings, as I recall, the St. Andrew Club would gather to discuss spirituality and prayer. On Tuesday night we had a seminar on philosophy under the direction of Fakhri Maluf, a Lebanese convert then teaching at Boston College. On the other nights we had poetry reading, dramatics, and the like. Daniel Sargent, a former professor from Harvard, helped us in our study of history, and for English literature we had the assistance of John Ryan (by now married to Mary Perkins, whom he had met through the Center). Professor Louis F. Solano of Harvard helped us study Dante in Italian. Thursday nights were special, because they were reserved for Father Feeney's weekly

Avery Dulles' godfather, Msgr. Christopher Huntington '32, and Bernard Cardinal Law '53 at the dedication of the Harvard-Radcliffe Catholic Student Center in 1991.

lectures on theology. The Center was vastly overcrowded that night, with people on the street leaning into the door and windows.

By the Summer of 1946 the Center was a beehive of activity. Scores of students became converts to Catholicism, and many others who had drifted away, returned to Catholic practice. Dozens of the young Catholics found marriage partners through the Center. A steady stream departed for seminaries and novitiates. In this honeymoon period few would have suspected the troubled future that lay ahead.

Before I left St. Benedict Center in July 1946 we had in press the first issue of its quarterly, *From the Housetops.* I remember going to the residence of Archbishop (later Cardinal) Richard Cushing to get permission to publish. Our delegation consisted of Father Feeney, Catherine Clarke, and two or three others. When we asked about censorship the Archbishop said, in effect, "You have my complete confidence. Censor each issue yourselves." Perhaps he named Father Feeney as the censor.

It would be for others to tell the story of how St. Benedict Center, in 1949 and later, got into conflict first with Harvard, then with the Jesuit Provincial, and finally with Rome and the archbishop. Its use of the adage "Outside the Church no salvation" became a subject of great contestation within the Church and beyond. But of all of that I have no firsthand knowledge. I remember the Center only as a place of youthful enthusiasm for the faith, exemplary Catholic conduct, and eagerness for growth in holiness. I look back on those first years with a certain nostalgia, somewhat as Luke, I suppose, looked back at the early Church in Jerusalem.

Rev. Avery Dulles, S.J., holds the Laurence McGinley Chair at Fordham University. One of America's leading theologians, Fr. Dulles' books include Models of the Church *and* Models of Revelation.

JOHN A. O'SHEA

John O'Shea, Harvard '13, wrote this recollection
for the Catholic Student Center in 1964.

I was a member of St. Paul Catholic Club, though, since I lived at home in Boston at that time, I was not too active in its daily affairs.

I have a rather vivid recollection that the Pastor and his assistants of the local parish church were under strict orders from Archbishop (later Cardinal) O'Connell, NOT to recognize, encourage or assist the Catholic Club in any way. So our "spiritual guidance" was slim and was taken care of by the individual consciences and faith of the Club officers and members and by their resolution to provide outstanding examples to our fellow college mates, of Catholic behavior, integrity, honesty, etc., something which was, in those days, a complete mystery to practically everyone but a Catholic. It was supported by dues and, in our case as previously mentioned, by the returns from that theatrical venture.

The number of Catholics in the college was not large, but I think a large percentage belonged to the Club. My belief is that the Club had been more or less dormant and little known until the students of that time tried to revive and reanimate it, with little or no encouragement from the Church authorities. On the contrary, disapproval. You see, at that time, Catholic students at Harvard, or any other college, were suspect as incipient apostates. Surprising that no effort was made to "redeem them."

THE CECILIAN GUILD
AND
St· PAUL CATHOLIC CLUB

Present

"The Commuters"

Plymouth Theatre   May 19, 1913

There was a great error in judgment, as well as an unnecessary loss of time, in not seizing the opportunity offered to the Hierarchy, by our efforts and desires, to revitalize a relationship which could result only, by example and contact, in an increased understanding and tolerance among our non-Catholic fellow students and people at large.

The interest, developments and ecumenical activity you mention is long, long past due. Experiences my wife and I had in later years, at the later reunions, among classmates among whom was a predominance of many members who had become Protestant clergymen, would emphasize that there had been a shameful loss of time and opportunity. The laity has always, probably with good reason, been discouraged by the Clergy, from any active participation in Church propaganda, etc., unless tightly supervised. I have found that there has always been considerable curiosity and interest in Catholicism especially among the Protestant Clergy who were precluded by embarrassment from going direct to the Catholic Clergy. A well-trained layman with his wider contacts was an ideal tool for dissemination of information.

What did the Club see as its purpose? Not so much the additional education in the faith. The needed cooperation, direction and inspiration was lacking. To inform the Harvard Community about the Catholic Church? Yes, but mainly by example and effort and intelligent information rather than by active proselytizing. To do social work? The average Catholic came from comfortable, but not wealthy, families. Many, like myself, lived at home in the Boston area and were not able to be too active in the daily activities of the Club. One important reason was to provide a means for congenial and sympathetic contact, especially for those away from home.

As a possible note of interest in the club affairs at that time, I have found an old program, which I am sending you, for a very successful performance at the Plymouth Theatre in Boston of a popular Broadway comedy of that time. The cast was made up of members of the Cecilian Guild of Back Bay, Boston—a group of Catholic young ladies, as explained in that program and of some members of the St. Paul Club. I was one of them.

What did the Catholic and the non-Catholic think of the Club? I do not think we "made enough noise," nor did we want to, to attract outside attention. Our influence was more in example and individual contact and behavior. Most of the Catholics, I might say "all" that I knew, were "practicing" Catholics. It became a matter with us, in principle, to prove to the non-Catholic (and even more to the cynical Catholic clergy) that a Catholic need not be "misled" at Harvard. I am sure that within the capabilities, financial and otherwise, the Catholic students were glad of the existence of the Club, and regretted its limitations. I suppose that those who were "climbers," as such a philosophy existed and will always exist, did not acknowledge their eligibility for membership.

What was it like to be a Catholic at Harvard? Just the same as it felt to be a Catholic anywhere else, at that time. There was certainly no visible nor invisible sense of being "marked." Frankly, at that time, we were emerging from the "hostile atmosphere" of extreme and bitter prejudice and antagonism long experienced by our Catholic predecessors.

It was still a time when the bitterly anti-Catholic organizations such as the APA (the American Protective Association) and the Watch and Ward

Society were in existence and viciously active. I remember, myself, such expressions of intolerance as ads which stipulated that "No Catholics, and No Irish, need apply." There was, of course, and there still is, acute but private feelings of prejudice inherent in the minds of our fellow students as well as fellow citizens. I, personally, did not experience and know of any unpleasant incidents. So, there really was no difference, as I stated before, between being a Catholic in Harvard or anywhere else. Of course, the person who went forth with a purposeful chip on his shoulder could expect a challenge.

Even among the non-Catholics there were the discriminatory niceties in even their own relationships: one private school to another, private schools to public schools, one frat to another, one Protestant sect to another; differences in financial capabilities, so on "ad infinitum." It is only when one becomes a "professional" this or that that there arises a feeling of discomfort or animosity.

Also, as stated above, the Catholic at Harvard could, at that time, have unpleasant experiences with the cynical, suspicious clergy of the Catholic Church. Their old "Ghetto" instinct prevented a sensible understanding of how the "true and faithful" Catholic could go or look anywhere, except within the Catholic confines, and expect to prove himself stronger than the alleged, but non-existent, perverting influences. In all my years at Harvard classes, etc., I never heard a disparaging or discourteous remark.

CATHERINE KEOHANE

*Kit Keohane was born in Ireland and came to Boston in 1914.
For many years, she worked at Radcliffe. She gave this interview in
November 1988, shortly before her death.*

I was born in 1906 in Rosscarbery, County Cork (Ireland). I was a twin, you know. But my sister died young. My mother was Julia O'Brien and my father was Cornelius Brady, and there was ten of us. Father died. He was a boss in the Benduff Slate Quarry in Barleyhill, Rosscarbery, County Cork. I came out here [when I was] eight years old. My mother didn't come for years after that. But I came to my aunt and uncle in South Boston.

Sure, I remember taking the ship over. Oh, I was dreadfully sick! They almost threw me overboard, I was so sick. I got better anyway, and I landed on Ellis Island. I was so young and I was so sick and I didn't know where I was going. I came to South Boston and I lived there until I grew up. I lived with my aunt and uncle. My sister lived in Newton, and she used to come in on her days off. I was in school of course, I was so small. And then I went to work for a very rich family in Newton, on Centre Street. They're all gone. I went to Saints Peter and Paul church in South Boston. Fr. Hurley from here went there. Now he's made pastor of Blessed Sacrament on Pearl Street. We had him here for quite a while at Saint Paul's.

After I was married, I lived at 38 Kinnaird Street in an apartment. There was a little store out front. Johnny was born on Kinnaird Street, and so was Joe. My neighbors on Kinnaird Street are all gone. But, there's a few left. There's a nice colored family still there—Mrs. Taylor was her name. The blacks and whites got along. I think the only place they fight is in Dorchester.

I worked up at Harvard for Radcliffe for a long time. I took care of the food with the girls, at the steam table. I worked on Ash Street, at the Graduate Center. One day, I was going by, and I was looking for a job, and I saw that the place was ready to occupy. So I went in, and I asked the girl at the desk. She says, "Come right in and I'll hire you right away." And she did. And I was there for years. She was an awful nice boss. I loved everyone at Harvard. I was at Radcliffe for so long. All the women who worked with me, they are all gone. Gertrude Earhardt, Mary Toner, they worked with me in the kitchen. Margaret McGonagle, she was the cook.

My children went to Saint Paul's School. They went from the first grade until they got out in the eighth. We had nuns then—all nuns. They were Sisters of St. Joseph. I remember Sr. Agneta, and Sr. Faulkner—she was lovely. They were awfully fond of my kids. We used to have processions every May. They used to put the red sash around their shoulders. . . . I remember the old church up at the corner. We had just moved in when the new church opened. Monsignor Hickey was lovely, but very strict if a kid didn't do what they should do. I remember the day he was waked up here. He was laid in state, you know, in the aisle of the church. We had Fr. Kenney, we had Fr. Collins. His folks in Ireland are as near to me as that wall. And the mother died, and the father was in Youville. I used to go see him all the time. Fr. Collins was the pastor after Msgr. Hickey. He was lovely. I saw him the other day at a funeral in fact. I told him he was getting handsomer. Do you remember Fr. Fratic? He's gone up to Precious Blood in Dover. He was my best friend. He used to come here and have a bite of lunch with me. I go to Mass every day, pretty near. I don't say the Rosary, I answer it. Saint Paul's was a rich parish. When the students came, some don't put a penny in the box. It's the parishioners that give. It was a good parish when Msgr. Hickey was here. You never heard him asking for money. We've had nice priests up here, and the nuns were friends. I loved them all.

The annual May procession was a highlight of the children's calendar.

GENEVIEVE MCGLINCHEY MATHISON

*Born in Cambridge in 1911, Mrs. Mathison grew up on Athens Street. Like
her two sisters, she attended Radcliffe, where
she graduated in the class of 1932.*

I remember the old St. Paul church very well. We had a choir loft
there and I sang in the choir for years. They put stained glass windows in. The parish rectory was down at the end of Holyoke Street.
Fr. John Ryan was pastor when my uncle [Fr. Joseph McGlinchey]
was assistant pastor of St. Paul's. He was a very fatherly man; there
was quite a large number of priests, five in the parish at the time.
He was very friendly.

The first pastor of St. Paul's was Fr. Orr, who came from
the north of Ireland. He was the cousin of Fr. Manasses Dougherty.
He was a very fine man, not too popular of course in the area, because there were different people from different parts of Ireland that
didn't like him; they came from the south of Ireland and didn't like
men from the north of Ireland. My mother and father were both
related to Fr. Manasses Dougherty; they were fourth cousins of his.

From St. John's in East Cambridge, Fr. Dougherty worked
up to St. Peter's, and started St. Peter's which was dedicated in 1848.
The first people married there were Hannah McGowan, Eliza
McGowan's sister. When she came to Cambridge, Eliza opened up
a school where people from Ireland would be trained by her, how
to set a table, how to make beds, how to act as a nurse or a governess
for people in the Boston area. I think she had always done that type
of thing evidently. She came out in 1850. She had bought a place
on the corner of what was called Brighton Street and is now called
Kennedy Street. My father remembered having his sailboat down
there at the pier. She was on the opposite side of the street from
the coal wharf, on the side where you have the Kennedy Park. It
was on the side which we used to call Murray Beach. It was kind
of dangerous, but we used to go bathing there.

[When the new church opened,] it was a very impressive ceremony. They had all the children there; we sang in the choir. In the
old church we sang at the nine o'clock Mass and at the eleven o'clock
Mass every Sunday. And I collected church debt for the pastor, and
brought my money up on Sunday afternoon very carefully—ten cents
per person each Sunday. I covered from Athens Street up to Holyoke
Street. It was called church debt.

And we sold chances for the carillon which nobody liked
because it rang every fifteen minutes. Harvard students didn't like
the idea because they couldn't study with that thing ringing every
fifteen minutes. We wouldn't run it, of course, from ten o'clock at
night to six o'clock in the morning. They didn't like the Angelus
either because that was disturbing their studies. You were supposed
to stop and say the Angelus at six o'clock in the morning, noon, and
six o'clock at night.

I went to the St. Paul's School. One half of the school was
separated from the other half by swinging doors. The boys were
on one side and the girls were on the other. No uniforms at that
school. Rarely did we have contact with the boys. We had sev-

*Andrew McGlinchey,
superintendent of
Sunday School and
trustee of St. Paul's
Parish. He was a cousin
of Manasses Dougherty.*

enty-seven girls in our class. St. Paul's High School did not last very long. I didn't go to it, because when they started it, there were only a very few people there, and it looked to my mother like it was not going to continue. It was very expensive to try to maintain. I don't think it lasted any more than two years. It was at the corner of Ellery Street and Mass. Avenue, next to the convent. It was a vacant building that Fr. Ryan had bought. It could not have survived because of the timing. It was just coming into the Depression. They didn't have a great deal of money in Cambridge in those days, because most of them worked in the dormito-

The handsome monument to Manasses Dougherty overshadows the rest of the Mt. Auburn Catholic Cemetery.

ries. They came down to Newport in the summer to work for wealthy families. They were almost all Irish families they were working for.

Professor McConnell had the choir. You were asked to go in the choir when you were in grade six. We sang in the choir in grades six, seven and eight. He was an organist, a very strict man. He wanted to make sure everything was exactly right. He had two daughters, one was in my class and one was a year ahead of me. They lived down in the house that faced Banks Street. There were no boys in the choir; they were altar boys. I don't remember any adult choir at that time. The adults were the ones who sang the solos at the funerals.

We [the children's choir] did every Easter and every Christmas: five o'clock in the morning, nine o'clock and eleven o'clock. We had three Masses. We didn't have any midnight Masses in those days. These were High Masses that you sang. They had vespers on Sunday afternoon at four o'clock. We sang for vespers, too. Our week was really cut out for us. We could not get in trouble, we were so busy going back and forth. And of course we took Irish stepdancing and we would go over and entertain all the people in hospitals, in St. Elizabeth's Home.

We sang at the parish missions, at the closing service at the mission. Some of the pastors would have preferred an adult choir, but Fr. Ryan preferred the children. I think the other choirs that would have been there sang at wedding Masses and funeral Masses on a paid basis. Joe Ecker followed the organist McConnell. He came with Fr. Hickey. He may have been in the last part of Fr. Ryan's term. My father said they had had an earlier choir. Probably, Fr. Ryan preferred the children's choir, after Fr. Orr died.

We had quite a few neighbors on Athens Street. Mayor McNamee was the man who came to live next to us in Cambridge. The McNamees lived on the first floor. Mary McNamee worked at the Reversible Collar Company, as one of the floor ladies. The fire captain was Capt. John Shea and they lived on the second floor of the McNamee's place. Down the foot of the street was Mayor Tim Good. And on the opposite side of the street was Mayor Thurston. On one very short street there were four mayors. The place was mobbed with politicians. Judge Burns [legal counsel to the S.E.C. under Roosevelt] was on the corner of Grant and Athens. He was very tall. His father was a conductor, a motorman. He went to B. C. and from B. C. he went to Harvard Law School. He got a Buckley scholarship to Harvard Law School.

Dan Buckley was going to leave his money to Boston College, but he had an argument with the pastor, and he decided to leave his money to Harvard. He went to Cambridge Latin and had graduated at the top of his class and if you graduated, as I did, at the top of the class you're supposed to get a Buckley Scholarship, but not the girls, just the boys. So all the people came down from Lawrence and Lowell to live in Cambridge, and they would go to Cambridge Latin for one or two years, and make sure they topped that class, and they would get a Buckley Scholarship. Dan Buckley went to work as an office boy for the Cambridge *Tribune*, and I think the man who owned the Cambridge *Tribune* didn't know he was Catholic. It was an anti-Catholic paper. At the time they were taking my grandfather's letters from out west, they didn't know he was a Catholic. They were about the gold rush and they published them. They thought at the time he was a Scotch-Irish Protestant.

At Radcliffe, I majored in chemistry, physics, and mathemat-

Like the bride, four of Genevieve Mathison's bridesmaids were graduates of St. Paul's Grammar School and Radcliffe College. Although pictures within the church were prohibited, this picture of her 1944 wedding was permitted since it was taken from the sacristy.

ics. After I graduated, I started to teach. I taught at Cambridge High and Latin from 1935 to 1945. I went back for my masters in physics at B.C. in 1943. Later on I got my Ph.D. at B.C. My sisters Anne and Grace went to Radcliffe. Grace got her doctorate in education in 1945. She was in school psychology and measurement. She was the first woman teacher at the Harvard Graduate School of Education.

Msgr. Hickey was a very nice pastor. He was a chum of my uncle at the American College in Rome with Msgr. Murphy. They were very formal, very precise people, very nice.

CATHERINE M. HANLEY

Catherine Hanley, Radcliffe '23, was Chairman of the Charity Board for the Radcliffe Catholic Club. She wrote this recollection in 1989.

The club was firmly established when I entered in 1919, much as the other undergraduate clubs, with officers, dues, program, scheduled meetings with speakers, and, of course, our chaplain, Father John J. Ryan, diocesan appointee as chaplain and pastor of St. Paul's.

The Radcliffe student body in the early twenties was 60% commuting, 40% resident. Fewer Catholics proportionately lived at the "dorms." Registration was about 400 students and Catholics numbered 40 students—10% (believed to be a quota). Who were these Catholic students? Like their non-Catholic classmates, they were mostly graduates of public high schools of Eastern Massachusetts, with a few from private prep schools—Catholic schools, few in number then, did not prepare for the College Board Entrance Exams required at Radcliffe and Harvard. A greater proportion of dorm girls came from private schools, and the Boston private schools were represented, even with an occasional Catholic.

The chaplain, Father John J. Ryan held a diocesan appointment as Chaplain of the Harvard Catholic Club and of the Radcliffe Catholic Club (probably two separate appointments). There was no connection, formal or informal, between the clubs in those days. All Radcliffe activities were separate from Harvard! Father Ryan was a great person—a man for all the elements of society. Like many members of the Radcliffe Catholic Club, he was a graduate of a Boston public school. Strong in faith, he lived easily in the pluralistic environment.

Religion at Radcliffe. The Radcliffe Christian Association, an all-college organization, held morning prayers daily at nine o'clock in Agassiz Living Room. My junior-class guide, a Boston Brahmin Catholic and member of the Radcliffe Catholic Club, belonged to and supported the Radcliffe Christian Assn. She suggested, only mildly, my doing so. But I didn't. However, the Radcliffe Student Government Association was in charge of orientation of new students (freshmen) and a most important aspect of this orientation was the assignment of a senior guide to each freshman. A prime consideration in the pairing was *denominational preference*! In such a group, with ten± Catholic freshmen bound in a wonderful way with their Catholic seniors, the membership of the Catholic Club was obviously facilitated. Of course, the system worked for Menorah too. And it was not always possible to make the pairings.

We had our board of four officers working independently but always with the chaplain to arrange our monthly meetings with Catholic speakers outstanding in their fields. On one memorable occasion we had the poet Dan Sargent, convert from Unitarianism, then a young voice in the literary community. Meetings were held in Agassiz Living Room, and Father Ryan always attended. A special annual occasion was an evening lecture in Agassiz Theater to which we invited family, friends and interested public. We also had a "charity board" consisting of a member of each class with the senior as chair. This encouraged Club members to participate in the weekly visits to Youville (then Holy Ghost) Hospital and arranged for a Christmas Party for the patients, who always showed cordial appreciation of our visits.

Our only purely religious, spiritual exercise was the annual mass and communion in the convent chapel of the Sisters of the St. Joseph, teachers at St. Paul School. Mass was followed by breakfast at the Harvard Catholic Club, arranged by Fr. Ryan. Of course, we were members of our various parishes and a strong spiritual life seemed to prevail among us—still does! The Emma Forbes Cary Guild of Radcliffe Catholic alumnae represents the spirit of the Club of earlier years.

Father Ryan loved the Radcliffe Catholic Club. Because of his long experience with youth he was at once one of us and still the stalwart presence of the Church among us. He liked the style of the Radcliffe girl and especially enjoyed hearing us sing the Radcliffe songs (particularly I remember "Cherry ribbon in her hair") after the communion breakfast. And he appreciated the thoughtful, educated, inquiring mind. In response to the questions on "higher criticism" of the Bible, Father Ryan gave us a course, one afternoon a week over some months, on the historical journey of the Israelites. His learning and his sharing of it left us so much his debtors.

It would be incomplete not to mention Catholic faculty—especially Professor Robert Howard Lord, a convert, of the distinguished team of Haskins and Lord who gave the big History of Western Europe course. Professor Lord later became Father Lord at St. John's Seminary. Professor J.D.M. Ford was chairman of the Department of Romance Languages and Professor L.J.A. Mercier was in his department.

Catholic students participated in the social life of the College and were notable for scholastic achievement—Phi Beta Kappas, cum laudes and magnas. In after years there were vocations and conversions.

We were classmates. Protestant and Catholic, Christian and Jewish, we pursued our goals with honest differences.

MARIE COSTELLO

*Marie Costello has always lived in Harvard Square. A graduate of St. Paul's
School and Radcliffe College, she gave this interview in July 1991.*

My name is Marie Antoinette Moakler Costello. They called me Marie
Tony for short. I was born in Cambridge on November 20, 1910, on
my mother's birthday. My mother was born in Cambridge on November 20, 1886. My mother went to St. Paul's school. She was in the
1904 graduating class. Her name was Marie Vittilene Clark. Her
mother was Acadian French, and they taught the girls to speak French.
Her father was Irish, although they were all born here, except for him.
He was brought over by another Irish family at the age of two. And
then his parents followed, and all the rest of his brothers and sisters
were born here. They lived on DeWolfe Street and Mount Auburn
Street. They were all born at home.

My grandfather died when he was fifty-five years old; he died
of a heart attack. He had a saloon on Palmer Street in Cambridge. He
never had a drink in his life. He took a heart attack on the kitchen floor.
They tried to put a spoon of brandy on his lips, but it didn't revive
him. But after Cambridge went dry in the 1880's or 1890's, he went
out of business. But then he went into bookbinding; he was a book-
binder. My father was a printer who worked for the University Press
and when it went out of business, he went over to Boston to work for

Marie Costello's grandfather, Daniel Clark, owned a saloon on Palmer Street.

Lincoln and Smith. He used to take us over there and show us. He did some very nice printing. Sometimes you used to see the funny papers, the colors wouldn't line up. My father thought that was terrible. He ran the press. The University press was where those apartments [Charles Square] are now.

Of course, we lived at 10 Eliot Street, right across the street. That was my grandmother's home for years. But I remember living on Chapman Street when I was two years old. I do remember that I got scarlet fever after eating crackers and milk. We had a wooden table with a felt top. I just kicked the thing over. You didn't go to the hospital in those days for scarlet fever. You just stayed home in bed. They put down the shades.

We lived on Hammond Street for a while. Those were rented apartments. Then we rented a place at 45 Dunster Street. J. Press is there now. Something has changed about it. But it still has that big yard in there. It was all covered with grass. The rest of the street was just the way it is now, except that J. Press was a house right to the end. There was a bakery there.

In the old days, in the teens, we used to shop at Dinny O'Brien's which is O'Brien's liquor store now, and Charlie McLane's, which was over where the Galleria is. Dinny O'Brien's was a regular grocery store. The little park was always there [on Boylston St.]. My mother's first job, her one and only job, when she got out of high school was selling gloves at Corcoran's in Central Square. Over the years, she always knew how gloves should fit. She knew old Mr. Corcoran and his sons.

In 1917, my parents bought 1134 Mass Ave and we lived down there. In the meantime, the house up on 10 Eliot Street, which was my grandmother's house, that house was sold and my grandmother came to live with us. Johnny Ross the undertaker was on Arrow Street, where that Russian tea room is now. And then right on our own block was Jack Cronin's store, a grocery store. And then the next one down was Dave Coughlan's funeral home. All they had was offices, maybe they had places to embalm in back. We never saw a hearse pull up. We were always buried from the house. My own father was buried from the house, and they put a wreath on the door. So, if you went by a house and you saw a wreath... I don't know when they started using funeral parlors. My father died in 1935, and my grandmother in 1941.

It was very nice [living on Mass Ave]. We had a very mixed neighborhood. Miss Donovan at 1130 rented rooms too, and Professor Allard—he was a French professor at Harvard—was her star boarder. We were of Irish descent, us and the Sheas and the Donovans. And then the Guffeys were WASPs; they went to the Baptist church. And then the Armenians came in the early 1920's. Up in that corner where Johnny Ross was, there were apartments with various people in them. There was Goldie Tannenbaum. Goldie was Jewish. And the people across the street, Emma Kirkland was Protestant. A girl from Halifax lived in our neighborhood. During World War One, a ship blew up in Halifax harbor, and she was badly scarred. There are lots of things I just know about because of the people who lived there. Nobody heard of the Armenian holocaust until recently; but I sure knew about it, because we knew the kids. There was an eclipse of the sun there in the early 1920's or in the late teens; we all went up onto the Shermans' roof to watch it.

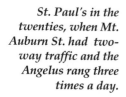

Captain Shea lived down on Putnam Avenue, and Putnam Avenue had some very nice houses in those days. He was the captain of the fire department. The Sheas were in city government a lot. They reminded me of the Sullivans. They had a printing place up on Mount Auburn Street for a while. Grace Shea sang in the choir; then Mattie Shea was a dentist; Charlie Shea was the city counsellor.

Of course, we all went to St. Paul's School. My First Communion was at the old church, the old wooden church. Inside it was very nice. They had the basement church, and you could go in there right off the street. You didn't have to go down any stairs to it. The church upstairs had the altar and all those things that were in St. Paul's basement church. The altar in the basement [of the new church] was the altar upstairs in the old church. The basement of the old church was always open, and my mother's cousins and Dan Brennan used to sneak in and play the Maple Leaf Rag on the organ. They had a great time. The priest wouldn't know. He was across the street in the rectory. Either that or he was listening. The old church was not all that much smaller. It was good-sized, it seemed to me anyways. The pews were the ones used in the basement of the big church. They were open in the backs. They didn't have any padded kneelers or kneelers that moved up either. When they had the missions, the Daly girls would be selling stuff down in the church, prayer books, statues, medals, rosary beads, candles and all kinds of religious articles and books. Well, I used to go upstairs and fish around for pennies on the floor, and I'd get eight or ten cents and then go down and buy something. I was an operator in those days! And I did it by myself. I don't remember my sisters being around.

Fr. Orr had the Irish accent. They tell stories about him. There was a lady who went to the rectory. She said, "Oh Father, my husband is a drunk, and he's doing this and he's doing that." And Father Orr would be going up the stairs saying, "God help him! God help him!" Thinking "Married to that shrew", I suppose.

St. Paul's in the twenties, when Mt. Auburn St. had two-way traffic and the Angelus rang three times a day.

The old St. Paul's at the corner of Holyoke and Mt. Auburn was enlarged significantly in 1890 and a new front and tower were added. On this block now stands the Holyoke Center, designed by parishioner and Harvard Dean Josep Lluis Sert.

At those two buildings down at the corner [at Ellery St.] was where they originally wanted to build St. Paul's church, but they weren't allowed. So they said we'll build it there next to the school. Immediately that 1200 Mass Ave, that big cement block, they put that up. They said that St. Paul's church would never be seen from Mass Ave. Whoever the developer, whoever put that up, that's why it was built. It was a spite block. Otherwise the church would have been down there, at the corner of Ellery and Mass Ave. But this proved now to be perfectly alright.

Oh yes, I remember Fr. Ryan. He was pastor when I was there. He was very nice, friendly. I remember at the little church down there, they used to have Field Day every year. Us kids would go to all the apartment houses all around selling chances, ten cents a book. Then at the Field Day, they would have the drawing. They would sell all kinds of things, a regular fair. They would have games and food. And the floor of the church was then a dirt floor, and they would have these trestle tables and light bulbs hung all around. The tables were just big wooden things on saw horses. I'll never forget the time Fr. Ryan was there having a little snack and a sandwich, and tea. And then someone said [with an Irish accent], "Look at Fr. Ryan there. He's saucering his tea!" In my days, when I was a kid, my mother when she had her tea, that was the way she would do it. She would pour any spilled tea from the saucer. But she said it's alright but you never do that on the outside. You can do it inside the house if you want. We were taught very sophisticated table manners.

The field day was the way to raise money before the church was built. Then after the church was built, they started having what they called the October collection, and that took the place of the field day. Instead of having fun and enjoying yourself, you just signed a check. We used to have something called the church debt society. We used to go around and collect a dime or a nickel a week. But they did that for years [after the church was built]. I remember them still doing it in the 1940's. I think my daughter was even a collector. There was a little card and you checked it for ten cents.

I think they liked Fr. Orr, apparently yes. In my day, you didn't like or dislike the clergy. As far as I know we all thought they were gods. In those days, you liked everybody, but there might be one guy you thought was strict, one you thought was stern, while another was funny or comical. Fr. Gunn was awfully nice to us kids. He had a little Ford car; he used to drive us around the block. We didn't have a car in those days. Then there was Fr. Murphy. We used to like him very much. He used to come around to test us, oral exams. He'd just come around and visit. We would stand up and he would give us little talks. I always liked Fr. Collins, he was in charge of the CYO. You know I liked him very much. Fr. Hickey was wonderful. He was a real brilliant man, a kind man. He'd been the superintendent of schools before he came to St. Paul's in 1925 I believe.

We had to sing Vespers every Sunday. We had to sing at the nine o'clock Mass, and the adult choir sang at the eleven o'clock Mass. There was a children's choir then. Starting in the third or fourth grade, you had to sing in the choir until you graduated. There were just girls in the choir then. The boys were the altar boys. My mother used to play the organ in the church for the Sodality. Not the big organ, they had a small organ downstairs. The Sodality used to meet there, on Monday or Tuesday night. They had missions and novenas. At Easter time, they had the processions.

I used to sit in the front seat when my kids were in the choir. One day this girlfriend had a sun dress right down to here, you know, no straps or anything. Those were the days when you wore hats and everything else, in the fifties. She was up there at the altar. You used to kneel down at the altar while they came around to give you communion. They'd go along. Monsignor [Hickey] gets to this woman, and I was next to her, and I could see him looking at her. He holds up the host. "Next time come more suitably dressed for church," very softly. Nobody did that [wore strapless dress to church] in those days.

Some of the people in the [adult] choir were Sadie Daly; she lived right next door to the rectory. There were two little wooden houses on DeWolfe Street. They used to use it as a clubhouse, for cub scout meetings, sewing clubs, women's clubs, all would meet there. But before that it was Sadie Daly who lived in that house. I guess she left it to the church. She was singing, and she would do funerals and things. Mary Downey, she was a singer in the choir. Joe Ecker, of course, the choir master. Hugh Currie, who went on to become the leader of the United States Army Band.

Every church would have an organist. We had a wonderful music teacher, Professor McConnell. He lived not too far away on

Like many homes, these on De Wolfe Street were demolished to build the Harvard Houses.

Mount Auburn Street. All the houses around were just loaded with people; they have one of those high rises there now. He was an excellent music teacher, so we were all well grounded in music. He was the choir master at St. Paul's; he played the organ, led the singing. I don't know how I got through school, but I did somehow, following around doing all those things. It becomes so routine. By the time the new church opened in 1923, I had been in school a long time.

We'd go across the street, there were a couple of families over there, and play in the church yard [the Baptist church]. I went to summer school there one summer, you know, Bible school. Who knew about the Bible? I was around nine or ten. The kids, the Shermans, went, so we wanted to go too. No, we weren't given a hard time by the [Catholic] church. The only time they give you a hard time is when you go to get married. When my sister got married, she had to get married in the rectory.

We used to pass this corner every day of our lives. And we used to skate or slide on these gratings, these granite blocks. The Sisters used to bring the lines along there. When we went home, we would walk down to the corner, where the kids could disperse. But when we came to our house, the kids could drop out of line. And we'd always skate on these grates. And the Sisters would make us stop. "Don't do that! Don't do that!"

I remember Sister Anna in the first grade, and Sister Bonaventure in the second. The nuns were awfully nice. Sister Mary Lawrence had the boys; we thought she was able to handle the boys. There was one that seemed a little crotchedy. But it never seemed to bother the kids. The education was very good. The English was important and done very well. Some history I didn't know about until I was at Radcliffe. The history would concentrate an awful lot on the explorers, you know Fr. Joliet, some kids in public school never heard of. It was a good school. Then we all went down to Cambridge High and Latin. St. Paul's started a high school around 1925, but we didn't sign up. It was down in the house beside 1033 Mass Ave. I don't know if they ever got it off the ground, or if any started it or not, or if people just didn't sign up. It was the same with Regis College. Regis College opened about that time. Most didn't want to go rushing out to Regis.

[I went to Radcliffe] because it was cheap. I wanted to go to Michigan. I would have loved to have gone away. Radcliffe was $400 a year. Not only that but you didn't have the travelling expenses, board and room. Quite a few at the college commuted. They had dormitories, but it wasn't until much later. The tough part of it was that I worked. An awful lot of us did anyways. That used to get my goat. I would leave Radcliffe around five o'clock to get in town. I worked at Schrafft's in Boston. [I majored in] chemistry, and I wound up in nuclear physics. That's when I finally got a job at MIT in the physics department. The main thing I was responsible for was measuring people who had ingested some radium. That is probably something that will never happen again. I graduated from Radcliffe in 1935. I've remained in contact with everybody. Yes, I go to the reunions. I've taken seminars at Radcliffe since, and extension courses. We used to take the extension courses when we were in high school. They were very cheap then, like $2.50. Now its $250.00! I went to college because I wanted to. We did what we wanted to do. My mother never put restrictions on us. She never taught us to cook. She never taught us to wash dishes. She never told us to clean house. She never told us to do anything like that. She would do the dishes rather than have us do them.

I remember the bells in the yard at Memorial Chapel. My whole entire life has been to school by those bells, you know, because I always went to school in Cambridge. My mother always called them the

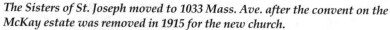

The Sisters of St. Joseph moved to 1033 Mass. Ave. after the convent on the McKay estate was removed in 1915 for the new church.

The 1930 Radcliffe Catholic Club's activities included a talk by the architect Charles Maginnis and visits each Friday to the Holy Ghost Hospital.

quarter-of-nine bells because they stopped at quarter of nine. They started at twenty minutes of nine and they went for five minutes. They still do it.

My mother graduated from St. Paul's; I graduated from St. Paul's; and all my kids graduated from St. Paul's. My grandchildren, too late. They went to the Houghton School. I had them go to high school at St. Mary's, and then St. Mary's folded. I have no credentials. St. Paul's is out the window. Cambridge High and Latin is out the window. And who's swallowing up Radcliffe? Harvard.

ELLIOT NORTON

Elliot Norton, Harvard '26 and a former President of the Harvard Catholic Club, is best known for his tenure as Drama Critic for the Boston Herald.
He wrote this reminiscence in 1989.

I graduated, as I think you know, in '26—sine laude.

At that time, the number of Catholics in the university was small and of these only about 100 belonged to what was called formally St. Paul's Catholic Club of Harvard University. We were, obviously, a small minority in an institution which had tended, in the not too remote past, to be rather coolly anti-Roman. I sensed no hostility during my four years, but rather a feeling of indifference to all religions. There was, however, though it was very coldly concealed, some anti-Semitism, which was even apparent in some areas of the faculty.

The Catholic Club was social rather than religious in orientation. We had a series of lectures during my time as president, one of which was given by President Lowell, another by U.S. Senator David I. Walsh, but our big event of the year was a formal dance at the Copley Plaza, which netted about $1200 for the treasury and made possible some improvements in the clubhouse.

President Lowell and his wife attended the dance as guests of honor and were much intrigued by the orchestra. We had imported from

141

New York—an action which stirred the Harvard Crimson to Page One excitement—Paul Specht and his orchestra, one of the famous Big Bands of the period, at a cost of $1000. In terms of 1989 dollars that would figure about $12,000-15,000 now. We were, of course, reckless.

In *The Fitzgeralds and the Kennedys,* by Doris Goodwin, I read not long ago that Cardinal O'Connell persuaded Mayor John F. Fitzgerald to send his daughter to a Catholic college, rather than Wellesley, on which she had set her heart. When I met His Eminence in the Spring of 1927, sent as a cub reporter to interview him, he gave no indication that my having matriculated at Harvard could be construed as an heretical act. He was friendly, and I remember most vividly, that while he would not consent to an interview, he wanted to talk about the Church privately, and told me, "We have now, after many years of trial, the basic needs of any church: churches, schools and hospitals. What we need now are scholars and writers."

The Cardinal, in the event that you didn't know this, was very friendly with President Lowell, and Lowell was not only friendly to us at the Club but was eager to get Catholics and Catholic scholars into Harvard. Professor Maurice DeWulf who taught a course in Scholastic Philosophy which I took, told me that "Mr. Lowell wants me to come back every year, but I find the travel too difficult, so I come on alternate years." DeWulf was a respected historian of medieval philosophy and a member of the faculty at Louvain University. When he was no longer able to travel, Mr. Lowell brought in Etienne Gilson.

There was at that time in Harvard a small but vital movement towards Catholicism, which had already brought into the Church Professor Robert Howard Lord of the history department and a number of others. Those involved in this attended small meetings of a group called Catholic Action, which met in students' rooms, with 15 or 20 students and some teachers present. I remember at one such meeting the guest was Father Bede Jarrett who at the time was head of the Dominican orders in England.

Historian Robert Howard Lord left his Harvard professorship in 1926 to become a priest.

As you know, it was while on the Harvard faculty that Father Lord became a convert and decided to give up teaching and become a priest. Near the end of my senior year, I met him coming out to Cambridge on the subway, what is now the Red Line, and we chatted. I remember when I asked him how he was going to spend the summer—this must have been May '26—he told me: "I have a sabbatical coming up, and I am going to use it at the Seminary (St. John's). I suppose it seems a little silly that I should have a call at the age of 41, but this is a good time for me to find out if it is real."

He went to the Seminary a few weeks later and registered as Robert H. Lord. They discovered who he was rather quickly and ordained him, as I recall, in one year. He was a remarkable man and in assessing what Harvard of that period did for the Church, it might perhaps be well to keep in mind that he came into the Church there and went into the Church from there.

The attitude of the Church itself towards us Harvard students seems to have been mixed. The pastor of St. Paul's, a Father Ryan, was amiable, and a curate named Father Gunn was more or less friendly. I may be doing them an injustice, but my impression in retrospect is that they and other clergy thought of us as poor little lambs that had gone astray. We survived.

FATHER FRANCIS GREENE

Father Greene was chaplain of the Harvard Catholic Club from 1932-43 and of the Radcliffe Catholic Club in 1936-7. He wrote this recollection in 1964.

The two clubs were conducted as separate entities, each having its own Chaplain. They were known respectively as the St. Paul's Harvard Club and the Radcliffe Catholic Club. Neither had any affiliation with the Newman Clubs of other universities, but we did keep in touch with several of them. Every September, immediately after registration day, we would go to the Phillips Brooks House and obtain a complete list of all Catholic students, both graduate and undergraduate. During those years the number of undergraduates was always in the neighborhood of 800.

The Harvard Catholic Club concentrated on the undergraduates, although we did notify the graduate students from time to time of some program we thought might interest them. I recall one year, about 1937, we formed a group of First Year Law students with the help of Judge John Burns (who had been a Law Professor, had served under Roosevelt as head of the SEC and was named Superior Court Judge). This group met several times. It was formed chiefly to help prevent failures among Catholic students in their first year of law.

As to membership, during the latter part of the 1930's we had a membership enrollment of about 200. However, all Catholic undergraduates were notified by mail about all meetings. Membership dues were $2.00 and used principally for mailing costs. The official seal of the St. Paul's Catholic Club was also the official seal of Harvard (Ve-ri-tas), surrounded by the words "St. Paul's Harvard Catholic Club." I was told that official permission was given by Harvard some years before to use the Harvard seal in this manner. Harvard Divinity School, the Protestant ministers who worked with the students, a rabbi and myself met for dinner at the Faculty Club to discuss students' problems as they affected us. These meetings took place three or four times a year.

I was appointed Chaplain in September 1932 to work with the students under the authority of Msgr. Hickey. The St. Paul's Catholic Club had its own clubhouse on DeWolfe next to the rectory. It is now the parish center. The students had not taken very good care of it for several years and it was in a sad state. There was the remains of what must have been an excellent Catholic library gathered by someone in the past. The Officers and active members were mostly all "day-hops" from in and around Boston. Very few of the resident students and those from out of the state took interest in the club. During this year we held regular meetings in this clubhouse. These took the form of discussions.

143

*Joseph Kennedy and Judge John Burns at a Harvard Class Day. Burns,
a graduate of St. Paul's School, Boston College and Harvard Law School,
was named Judge at age 29.*

However, they were not very well attended. By this time, in the history of the club, an accent had fallen almost exclusively on the social. The biggest event of the year was the Annual Easter Ball, a very formal and elaborate dance, held in one of the large Boston hotels. These were very well attended, but not exclusively by Harvard and Radcliffe students. These dances had a certain air of "society" about them and they enjoyed great favor with Boston people. They were very nice dances and I fear that they gave St. Paul's Catholic Club a reputation outside Harvard which it did not merit. We discontinued them around 1936.

At the beginning of the school year of 1933-34, we closed the club house on DeWolfe St. Msgr. Hickey fixed it up for the parish center. It was not serving the majority of the Catholic students. We then transferred our regular meetings to a room in the Phillips Brooks House. We had both discussion meetings as well as guest speakers. The attendance and the type of student were better but did not come up to our expectations.

The following year, we asked for and received permission from the Harvard authorities to use the various common rooms in such houses as Winthrop, Eliot, Adams, Lowell. We used a different common room for each meeting. We used guest speakers for the most part. The change to the common rooms seemed to answer our problems for the most part. Attendance was always satisfactory. Moreover, we succeeded in getting a fine representative group of students. We continued this plan for the next several years until the coming of the war years made [it] impossible.

In 1935, in addition to the above, we added an Annual Communion Breakfast with Mass in St. Paul's Church followed by breakfast in the Harvard Union. I remember that one of the first places our present Cardinal Cushing spoke publicly after his consecration as Bishop was at one of these Communion Breakfasts. In the Lent of 1937 we added a Lenten Course

The 1955 Harvard Catholic Club retreat at Campion Hall, North Andover.

with six weekly meetings in one of the common rooms. I recall in that Lent the Rev. Francis Keenan, then Secretary of the Marriage Tribunal and professor of Moral Theology, gave the students a course on "Christian Marriage." These proved worthwhile.

In the fall of 1937 we tried a very ambitious program by inaugurating a series of Catholic Lectures to be held, with the permission of the Harvard authorities, in the lecture hall of Emerson Hall. I remember having such men as Rev. Martin D'Arcy, chaplain at Oxford, England, who was visiting Cambridge at the time and Thomas Woodlock, well known Catholic lecturer and Editor of the *Wall Street Journal*. We were unable to keep them going long enough to see if this idea would catch on. Again, the attendance was satisfactory. (We got the idea from the previous year of 1936 when Etienne Gilson gave the Goddard lectures in the same hall. These lectures lasted thirteen weeks, yet the hall was overflowing every week. Mr. Gilson was an outstanding Catholic philosopher.) While we did not come near to have an overflow crowd we thought the results worthy of the effort.

The lack of funds was the big handicap. The dues went almost entirely for mailing costs. We had no success in interesting others in the problem of Catholics at a secular university. The stock answer was that "they should not be there."

We continued our meetings in the common rooms, but 1938-39 were years of uncommon turmoil. War was in the air and a great movement of student organizations on the various college campuses was directed toward peace rallies and peace marches. There were many such groups at Harvard. They made great efforts to have us lend them the use of our name, but we had been forewarned and as later events proved most of these student groups were "front organizations."

Following were the war years and we had to discontinue the format of our club events. With the encouragement of a sizeable group of Notre Dame students then at Harvard Business School, we tried a series of monthly Holy Hours at St. Paul's Church. Whether it was the gathering clouds of war, we did have some success with these.

Perhaps the following items may not belong properly in a History of the Catholic Club, yet they are the better memories for me and were, to us at least, visible fruits. I refer to the number of wonderful converts we had from among the students during the 30's. I have the names of twenty Harvard students and two Radcliffe girls who took instructions and became Catholic. Two of these Harvard students to my certain knowledge became priests—Rev. Henry Sims, now in the Diocese of Portland, Maine; Rev. William Macomber, S.J., now in Iraq. We had such converts as John Cort who joined the Catholic Worker movement and the Catholic Trade Movement. He is now a Papal Volunteer in South America. There are several of similar calibre whom I remember. It may be of interest in your historical search to know that the late President John F. Kennedy was an officer in 1939-40. [Editor: This last item has not been substantiated by the officer lists for that or preceding years. Perhaps, Greene has confused John with Joseph who was Secretary in 1935-36.]

When war did finally break out in 1941, Harvard to all intents and purposes became a war college. Practically all the students were in training and under army discipline. I remember seeing them march daily in companies to class.

St. Benedict's Center

From 1940 on the story of the St. Paul's Harvard Club is linked up with the story of St. Benedict's Center. Although we spoke of it as under the St. Paul's Harvard Catholic Club, little by little we ceased using the name and referred only to the "Center." The Center developed almost like an answer to a prayer. In its healthy years it was almost a perfect answer to the Catholic student problem. Perhaps you might like to read a few historical side-lights about its beginning. Around the year 1938, a small group of people, some of them students, organized a club called St. Andrew's Guild. As events later showed it was for their own edification, the study of liturgy and reading the Divine Office in common. I was not aware of this group until a mother of a Radcliffe girl came to me with an invitation sent to her daughter. The wording was very vague and could have been very misleading. I sent for the boy who signed—a certain Fred Farrell whom I knew very well. He came to see me with a Mrs. Catherine Clarke. That was the first time that I had met her. I found that their aims were of the best. I pointed out to them that work of a Catholic nature among the students must be done in and with the official Harvard Catholic Club. They agreed to do so. Meanwhile they had scraped enough money to rent a vacant store directly across from the church on a "until someone wants to lease it" basis. At first the meetings were confined to members.

A short time later, through the influence of a Third Order member of the Benedictines the name was changed to St. Benedict's Center and it very quickly evolved into a meeting place for students. Because of the nature of the times this seemed to be a perfect answer to our problem. Msgr. Hickey assigned me as Chaplain of the Harvard Catholic Club to supervise its activities and thus give it some official standing.

At this point Fr. Feeney was only a visitor and guest of Mrs. Clarke. He was on sick leave living at Boston College High School. In all my time at the Center we had money trouble. Christopher Huntington, a convert and at that time a dean of Freshmen and now a priest in the Diocese of Washington, D.C., and Avery Dulles, who had been baptized a short time before by Fr. Quain, S.J. in St. Paul's Church, began to help financially and even after they entered the service they

*Radio star, poet and wit, Leonard Feeney, S.J., added great
vitality to the St. Benedict Center but also led to its downfall.*

continued to send money for the rent. Also, Msgr. Hickey, feeling as I
did that this project promised so much, also volunteered to help. (It
will always remain a mystery to me where Fr. Feeney got all the money
he had during the days the Center was under Condemnation. We
had none when I was there.) From the beginning the Center was a
success. Mrs. Clarke, who seemed to have all the time she wanted,
served as a kind of unofficial hostess. She was there every day, at
first only in the evenings but later from 10:00 a.m. to midnight.

An excellent program of evening lectures and talks developed
so that there was something going on almost every evening. For example, a certain John Ciampi gave a course on the Divine Comedy of
Dante, a Fakhri Maluf gave a course on Christian philosophy and Father Feeney started a course in theology particularly on the Holy Eucharist. These lectures proved immensely popular, particularly Fr.
Feeney. He spoke to an overflow crowd every Thursday night—so
much so that we seriously considered moving his lectures into the
school hall. Many other well known figures came to speak. For example, we had the famous "Copey" of Harvard for one of his famous
readings. There is much more I could say on this particular point but
the above will give you an adequate idea of the work of the center. One
of the best features of the center was a custom that grew up of the students dropping in after classes. That gave us an excellent chance to
meet and speak with the students on a basis more personal than a formal meeting. Either Father Feeney or myself, sometimes both, would
be there every afternoon to meet them.

Things were developing so well that Msgr. Hickey, after dis-
cussing the matter with me and others, decided to ask the Jesuit officials
to let Fr. Feeney work at the Center by official appointment and this

*The Catholic Club's
crest in the sixties
displayed the sword of
St. Paul and Cardinal
Cushing's motto "So that
they may know you".*

was done around 1941 or 1942. Fr. Feeney was largely unassigned
due to sickness.

From the beginning the Center enjoyed wonderful success. A
Mrs. Francis Gray, a convert who sponsored a salon for converts at her
home, gave (or loaned) an excellent Catholic library. At first only
Harvard and Radcliffe students frequented the Center but very shortly
students from other colleges started to come as well as some who had
no college affiliation at all. Neither Msgr. Hickey or myself liked this
trend but not much could be done about it as long as our own students
kept coming. To avoid making it any worse, we vetoed an offer made
to us to have a story with pictures in the Sunday Magazine section of
the New York Times. As a matter of fact, looking back now, it was
these outsiders from whom Fr. Feeney drew his following in the bad
days to come. Few if any Harvard or Radcliffe students stayed with
him when the trouble began.

During the three years I was associated with the Center, I never
heard Fr. Feeney discuss the matter on which he was later to break with
the Church. As a matter of fact in the year following my departure,
Christopher Huntington wrote as following from Rome. "The most
wonderful thing has happened. I have not fully grasped and never
surely will. I had a special audience with the Holy Father who took
particular pains to let me know that he would be most happy to give
St. Benedict's Center his blessing. The document on which the blessing
is written will be sent to the Center by way of Bishop Cushing....I was
the last one in line. He said to me 'Oh yes you are from Boston.
You have a foundation there and you have written a memorandum
which I have read'...The Holy Father repeated several times that he
was especially happy to send his blessing to the center." (Sept.1940).
I am citing these above items of information to show what a sad
thing the defection of Fr. Feeney was and what a wonderful movement he ruined. It was not until 1947 that strange things began
happening at the Center. Some of my friends would report to me
their disappointment. Fr. Fitzpatrick was highly disturbed but he
had to leave since his time to become Pastor had arrived. After that
matters got beyond control largely because of the intransigence of
Fr. Feeney and Mrs. Clarke.

MSGR. JOHN TRACY ELLIS

Msgr. John Tracy Ellis, the distinguished historian of the American Catholic Church, entered that field in the summer of 1941 when he was asked to take over Peter Guilday's graduate courses at Catholic University. He was given a year's absence to prepare himself for the unfamiliar subject, and it is revealing that for such a topic he decided to spend most of the leave at Harvard, auditing courses and using Widener Library. Soon after arriving in Boston, he had a lengthy interview with Cardinal O'Connell, who told him "I understand you have come to study at Harvard. We shall do everything we can to make your stay pleasant, but remember, you are a priest first; don't try to be a Harvard man."

In 1974, Ellis gave the third annual Thomas T. McAvoy Lecture at the University of Notre Dame, entitled "A Harvard Interval." Parts of that lecture are reprinted here by permission of the Review of Politics, *where it appeared as "Fragments from My Autobiography, 1905-1942" (vol. 36, October 1974). In another part he also recalls conversations with Heinrich Bruening, the devout Catholic who had been chancellor of Germany in the Weimar period and then, after a narrow escape from Hitler, professor of government at Harvard.*

From my arrival at Harvard I had been repeatedly interrogated about the Church's teaching and Catholics' belief and practice on one subject or another. "It's your own fault," interjected Professor Schlesinger, who maintained that since I was approachable and easy to talk to, as he put it, "people are seizing the chance to question you about things Catholic that they have been wanting to know for a long time." The questioning continued on through the remainder of my stay. If it was not a student group it was a single inquirer.

Ellis was invited to dinner at the illustrious Society of Fellows, in the company of President Lowell, Alfred North Whitehead, Arthur Darby Nock, and the 20-some handpicked young men of promise whose number included two Catholics who had earned A.B. degrees at Harvard, one of Polish descent and one of Irish descent. During my conversation with President Lowell the old gentleman reminisced in a manner appropriate to one of so impeccable a Brahmin background, dropping a few names on his own as he chatted about his acquaintance with people such as Woodrow Wilson, Cardinal Mercier et al. At one point he remarked, "Years ago we wanted to give one of your professors of church history an honorary degree; he refused, and it was not for a long time that we found out why—Cardinal O'Connell would not let him take it." I replied, "That feeling has now changed, I believe; it is water under the bridge," whereupon the octogenarian declared, "Yes, and it was good water, for it purified the stream."[2] I had been told that the cardinal's attitude toward Harvard had mellowed somewhat in recent years, perhaps not uninfluenced by the honorary degree that he himself was awarded there at the commencement in 1937.

At the present time it would be no task to suggest the names of young Catholics who could meet the standards set for the Harvard Fellows, but in 1942 the type was not in plentiful supply. The difference was in part explained some years ago by the Harvard historian, H. Stuart Hughes, in contrasting the Catholic graduate students in history at Harvard before World War II as "few in number, mostly undistin-

guished, and on the margin of intellectual exchange." At the time
he wrote (1966), however, he said his Catholic students were "some
of the very best I have, they are right in the center of student life,
and they do not hesitate to discuss the most prickly topics frankly
and cordially."

Were I asked what were the most lasting impressions left with
me after those months in Cambridge, I would unhesitatingly reply it
was that academic community's extraordinary courtesy which seemed,
as it were, to encase its equally extraordinary habits of study. Again
and again I have asked myself why at Harvard, as at Brown a quarter
century later, it should have been so marked a characteristic of practically all those with whom I had contact. I never arrived at a more satisfactory explanation than that it was the external manifestation of a
very old and highly valued tradition inherited from an age of deep religious consciousness when good manners were predicated in no small
measure on good morals.

*Lunching one day with the History Department at the Faculty Club,
Ellis met George La Piana, Professor of Church History at Harvard since 1916.*
I had known his name for some time, both as an authority in the early
centuries of the Christian era and as one of a considerable number of
Catholic priests who as professors in various seminaries and institutions
of higher learning had either voluntarily resigned or been dismissed
from their posts in the aftermath of the antimodernist decree,
Lamentabili, and the encyclical, *Pascendi Dominici Gregis*, of 1907.

Since my arrival I had heard nothing but praise of La Piana's
courses and public lectures, and that from local priest acquaintances such
as Francis V. Murphy, pastor of St. Peter's Church, Cambridge, who told
me of having attended La Piana's lectures at the Lowell Institute one year
and found them admirable in every respect. At the close of the luncheon I
made a point of going over to bid him good-bye when he quietly smiled
and said "Remember me to Mr. Guilday." If I had been unaccustomed to
hearing my former professor referred to as "Mr.," on second thought I realized no offense had been intended, for at Harvard everyone from President Conant on down was called "Mr."

It is pleasant to record that nearly two years before George La
Piana died, incidentally on his 93rd birthday (February 28, 1971), he
had been reconciled to the Catholic Church by Richard L. Foley, priest
of the Archdiocese of Hartford, a Harvard doctoral alumnus, who at
present is Dean of the North American College in Rome. The funeral
Mass was offered at St. Paul's Church only a stone's throw from the
Harvard Yard that he had first traversed 55 years before. It is possible
that La Piana may have been the final survivor among the priests who
more than a half century previously had been involved in the controversy over modernism.

During all the time at Harvard I carried on the business of the
secretary of the American Catholic Historical Association and editor
of its journal, the *Catholic Historical Review*, which posts I had assumed
the previous year. The Boston-Washington mail service must have been
more efficient than is the usual case these days.

For the knowledge gained, the intellectual stimulation afforded,
and the interesting people encountered, I was ever after grateful to what
I have called a "Harvard interval." I count it one of the most enriching
and rewarding experiences of my academic life.

FRANCIS BANE, D.M.D

Frank Bane sang in the boys' choir in the thirties and forties. A graduate of Boston College, he now practices dentistry in North Cambridge.

I was born at the Mount Auburn Hospital. I was raised at 53 Ellery Street, just down the street from the old fourth and fifth grade girl school of Saint Paul's. It was on the corner of Ellery Street and Massachusetts Avenue. It was an all girls building. No boys were allowed there. For some reason or other, they had an overflow of young girls in those days, and they utilized that building there on the corner of Ellery Street and Mass Ave.

My father first worked for the old Boston Woven Hose. He worked there during the Depression years. Probably in the thirties, he began working at the Riverside Press. He worked there until 1958 when he retired. There were many people from Saint Paul's who worked there. Esther Murphy, who lived in the apartment house right next to Saint Paul's convent. John Droney, who was the District Attorney, his sister, who is still alive, she worked at the Riverside Press, too. They were all good Saint Paul's parishioners.

Ellery Street was considered the aristocracy in some sections, because we had the White family, who lived diagonally across the street from where I lived. Joe White was the founder of White Fuel Company. It's a misnomer to say that Ellery Street was the aristocracy. It's only the fact that it was out of Kerry Corner's grasp by about two blocks. It was a combination of three-deckers. There was actually a six-decker right next to the house that I grew up in, which was a three-decker. The Whites lived at 60 Ellery Street, which was a house that was built by Joe White after he had amassed quite a bit of money. Joe was a very, very wonderful guy. Thought nothing of giving money to the parish, Saint Paul's, and the Jesuits. Mrs. White was very, very gener-

Frank Bane stands above the rest of the St. Paul's boys choir, ca. 1950.

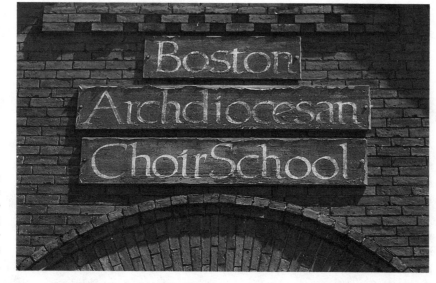

*Out of the St. Paul's
parish choir grew the
Archdiocesan Choir
School, founded in 1963
by Theodore Marier
with twenty-five
students.*

ous. Her son went on to become a Jesuit later in life; that was Bobby White.
John White was captain of the hockey team at Cambridge Latin, went on
to MIT (Massachusetts Institute of Technology), and became captain of the
hockey team there. He's a brilliant guy now; he's a lawyer out in Dedham.
Joe White, the son, graduated from the Naval Academy. Tommy White,
who we call Hinkey White, who is probably now about seventy-two,
he was John Kennedy's roommate at Harvard. Everybody claims to
be John Kennedy's roommate at Harvard, but this is the one and only
real roommate. You can verify that. He was the fundraiser for John
Kennedy when he ran for Senate and for President. He's head of the J.
F. White Construction Company now, which built and enlarged Route
2 and 128. That was where Ellery Street gets its name, the aristocracy.
But it really wasn't. On Ellery Street, there were many just average-
type families, immigrant families.

I graduated from Saint Paul's in 1943. Yes, I was in the choir. Sister
Agneta was the choir-master, probably what we called her, but she was
the Singing Nun of Saint Paul's. She was rather a stern disciplinarian. But
she could recognize whether you had a good voice or tonsils, or whatever
she considered adequate for her selection to the Saint Paul's Boys Choir.
Every fourth grade class of boys would be paraded down on a Friday
morning early in September when school started, down into the hall, the
great, big hall and auditorium in the basement of Saint Paul's school
building. We'd all be selected one by one to go up, and she would intone
the piano, you know, go up the scale with her. She would decide then
whether you were quality type of voice or you were dismissed back upstairs. Of course, the boys would enjoy it because we would get out for
that hour. Some of the other nuns weren't too happy that we would get
away from Religion. That was first period at Saint Paul's. Anyway, if you
were selected, every Friday morning you had an hour free. You went
downstairs and sang. We learned the Latin. One great thing about it was
that you learned how to sing the Latin Mass.

They sang the whole Mass then. We were on the altar. We would
parade in with the altar boys. We used to call them sitters. They used to
sit on the other side to balance of the altar. And it would be about forty or
forty-five choir boys, and they'd have forty altar boys, maybe a few

*Former Cambridge
Mayor Walter Sullivan
and Harvard minister
Peter Gomes demon-
strate an amicable
meeting of Town and
Gown at St. Paul's.*

less, maybe thirty-five. But quite a few sat on the opposite side of the altar from the choir boys in order to balance it off, because Monsignor liked to have everything just so. He encouraged Sister Agneta to teach the boys the Latin Mass.

Now we started out just as a boys' choir. At that time, Mr. Ecker was the leader of the men's choir, and there were no women at the time, they were up in the choir loft with the organ. Mr. Joseph Ecker, who came from Belmont, was a fine, big, strapping guy, and he had a wonderful voice. Ted Marier, who was the famous successor of the boys' and the men's choir, the Choir School Director and Founder, was the organist. That was when I got my first introduction to the Saint Paul's Boys' Choir. We used to practice with the men's choir, which was led by Mr. Ecker and the organist was Mr. Marier. We would practice the Tenebrae, Holy Week services, with them once a year. At Christmas, we would join together for some of the service. We were way ahead of the times with the Monsignor, because he insisted that the Mass be sung at Saint Paul's. I don't think that any other churches in Cambridge or in the surrounding area had such an elaborate choir. But it was the boys' choir with Sister Agneta, and the men's choir, they were separate, and later on, in later years, as you well know, it became unified under Mr. Marier.

The concept of the boys' choir started before my time. I believe Sister Agneta was the founder of it. I think she originated the idea because she gave piano lessons. To my knowledge, I don't remember anyone else ever being mentioned. Sister Mary Agneta was born of Irish parents from South Boston, of all places.

In those days there wasn't participation by the parishioners. Everybody had a missal, Saint Andrew Daily Missal. The congregation knew the Kyrie, the Credo; they knew the Sanctus, but they didn't sing it. The men's choir would sing it with us. But we carried it. We would sing the responses. The men's choir wouldn't sing the responses.

Yes, there was a big turnout at the Mass. In those days, Monsignor Hickey prided himself on the eleven o'clock Mass at Saint Paul's. I can remember that the ushers were always selected as young, college-type men, and were young, in their twenties, late twenties, and they had to wear tuxedoes. They had to wear a full tuxedo every Sunday. My brother Joe was one of them. He had to wear tails, full-dress tails. Monsignor Hickey, he bought them the outfit, and every Sunday there was probably six of them. You know, they had to show up, and two of them did the main aisle. They ushered people into the pews. It was almost like an honor to be able to sit up front. People would come early. And that Mass was jammed. The likes of it you don't see that today. But, it was like a tremendous commencement, graduation-type Mass. It was routine for Saint Paul's in those days. People were from Brattle Street, you know, prestigious people, like the lawyers and the doctors, the politicians. They would vie for the seats and they would be ushered down. You didn't have any particular seat. There was no rank. First come, first serve. It was very orderly, very orderly. That was in the forties and fifties. Of course, the War put a dent in it for a while. After the War they reinstituted it, but that type of Mass went out in the fifties I'd say.

Monsignor Hickey was a wonderful guy. He was the type of guy who was very, very serious, very religious, very dedicated. I can remember to this day, when he gave a sermon about money, he would get up and close his eyes, and would say, "Now this is very painful for me." And he would always keep his eyes closed. He was the old-school type of a parish priest. He believed in the priesthood, was like a hierarchy. He had a wonderful group of priests around him: Father Greene, Father Hayes, Father Kenney, Father Collins. Joe Collins, he was a wonderful, wonderful guy. Father Collins was a regular, athletic type of a priest who related well to the younger boys and men in the parish. Whereas Monsignor Hickey was a more academic, intellectual leader type of a parish priest, very stern, very well-respected, but more into academia than he was into the everyday parishioner's life. But, he was truly dedicated to making Saint Paul's the number one parish in the archdiocese, and I think he did. He was very stiff, if any one word, very stiff, but dedicated, a fine religious example to everybody. The one thing I thought: he could relax just a little bit. But that was his approach, and that was the approach of the Church in those days. The prime example would be Cardinal O'Connell, and I think he patterned himself after Cardinal O'Connell. You know, he [Monsignor Hickey] expected you to live up to that. I think he was a man ahead of his time, for an Irish Catholic. But he certainly gave a good example.

I remember the athletic activities very well. Saint Paul's CYO had a basketball team. They always had a group of the altar boys and

Monsignor Augustine Hickey, Vicar General of the Archdiocese, was pastor of St. Paul's from 1925 until 1965.

the choir boys. One priest was assigned to the altar boys and to the choir boys. Every early summer, right after school finished, they'd have a big outing down at the White's in Hull. It's a lovely home right on the water in Hull. Father Collins and Father Greene would pile everyone into one of Mike Sullivan's big, big trucks. It had an open cover on it. They would peel the cover back and everyone would hang on for dear life. There would probably be sixty or seventy altar boys and choir boys in that truck, and there might be two trucks some summers. And away we'd go down to Hull, and we'd have a big outing for the day down in Hull. Joe White would pay for it all, and Mike Sullivan. They'd take us over to the amusements at Nantasket. It was wonderful.

They had a dramatic club there for the young high school and post high school, not the college people as much as the people who were out working. They would put on dramatic events, like shows, in the school hall, and that was a very, very big thing. They also had a lot of dances for that age group. That was prior to World War Two. I was ten, eleven years old. So that went out with the War, but then after the War that never took flight again.

The Holy Name Society was very, very big. I can remember one time with the Holy Name Society, after the War, that we went on and had a candlelight vigil march on Fenway Park. That was considered the high point of the parish. We also had a tremendous group of Knights of Columbus. I have a picture of it. There must be three hundred in the Saint Paul's yard, between Saint Paul's school and the church. It was just loaded, probably three-hundred-fifty men. They were all the Holy Name Society and the Knights of Columbus, Saint Vincent de Paul Society.

The Christmas play was really the high point of the year. They'd start practicing for it probably in November, to what I can remember. The one who got picked to be the Blessed Mother was, Anna Tobin in my year, usually not only the prettiest, but also the best student. It was a combination of both. She was probably the A Number One gal in the eighth grade. Saint Joseph was always the tallest and the best-looking guy. And then there were the Wise Men. I never got that. Then you had to have the choir boy who sang the solo by himself, for the Annunciation of our Blessed Mother having the Baby Jesus, that was a big thing. Then you had the shepherds. I wound up as a shepherd. So, if you made that play, you were really made cool. It was the big thing because you didn't want to be in it because of the social pressure; you wanted to be in it because it was such fun. They would have rehearsals after school. Everybody in the sixth, seventh, eighth grades participated. We would rehearse in the afternoon, after school. Nobody really minded staying after for it. It went on and on. In Christmas week, they'd have it on the last Friday of the school year before the Christmas break. Everybody came. They would have one for the school children in the afternoon, and then they'd have one at night for the parents. And then they'd have one on Saturday afternoon or night for the people who couldn't come on Friday night. It was great. And the singing was really terrific. Sister Agneta put that all together. And that was probably the biggest, biggest social event of the Christmas season. Not to say, the eleven o'clock Mass was always the most important. But this was for the entire parish, and it was more a social gathering.

We graduated in church. When we came along in '43, I think they had phased out the graduation play, and they were graduating us in the church. I know we had to have a dark, black suit or navy-blue suit with a white shirt and a red tie. We graduated in the church, upstairs.

Zuby Zubrinski went to Saint Paul's. Now Zuby Zubrinski came from Kerry Corner, OK? And it shows you how wonderful Kerry Corner was. Zuby was a young American boy of Polish descent. His father had died, and he grew up at Saint Paul's. He was just one of the gang. Everybody loved Zuby. Zuby went to Cambridge Latin. Zuby was the big hero, baseball player. He was four years ahead of me. He was the funniest guy on two feet, and he was a tremendous athlete. He always looked back on Kerry Corner, as he was one of the Saint Paul's Irish boys. And he's a teacher to this day down at the Longfellow School.

Michael Sullivan, I knew him well. He ran the trucking business, the Michael F. Sullivan Trucking business. He had the garage right in back of his house. My brother Joe drove one of his trucks with Edward, Edward Sullivan, the Clerk of Courts. Mike was a close friend of my family's, and I knew him well. He actually had Donuts, Edward and Walter drive the trucks for him. He was around for years. He was charismatic, fiery, straight-forward, almost like a Harry Truman. He'd call things just the way the were. He spoke exactly what he thought. He was a fine gentleman. There's another example of the Irish. He didn't have a great education, but he worked for the people, on Kerry Corner and Cambridge. He would do anything for you, just like Edward and Walter. They're much more polished. The father had a way about him. He was very intelligent. He was anti-, town versus gown. One famous story about him. He picked up in the dump, the City of Cambridge dump, where his trucks would empty the refuse from the Simplex Wire, he had a big contract with them. One day, he found in the dump, the Revolutionary War Memorial that is now down on the Common I believe. It was engraved, it was a stone. And for some reason, somebody had taken it down off the Common, and had dumped it in at the City of Cambridge dump, and he happened to be with the trucks, and he found this. It was engraved to General Washington taking command of the army in 1776, the Continental Army, on the Common. My God, he found it, and he was dumbfounded that somebody would just discard this. So he went to the next meeting of the Cambridge City Council, and they were having a discussion about refurbishing something about Patriot's Day or Memorial Day. He brought it out that somebody had discarded this. And I guess that somebody was a famous politician of the Yankee heritage, and he embarrassed the heck out of him. That's a true story.

After 1880 a new wave of Irish immigration formed the "Kerry Corner" community around Flagg, Banks and Cowperthwaite Streets.

KERRY CORNER REUNION

✿ MAY 29, 1962 ✿

ELIOT BALLROOM
CAMBRIDGE, MASSACHUSETTS

The Riverside Boat Club was originally started by the Irish-American people of Cambridge just as a center for exercise. Some of the guys had rowed in shells over in Ireland. They came here and they settled in Cambridge, and they built that boathouse. Guys like Facey and Power and Faulkner and Shea and O'Brien, and they built that boathouse. It was right near the Riverside Press, but it had no connection. I rowed there for years.

Saint Paul's is a unique parish. It had Brattle Street, it had Kerry Corner, and it had Ellery Street. The aristocracy in Saint Paul's parish was Brattle Street, where you had Doctor Barnes and the Harvard University professors who were Catholic. That's the academia, and I think Monsignor Hickey really thought that was where we should be moving. Then you had the Kerry Corner group where they were striving to get an education. The thing about the Irish was that they could see that education was the only way out of the ghetto, out of South Boston, out of Kerry Corner, in order to improve yourself. But Kerry Corner was probably the best area to be brought up in Cambridge or South Boston, for the Irish. The people were united; they worked together. If somebody was in need, they always shared and took care of each other. But there were different aspects of Saint Paul's parish, and I think they always seemed to have a priest who was able to relate to every district.

"The Riverside Boat Club was originally started by the Irish-American people of Cambridge just as a center for exercise."

JOHN CAULFIELD

*John Caulfield '50 was captain of the Harvard Baseball team
and for many years Principal of the Martin Luther King School.
He gave this interview in February 1989.*

We came to live in the community in 1940. Before that, I had relatives living there, the Keohanes. We were up around the Agassiz grammar school. My father was a janitor on Wendell Street by the Agassiz School. In 1938, he died, and in 1940, we moved down to Banks Street, at sixteen dollars a month rent. People can't conceive of that now. It was a four-family house, 218 Banks (Street). Then we moved in the next summer to 118, corner of Flagg and Banks Street, across from the Corporal Burns Playground. In the winter-time, we had two rooms, the kitchen and the front room. I slept in the kitchen. Remember the big, black stoves with the oil bottle? That was the heat in the kitchen. There was a little space heater in the front room; the front room was really a big bedroom. The first one to bed got the best piece of the bed. Life was good though. But everybody in the neighborhood knew everybody, and everybody's door was open. I can remember when we had no food. My mother was sick. Charlie Sullivan, a close friend, lived on our street, and his mother sent him down with chicken soup. That was common. It was one big family, that's what it was.

No, my mother didn't work. She was home all the time. She worked a little bit. You see, my father was in World War One, and we used to get a veteran's pension, fifty-two dollars a month, which paid for everything, food, clothing, rent, everything. So we really had nothing. I know without a doubt, but I can't prove it, that I was the poorest kid at Harvard when I was there. But you see, at that time there was the Buckley scholarship. Any kid who came out of Rindge Tech or Cambridge High and Latin, and could pass the college boards, could get into Harvard a year free. And if you kept a minimal grade, you could keep renewing the scholarship. There were nineteen kids from Cambridge High and Latin the year I got in, all Buckley. I don't think it exists anymore. There is a Cambridge scholarship, and now eligible for it are parochial school graduates as well, and no longer can you get the whole thing. The tuition when I went was four hundred dollars.

My mother valued education. I can recall as a little kid having breakfast in the morning, and she would say, "Oliver wants more." Oliver Twist. She always told little bits of the classics, as I tried doing with my eight kids. We'll be riding along someplace and we'll see the flying horse. "What's its name?" "Pegasus." Any chance that you can get, pour a bit more into a kid's brain. She was always doing that. She loved classical books. She was a unique woman. In 1949, we planned her wake. Remember that blood disease she had? Monsignor Hickey, over a six month period, acquired forty pints of AB negative blood to keep her alive. They took her spleen out finally in the spring of '49, and she enjoyed good health until she passed away in 1984. She was truly a saint.

Monsignor Hickey was the pastor at the time I was a child—the "Spider", Augustine F. Hickey. He was a little guy, but when he came around, everyone scattered. "Here comes Gus. Here comes Gus." He was a little guy, but a gentleman and a spiritual giant. If anybody was poor in the parish, he used to bring food and baskets to the families that needed it. If somebody was at the front door of the parish—there's a store, now its called Cremaldi's, on Putnam Avenue. It was McCarthy Brothers forever and ever—and he'd say to someone, "Go get an order from McCarthy's and send me the bill." If there wasn't any money, there was never any tuition for school. The backs of order sheets from companies, the blank backside, they used it for paper. So there was no tuition.

I finished Harvard in 1950, and then I taught at Rindge Tech, I taught algebra and geometry for a year. Then I got appointed to the Thorndike School in East Cambridge, where I taught the sixth grade for nine years. Then they began foreign languages in the elementary schools—FLES. I had majored in French at Harvard, I studied Italian and Spanish as well. I studied Latin at CHLS. I like languages, the words. So this thing opened up, and I said, "I'm going to get into this FLES program." Because after a while in the same classroom, the walls begin to close in a little bit. So I did that for ten years, traveling around the schools. Then, on May 1, 1969, I was appointed principal of the Houghton School, which then became the Martin Luther King School now, on Putnam Avenue. Doris O'Connor, who was my secretary for five years, lived on the other side of Banks Street. So we both came from the same neighborhood. The irony was that my whole life was spent first at Harvard and then at the King school, all in the same community.

[The area around Howard Street was a traditional black community.] It always was. That's called the Coast. There would be seven hundred children at the Houghton school. There was a large number of people with Canadian background from Nova Scotia. I didn't realize it until I got down there. Kerry Corner was at the corner of Flagg and Banks Streets. My front door was an old wooden barroom front door. That was Kerry Corner right there. Well, there were barrooms way back in a lot of the houses. Way back. A lot of houses had a little "how-do-you-do" where you could buy a beer. Walter, one time, mentioned they used to have boxing matches on Putnam Avenue right near the school, where the projects are now roughly, the Putnam Gardens project is now. Then there was the War Field. There was a little green right off the square, parallel to Mount Auburn Street where Banks Street goes off Mount Auburn. Well, between the two in the back was a big, open area called the War Field. That is now all developed. On the other side of the War Field, was a little Green St. which paralleled Mount Auburn Street and came in off Putnam Avenue perpendicularly, and there was a big block. The Keohanes lived there a while, 702. It was called Kerry Corner because of—I don't know how accurate this is, it's a story: Fred O'Connor believed that his grandmother, an Irish immigrant who had settled in Brookline then came to Cambridge, gave the corner its name around 1916. At that time, all the greenhorns were coming in, she looked out the window one day and said, "My God, they're all Kerrys!" That's allegedly one story. The other side of Mass Ave, Trowbridge, Ellery and Dana Street, I suppose you can call it the parish aristocracy—the Whites, the Burns, the Noonans. They had more of a professional background, better off financially.

I remember the Riverside Press. My sister, Margaret, worked there. Everyone in our neighborhood worked for either the Riverside Press or Harvard, because they were the two great sources of employment. The Riverside Press was well staffed by Kerry Corner people. They had a bin of books that were not a hundred percent right, but they were fine. You could get a textbook or a resource book, some of the books were worth eight, nine, ten dollars. You could build a whole library at home for a couple of dollars. They went for ten cents.

I have noticed tremendous changes in the neighborhood over the years. I wrote an article for the parents when I first went to the Houghton School, of the neighborhood when I was a kid there, and then when I was an adult. Well, its tragic to see that Mass Ave is a canyon. The open spaces are all now filled. There are townhouses on Surrey St. behind McCarthy's store. In every square foot, they stick a townhouse, and they get fabulous money for it. When we think back, when we didn't have a dime. I used to pay a dime for a gallon of oil from Sammy Goldstein's store, which is now part of Mather House on Flagg Street, to keep our own black stove going. And the community itself, all the families are gone. All the three-deckers, which would average four or five kids per flat, pouring up to St. Paul' school. It's all gone.

SIDNEY CALLAHAN

Sidney Callahan was a member of St. Paul's in the late fifties, while her husband Daniel pursued a doctorate in philosophy. A frequent writer on Catholic issues, she now teaches at Mercy College in Dobbs Ferry, New York, where she gave this interview in 1988.

We had started an informal graduate school Catholic Club. We invited people and speakers. We didn't have any money, so they would stay with us and sleep on our floor. We would have meetings and informally started a graduate colloquium. We had the Abbot of Portsmouth Priory, Aelred Graham. We had Dan's old professor from Georgetown, Tom McTighe. We would corral anyone we could. Maybe we had John Cort talk about labor, he was certainly a part of that group.

We were worried about the undergraduates because we felt that they needed more care and sustenance, so I think we even got some people to arrange a champagne party for the Radcliffe and Harvard Catholic Clubs because we thought they should really get together and shouldn't be as alienated as they seemed at that time. Well, we were definitely against Harvard Catholic men marrying women beneath them; we were on the side of educated women, trying to foster these matches. We were on the side of marriage, too. Marriage and child-birth were very big in those days.

You still have Bob Kiely, Master of Adams House, and his wife Jana. She was one of the graduate students at this same time. They were an unmarried group and we were very interested in their affairs of the heart. That was great fun, since Dan and I were sewed up and married, but it was fun watching the other people. We had lots of parties, in none of which we could serve anything except non-alcoholic things because we didn't have any money.

The parish clergy were very kind to us and we used to go to daily Mass. Msgr. Hickey had a wonderful choir, it was a full, beautiful, wonderful liturgical experience. And he was a very holy man, I think. We lived right where the new Quincy House is, right on DeWolfe Street. We were evicted in order to build that new dorm. We were there a long time, from the fall of '56 to the fall of '61. It seemed like a lot longer time because time goes much more slowly when you're

Christopher Dawson, the first Stillman Professor, and Cardinal Cushing.

young and having babies and trying to get through prelims and so forth. We had, during that time a little discussion group on Protestant theology. It was a very interesting little group. We had John Noonan, Dan and myself, Mike Novak, Harvey Cox, John Rielly who directs a foreign policy association in Chicago, Mary Lou and John Ratté, and we all read Protestant theology and discussed it. We tried to develop ourselves intellectually. Because Catholics were not assimilated and were somewhat persecuted and of low status at that time, we had to give each other a great deal of emotional support. Certainly the families did that with each other because we were all poverty stricken.

At Bryn Mawr, I was a convert; it was like voluntarily contracting leprosy as I recall. Catholics were used to being scorned at that time because the reigning secular wisdom was straight out of the '20's and '30's. Freud was in the saddle, and even B.F. Skinner hadn't quite emerged yet. But the Freudian explanations, reductionism of religion, were very strong and the other dogma was a triumphant atheism which just took for granted that religion couldn't be true so why should anybody waste any time.

And also very important — I should mention this — Agnes Bourneuf had a Catholic bookstore, named Thomas More, and she would have book parties, that would bring Catholics together. I remember Wilfred Sheed spoke; we all came to that party. That would be another way you would meet the Catholic community.

I've always felt that the great strength of Catholicism was its sacramental life and community life, and it will tide you over for a while, but you still have to know why you are doing it or you'll stop doing it. That's my basic insight, if you don't have an idea what prayer is, or even an idea of what prayer might be accomplishing, or the function of prayer, you stop praying. You need to have that intellectual component of one's faith. It's very important.

One other thing that happened at this time was that Christopher Dawson came to the divinity school, the first Catholic professor ever in the divinity school. Chauncey Stillman had set up the chair and when Dawson came he turned out never to have taught, totally a nineteenth-century person, and Dan, my Dan, was his assistant. He got six or seven students. Anyway, that led to a whole further entree into Catholic circles and the Catholic world because everybody wanted to hear Dawson. He was wonderful, he wrote like an angel but he couldn't speak. Anyway that led to more little parties, going to people's houses where he was the honored guest. I do remember knowing people at Boston College, Fr. Sweeney who was a very important figure in Catholic literature. There was some connection there as well. In an interesting way, all the Catholics felt that they just wanted to know all the other Catholics and made efforts to get to know them, at least we did. So any priest who was coming around and studying we tried to get to know, this was before the Jesuits came to Weston. But Jesuits did come and study and then of course there was one tension which was with the Opus Dei people. Opus Dei had had it all sewed up when we first came. They courted everybody who arrived and then those people who did not go the Opus Dei way, went the other way which I would consider the Benedictine way. It was an interesting time.

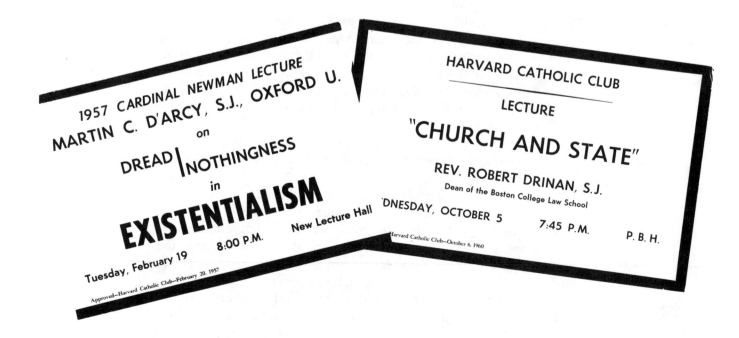

1957 CARDINAL NEWMAN LECTURE
MARTIN C. D'ARCY, S.J., OXFORD U.
on
DREAD | NOTHINGNESS
in
EXISTENTIALISM
Tuesday, February 19   8:00 P.M.   New Lecture Hall
Approved—Harvard Catholic Club—February 20, 1957

HARVARD CATHOLIC CLUB
LECTURE
"CHURCH AND STATE"
REV. ROBERT DRINAN, S.J.
Dean of the Boston College Law School
'DNESDAY, OCTOBER 5   7:45 P.M.   P. B. H.
Harvard Catholic Club—October 6, 1960

REV. JOSEPH I. COLLINS

Fr. Collins was pastor of St. Paul's from 1965 to 1971,
after serving twenty years as an assistant.

In August of 1946, I came back to the U.S. after spending twenty months in France and Germany during World War II with the 89th Infantry Division. It was sometime in September that I got the letter from Cardinal Cushing, it was actually signed by Bishop Wright, assigning me to St. Paul's and as the chaplain at Radcliffe College. I was there from October 9, 1946 until September 1, 1971—for 25 years.

I lived with Monsignor Hickey for sixteen years. He was assigned there in 1925 and he stayed for forty years, leaving the parish in 1965. He was a very small man and he used to say to me "You don't know what it is to go through life looking up to people." He was only about 5'2". He was very prim and proper. He used to wear spats and he wore a straw hat. You could always tell when fall came and when spring came. As soon as fall came he put the spats on; as soon as spring came he took off the spats and put the straw hat on. At one time in a magazine called *The Protestant* there was an article entitled "Hickey Over Cambridge" and it criticized the influence that Msgr. Hickey had in the city of Cambridge. Because he was very active with the Red Cross and with the budget committee and all civic activities and he was also the Vicar General of the Archdiocese of Boston. At one time he was the superintendent of Archdiocesan schools. All the people who were my age or who had been in school when he was the superintendent always used to fear Msgr. Hickey's examinations because he used to have his exams for all the children at a certain time of the year.

He was very conscientious about his work as pastor and used to say the 8 o'clock Mass every Sunday. We'd go over to help out before Mass and he would be sitting there with his sermon written out in his hand. He used to write out his sermon every Sunday. He was famous, too, with children long before the liturgical movement began to blossom. He used to go to the children's Mass every Sunday and walk up and down the aisle and tell the children what part of the Mass it was and why that was a particular part of the Mass and explain all the different sections of the Mass. I've heard children who were at these Masses explain how helpful the instructions of Msgr. Hickey were to help them get an appreciation of the Mass.

Msgr. Hickey's sermons were very liturgical and he would talk about the text of the Masses, of the epistles and the gospels. There was one Harvard professor, I don't know who he was, but he was alleged to have said that if you want to hear the last of the great Puritans go down to St. Paul's Church any Sunday at eight o'clock and listen to Msgr. Hickey. I would say he was a very conservative man as far as theology is concerned and as far as the practice of the church is concerned. But he did have an ecumenical spirit because he did get into all the different civic activities.

Another interesting point is that when this building, Regina Cleri, was finished, he called me one day—I was over in my office, I was chaplain at the time—and when he came into the office he told me he had just sent his letter of resignation to the Cardinal and he was going to be the first resident of Regina Cleri and that was in 1965, when the building had just been completed, and he was the first one to come

*Rev. Joseph I. Collins,
priest, pastor, and student
chaplain in Harvard
Square for 25 years.*

here to reside as a retired pastor. And he said he had recommended
to Cardinal Cushing that I succeed him but in the meantime the Cardinal had appointed someone else. I told the Cardinal I wasn't pleased
with that assignment. "What are you going to do about it?" I said,
"Why don't you appoint me the administrator? (laugh)." Because I felt
that the particular person he had mentioned he was going to appoint
didn't seem to have an interest in the choir nor in the liturgy. These
were the two great things I felt were necessary for that parish. He finally agreed with my suggestions.

But I had sixteen very happy years with Monsignor and also with
the priests with whom I lived. Fr. Fitzpatrick was transferred in January
of 1947 and a Fr. Charles Murphy came. And the four of us—Murphy,
Sullivan, Kenney, and Collins, and Hickey—the five of us were there from
1947 until 1954. Then in 1954 Sullivan was made a pastor and another
young priest named Charles Sheehy came. He was very popular with the
youth and with all the people; he was very active.

I was in charge of the Catholic Youth organization. We used
to have four aspects to it. There was the cultural, the social, the spiritual,
and the physical (which would be basketball and baseball.) We used
to have basketball and baseball teams that would play with all of the
different parishes in the area. And I had the Radcliffe Club. I used to
go up there two or three times a week, because I was part-time, and
Fr. Kenney had the Sodality, and Fr. Sullivan had most of the work in
the Rectory inside making assignments, and Fr. Murphy had the Holy
Name Society. Sodality of course would work with the women of the
parish and develop their spiritual life and the Holy Name would work
with the men of the parish and develop their spiritual life. And they
would often have social activities. And once every year we would—
the four curates as we called them—would take the census. The parish
was divided into four sections and we'd go out every day for a month
visiting every home in that parish. We had a card for each home with
the names of the parents and the children, where they would go to
church, whether or where they were baptized, whether they were going
to Catholic school or public school, whether they were going to CCD
classes. Then after the census we'd have a mission. Some of the

Paul Hotin leading a group of students in a concert of recorder music for the pastor, Msgr. Hickey, and the principal, Sr. Margretta, C.S.J., during the choir school's first year.

religious order of priests would come in and spend a week or two having missions. In the old days they'd have a men's mission and a women's mission and the church would be filled with the men and women of the parish.

The school hall was where we had all the activities—and of course the lower church was a church, there was no hall there—and we used to have meetings in the rectory as well. But under Msgr. Hickey very seldom did a lay person come to the dining room table. It was reserved for the priests and we each had an office in the rectory for when people would come in to arrange for marriages, to arrange for baptisms, or when people would come in for counseling. And of course there'd always be funerals, and preparing children for confirmation.

When I arrived there in 1946 we had 22 teaching sisters and over 600 children in the school. We used to have a section of the school up on the corner of Ellery Street and Mass. Ave. where the convent was (at 1033 Mass. Ave.). Then as the numbers dwindled we had to raze the building up there. And when I left in 1971, there was no school and no sisters. There was the choir school, but the parochial school had discontinued because there were no children. The reason for the decrease in numbers was the expansion of Harvard and M.I.T. The people with children all moved out so most of the parish now is students. The choir school began in 1963. That was 25 years ago. Dr. Marier came to Msgr. Hickey and asked him about it. He finally agreed to it. I was the chaplain of the school and worked with them, and then when Msgr. Hickey retired I became the pastor eventually. First I was administrator from 1965 to 1967. This letter up here is the one that I keep which appointed me the pastor January 25, 1967. That date was interesting because it was the Feast of the Conversion of St. Paul.

In the fifties, I used to have meetings with the graduate students in what was called the Clubhouse right in back of the rectory. It was an old family house. It had a basement and a first floor and a second floor, but it was a place where there was buzzing activity. There was activity every day, along with the hall in the school. But this clubhouse was more a parish center than the school, since the school was mostly for children. But we used to have the meetings there of the book club and of the Tekakwitha Guild, ladies who used to collect clothes, repair them

A meeting of the officers and friends of the Harvard and Radcliffe Catholic Clubs, 1961-62. Seated left to right: Theodore Marier, Carla Marceau, George Francis, Timothy McCaffrey, Rev. Joseph Collins, Peter Solomon, Rev. Edward Murray, Lenore Pardee, John Dunn (then Secretary of the Club), Marijo Miller, Robert Fugere. Standing left to right: unknown, Shelley Jankowicz, John Brandl, Austin Winkley, Eileen Maher, Rev. Christopher Huntington, Philip Leavitt.

and give them to the poor. We also had the St. Vincent De Paul Society there. Different committees of the Sodality and the Holy Name would meet in the clubhouse. Sometimes kids would come over to practice. The Girl Scouts used to meet there and the Brownies; Boy Scouts used to meet in the school hall.

In 1954, Fr. William Porras, a priest of Opus Dei, was appointed chaplain for Harvard; he resigned in 1960. I was sitting in my office with John Boler who was a philosophy student in the graduate school. I got a telephone call from Msgr. Sennott, who was the Chancellor. He said, "Joe, Cardinal Cushing would like you to be the chaplain at Harvard full-time." "Well, alright I'll do it." I turned back to John Boler and said, "John, you're the first one to know that I have been assigned as full-time chaplain at Harvard. So he congratulated me and I said, "Have you got any suggestions?" and he said, " First thing, you ought to start a Mass at 5 o'clock every afternoon." And I think that Mass is still going. That was in June of '60 and I took over full-time in September of 1960.

We didn't have any place to meet so I used to go up to an office in Phillips Brooks House. I shared it with some of the other chaplains of other denominations. So I said to Msgr. Hickey, "Gee, we're not using that part of the school." In fact, we used to have four classes in that building that is now the Center, 2 first grades and 2 second grades. The numbers were diminished, so the building was vacant. I said that we ought to make a center for the students out of that. So I called an architect and asked him what it would cost to renovate it and he said about $5,000. We had a contractor come in and put out bids. I had told the Cardinal in writing, Cardinal Cushing, that it was going to cost $5,000 to renovate the Center. So one day we had a meeting with the Cardinal and all the pastors and all the priests, and Msgr. Hickey came with me. In the meantime, I had received bids for the renovation of the Center, and the lowest bid was $50,000. So, I had to tell this to Cardinal Cushing when the meeting was finished. The two of us went up to the Cardinal. "Your Eminence," I said, "I made a mistake when I sent you that note. I forgot to add a zero to the cost of the renovation." So he said, "Bob," (Msgr. Sennott was the Chancellor), "come here a minute. Joe is going to renovate that building over there. It's going to cost $50,000. I know one of these things is expensive, so I want Joe to send you all of his bills, and you pay all the bills." So that's how it began.

We did renovate the place. In fact, Dean Sert, who was the dean of the Graduate School of Design, designed it. There was a fellow by the name of Powers who did the material construction. By the time we finished it was over $80,000 to build the Center. I'll never forget it was dedicated March 7th of 1961 and the Cardinal came over. We had Mass in the church and after Mass we walked over to the Center to bless it. When we got to the door he looked at it and said, "Gee, it's kind of small." So we went up and he blessed the Center. It became a very, very active place for students, not only the undergraduates but for graduates from all the graduate schools and also from Lesley College. That was the beginning of the Center; Jose Luis Sert was the architect. He was very active. He was at the church all the time and he was on our board of directors.

There was always a little conflict. We had the three aspects of the parish. First of all the parish itself, and the students, and the choir school. During the Middle Ages you had the Town, the Crown, and the Gown. We didn't have any crown, but we did have the town, the townies as they called them, who were the local parishioners, and the gown of course would be the University.

What kind of energy did the Vatican II Council create in the parish? Oh! In 1948 we had the liturgical conference, Liturgical Week, here in Boston. I was the local secretary. At the time Msgr. Hickey was ill, but he should have been the chairman. They had Msgr. Finn as the chairman. This was held in Mechanics' Hall in Boston for four days. Many of the ideas expressed there were implemented in Vatican II. We were the first parish to have the Easter vigil at night and it was on television, and we had some baptisms too. We started at 10:30 and didn't finish until about 1:30 the next morning. Msgr. Hickey was the celebrant, Fr. John Sullivan the deacon, Fr. Murphy was the sub-deacon. Fr. Kenney was the master of ceremonies, and I was in the pulpit explaining all the activities that were going on and the different aspects of the Easter vigil: starting with the darkness and the lighting of the candle, and the singing of the famous *Exsultet* . We had a choir and the blessing of the water for baptism. I have a copy of this on film, but there is no audio. It was the first time it was celebrated at night. I have always had a very special interest in the liturgy. In fact I was the secretary of what we called the Sacramental Apostolate. We published a newspaper called *Mediator* five times a year for the different seasons. We used to send it all over the world.

We did our best to implement all the decrees of the council. One time we painted the church; it cost $30,000 to paint the interior of the church—well it was after Msgr. Hickey, so it would be after '65. But we didn't touch the lower church at all; that was done after I left. They took out the altar and the benches and the confessionals.

President Pusey, did you deal with him much then? Oh yes, I used to see him lots. I used to go over to Memorial Church and lead the

Cardinal Cushing received an honorary degree from Harvard in 1959, but disappointed the crowds by wearing simple black.

morning prayers there at quarter of nine, three or four times a year, because I was a member of the United Ministry. I was secretary one year, treasurer another, and chairman another. He and his wife would be present at the service. But I did see the Puseys often— they used to walk and talk. When Msgr. Hickey left, the one thing he wanted to do was go up and say goodbye to President Pusey. He called to make an appointment, the two of us walked over one day. We sat in the President's office. On the wall was a huge map of Greater Boston. Before we sat down President Pusey said, "You know, a lot of people think that Cambridge is not at the center of Greater Boston, but that's not true. You look at the map, Cambridge is at the center of Greater Boston." I said, "That's true, Mr. Pusey, but you know St. Paul's is right at the center of Harvard and Boston is the Hub of the Universe. So St. Paul's is really at the hub of the Universe." He was a charming man and we enjoyed him very much.

Did the Harvard and Radcliffe groups have much contact? Bishop Riley wouldn't let them have any contact. They used to go into adoration at the Shrine of Perpetual Adoration at St. Clement's. He wouldn't let the boys and girls go together, so they would go separately. I used to go over to Radcliffe two or three times a week. I would talk with them, I had Masses in some of the Houses. Mrs. Bunting didn't like that very much, because she didn't want to have any specific religious activities on campus, especially worship.

Who was active of the Harvard Faculty? Well, of course, Bob Kiely and his wife. The Master of Leverett House was John Conway. His wife Jill became the president of Smith College. They are living down in Milton now, too. She was a convert. There was Jim Kerr from Australia. Prof. Francis Rogers was very active as well. Of course, Dean Sert, and we had several fellows at the Law School, like John Mansfield. From the Business School we had Joe O'Donnell and a fellow by the name of Tom Raymond who was very active. There weren't many Masters who were Catholics. But there was also a senior tutor in Quincy House, Paul Sigmund, who was in history and was especially interested in Gallicanism.

The St. Benedict Center was right in front of the Church. In the summertime we could look right out the door when we were in the pulpit and we could see the Center. We used to go over there frequently Saturday nights after confession, just to listen to the talks. They always had interesting people. Theodore Chandler and Daniel Sargent were often there. Daniel Sargent had written much once about Thomas More, and I think he was an interested intellectual who was concerned about the students and wanted to provide some help. He used to lecture too, I believe.

When Cardinal Cushing got his honorary degree, how did that go? They had several dinners. I wasn't at the dinner though. I don't think Msgr. Hickey was either, because Msgr. Hickey was never favorable toward the university. The St. Benedict's Center protested his receiving a degree. In fact, they picketed Lowell House where they had the dinner afterwards. That was in the early sixties.

Bernard Law—did you know him as an undergraduate? Very well. Cardinal Law came to Harvard in 1949 and one of the first things he did was join our choir. He used to sing in the choir all the time with Mr. Marier and he used to visit the rectory frequently. I got to know him pretty well; he was Vice President of the Catholic Club when he was a senior. When he was appointed Archbishop of Boston, I went to the airport terminal to meet him the first day he came, and when he came out of the airport terminal he saw me and he came over and gave me a big hug. And the first thing he said was, "Joe, who would ever believe this?" We did see him frequently.

Josep Lluis Sert redesigned one of the parish school buildings into the Harvard-Radcliffe Catholic Student Center in 1960.

JANA KIELY

*Jana Kiely is Director of Religious Education at St. Paul's and Associate
Master of Adams House. In 1989 we asked her to write this recollection about
her first years in Harvard Square as a Catholic graduate student.*

My first contact with St. Paul's was a Mass in the Lower Church in
September, 1958. The entrance to the crypt was from De Wolfe St. On
that day Msgr. Hickey was the celebrant. I had come fresh from St.
Séverin and the Centre Richelieu in Paris, the two student parishes
where what were to be called Vatican II ideas were then brewing. At
St. Séverin, already in the late 50's, the congregation surrounded the
altar and was actively participating. The sermons were moving, rivet-
ing pieces of oratory, founded solidly on the scholarship of the École
Biblique de Jerusalem and breathing with the social concerns stemming
from the worker priests movement. The Centre Richelieu, the student
parish of the Sorbonne, was the most exciting part of my Sorbonne
education (which otherwise consisted of slightly old fashioned biology),
with its eight priests (among these eight priests was Jean Marie Lustiger,
now Cardinal archbishop of Paris), excellent courses in Scriptures and
Theology, wonderful retreats, and the famous pilgrimages to Longpont,
Sacré Coeur and Chartres; people like Camus coming to discussion
groups, and Père J. Daniélou teaching. It was in this atmosphere that I
joined the Church as an adult. I came to Harvard as a graduate student in search of more exciting biology, but my first question was,
"Where is the Catholic Student Center and the Catholic Church of
Harvard?"

So, I found St. Paul's and Msgr. Hickey celebrating Mass, seemingly for himself and by himself, while the congregation recited the Rosary
for themselves and by themselves. I knew nothing in those days about the
Irish Church of Boston. Only much later did I come to know and admire

*Fr. Joseph Collins officiating at the marriage of Robert and Jana Kiely in Prague. The Kielys are now
Masters of Adams House. Jana is Religious Education Coordinator for St. Paul's.*

their great accomplishments, their deep Christ-like concern for their people. That first day, all I could see was the lack of intellectual curiosity and enthusiasm, a certain narrowness of spirit and an unabashed, condescending paternalism. With no further questions, I got up and left the church. It might have been my walk out of *The Church*, but it so happened that as I was going up those stairs to De Wolfe Street a young woman was coming down. She gave me a big smile, full of loving cheerfulness. I suddenly found my first reaction petty and I followed her back to Mass into the lower church of St. Paul's.

On Sunday I discovered the 11 a.m. Mass with Ted Marier and the Choir, (which I joined on the spot). A new face of St. Paul's opened to me. I found the Church, especially the inside, upstairs, extremely ugly, to the point of unpleasantness, but closing my eyes I could hear wonderful music; the Gregorian would take me back to Solesmes (France), the hymns, so many of them from the Protestant hymnals, would answer to my Czech Hussite background and plant me firmly on the soil of my newly found home, the Pilgrims' land.

A final memory of my arrival has to do with the first meeting of the Radcliffe Catholic club at 6 Ash Street with the Radcliffe chaplain, Fr. Collins. He indeed was my door to the Church in Cambridge; his cheerfulness, his great love of people, his human warmth, all of this made up for the lack of intellectual probing and theological excitement. Besides, all of that came later too, as the people he so warmly embraced moved his parish church. At that meeting of the Radcliffe Catholic Club, tea was served, cookies were passed, jokes exchanged about meeting Catholic Harvard boys and mixers planned to facilitate this seemingly unique purpose of the Club's existence.

I could not believe my eyes or ears. After all, I was looking for the Harvard-Radcliffe version of a student parish, the Cambridge Centre Richelieu. As the meeting was drawing to a close I felt a sinking feeling, almost of despair. Where to now? I began to pray to the Holy Spirit and then suddenly a simple, small suggestion came to me. "Could we meet once a week for Mass and breakfast?" Fr. Collins, who loved us all already, enthusiastically recorded this proposal. It was voted on the spot. In my mind this is the beginning of the Student Mass at St. Paul's. Yes, indeed, there was then a student Mass at PBH, celebrated by Fr. Porras the Harvard Chaplain. That was off limits for most of us. Later that developed into a much more inclusive Harvard Mass with Fr. Richard Griffin, but the Catholics who kept swelling the ranks of the student population in Cambridge looked to St. Paul's as their parish; PBH remained off center.

The daily Mass at St. Paul's was at that time at 7 a.m. Through Fr. Collins we petitioned the pastor, Msgr. Hickey, to have the Student Mass on Saturday at 8 a.m. (not a very bold suggestion). The response came swift and direct, "I am there everyday at 7 a.m. If they want to come they can be there too." So we did go at 7 a.m., every Saturday, often half awake, once directly from a party at the Signet, where we had danced, mostly Scottish dances, *all* night long. After Mass we met at the Club house, a yellow wooden house on the parking lot behind the rectory.

The group grew. It was made up mostly of graduate and some undergraduate Radcliffe and Harvard students, law students, business school students. The breakfasts were wonderfully lively discussion

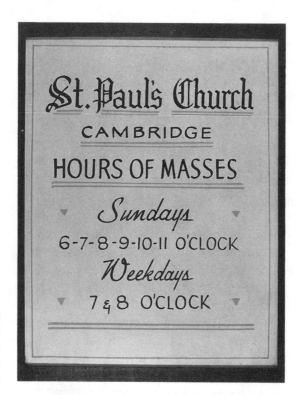

Hanging in the Student Center in 1963 was the schedule of parish masses, with many convenient times.

times, where we talked about everything, from Jacques Maritain to John Courtney Murray, from Evolution to the immana of Christ in Eastern Religions. We organized lectures by visiting scholars. I remember very clearly Barbara Ward, Lady Jackson, being given a brilliant, flowery introduction by Jeremy Adams, then graduate student in history. We often met at the home of Christopher Dawson on Ash Street; he was the first holder of the Stillman Chair. I remember in fact the discussions around the establishment of that chair.

With my French background I thought the Student Center should be totally independent of the University and organize its own curriculum, designed to bring up the Catholic Students' religious education to the same level as the rest of their Harvard education. I remember how surprised and intrigued I was when many (Dan Callahan in particular) argued that Harvard was too absorbing, and the only way to religious education could be through courses that would be part of the regular curriculum. As I became more familiar with Harvard I understood more and more the wisdom of that argument. The person who certainly understood it best was my husband, who later worked for the establishment of the Religious Studies Major and began to teach in the English Department the Bible as well as courses such as the "Literature of Christian Reflection" with Robert Coles.

Back in the 50's our efforts at religious education led us to Regina Laudis. I was introduced to Regina Laudis Abbey by John Noonan, who was a good friend of the Lady Abbess (at the time, the prioress Mother Benedict). He was sure I would love the place and one day he gave me a ride there. He was on his way to New York and dropped me off one night after dinner in front of the cloister walls. It was a beautiful spring night. The moon was shining above the walls. There was absolute peace. I was mesmerized. Soon I was bringing our

Marie-Claude Thompson, founder of the Earthen Vessels tutoring program, distributing the Eucharist.

whole group down for regular retreats and lectures by Mother Benedict on liturgical and theological developments. Back at St. Paul's we would sing Compline, that we had learned at the Abbey. I discovered Ted Marier's connection to Regina Laudis and I was again full circle home. Fr. Collins almost always came with us, and for all of us this association meant real spiritual growth.

A young philosophy student joined us then; he had left the seminary where he had been since childhood and he was not too happy with the Harvard Philosophy department either. He burned with ideas and ambition; he wanted to write. At St. Paul's, he started a magazine called The *Current*. His name was Michael Novak.

One day he asked me to contribute to the *Current*. I too was burning with ideas and a certain kind of ambition, ambition for the development of the Catholic Student Center at St. Paul's. I wrote "You are the Salt of the Earth" in which I pleaded for a chapel and a student center. When finally Sert and Solomita rehabed a part of the old school into what was at the time a beautiful Student Center (later in the sixties, it got trashed), I saw it as an answer to prayer. However, the chapel was missing. Still now, I consider the chapel the most important part of the building project we are currently giving birth to.

Along with Fr. Collins the person I would most want to re-member is Agnes Bourneuf. The Thomas More Bookstore is probably, with the Choir School, the most important part of the history of Catholics at Harvard. The bookstore was the true intellectual Center for Cambridge Catholics as long as Agnes was there. She knew every book in her store and almost everyone in the community. To drop by was to learn in a few minutes what new books have come out, what new ideas were churning. It meant also a few minutes of peace in the middle of Harvard Square, a cup of tea, a good conversation. Agnes radiated intelligence, good cheer and peace of mind. Her ladylike composure surely contributed to my picture of her as the "grande dame" of the Cambridge Catholic community.

THE HARVARD AND RADCLIFFE STUDENTS OF 1963

*In Spring 1963, the editors of the CURRENT devoted an entire issue to the theme
of Catholics at Harvard. The lead article, which follows in reduced form, was
entitled "The Present Position of Catholics at Harvard." It was based on a survey
of 800 graduates and undergraduates which produced 176 responses.*

"Harvard is too self-conscious, and Harvard Catholics are
worse." So wrote a first-year graduate student in history on the ques-
tionnaire which The CURRENT sent to its local readers in January. If
any other proof of the charge is needed, this issue of The CURRENT
can provide it well enough, since for the first time in its short history
The CURRENT is devoting an entire number to a single theme, and
that theme is the experience of the Catholic student at Harvard.

We are convinced that Catholics belong at Harvard. We make this
a challenge, for there are many, particularly Catholics, who would deny it.
The following statement says very well what we have in mind:

> When Catholic educators vent their ire on "secular universities,"
> they in effect push Catholic students out of "their" Church when
> they leave the Catholic educational system, or may seem to give
> that effect. The Catholic student goes on thinking he has made a
> decision against Catholicism. Father Ellis once said here that
> there are Catholics in a university like Harvard because it fit
> their intellectual needs better than anywhere else, because
> Catholic universities don't offer the same quality of education or
> scholarships as Harvard. Catholics who came to a place like
> Harvard are intellectually curious; pat answers aren't going to
> satisfy them; and Harvard is probably a better place than most
> for them to go.

This was said by a student of history who has spent six years at the
university, four of them at Radcliffe and two more in the graduate
school.

We can make no claim to scientific rigor or statistical preci-
sion in this survey. There was no control group with which to com-
pare the answers of the Harvard Catholics, and the questions were
admittedly general. Their very generality, however, permitted those
responding to say what was on their minds. What from our point
of view was most important is not the numbers but the qualities.
We were not at all interested in such neat (and meaningless) statements as "x% of Harvard Catholics lost their faith in the freshman
year from reading Nietzsche." What we wanted was a test of attitudes, a sense of the believer's strains and his successes, an insight
into the things that concern him most deeply. These things do not
yield themselves easily to statistics. In the interpretation of our survey presented in this issue of The CURRENT, we have tried whenever possible to let the students speak for themselves. Their comments are disarmingly frank, widely varied, and often tinged with
the irony that seems to come naturally to the Harvard student.

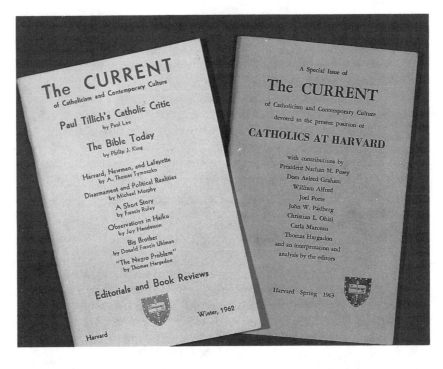

The editorial policy inside each issue: "Published by Catholics at Harvard, the CURRENT rejects the division of temporal concerns into the 'secular' and the 'religious'; it is interested in the whole range of earthly things, for everywhere lie traces of God."

ARRIVAL AT HARVARD: RELIGIOUS I.Q.

"If you are not confirmed in basic fundamentals when you come here, I might expect that you would run into much trouble." A second-year graduate student in physics wrote this, and with magnificent understatement he focused on one of the major causes of difficulty for many a Harvard or Radcliffe Catholic. If our survey is any reliable index, a sizeable number of Catholic students arrive at the university not at all well informed about their faith. Asked to characterize their "intellectual background in religion" upon coming here, 176 Harvard and Radcliffe Catholics gave answers which the editors interpret as follows: 52 replied "poor," and another 52 "fair." Only 37 termed their background "good" and 26 "excellent." Nine other answers which defied categorizing, filled out the total. In quantitative terms, 83 had no formal Catholic education before Harvard; 10 had less than 4 years; 38 had four years or more; and 45 had more than eight years. Almost half of those answering, then, had never attended a Catholic school at any time in their lives.

Here are some of the answers we received on the first question, "How would you characterize your intellectual background in religion when you arrived at Harvard?"—

" From grades 1-7, I was taught catechism by Sisters of St. Joseph (God made me to know him...). During grades 8-12, I received what I considered an excellent background in religious training from priests in a Catholic day school: Church history, theology, apologetics, the Mass, etc."— HARVARD FRESHMAN IN MATHEMATICS

"Rather poor—I knew all the conventional things but none of the deeper philosophical tenets of the Faith."— HARVARD SOPHOMORE IN ENGLISH

"Rather good, especially in the historical and liturgical areas; most of it self-acquired."— HARVARD SOPHOMORE IN CLASSICS

175

"I have had a Catholic education up to my finishing college, although I cannot say that theology on the college level was much greater than in high school, but that is due to the college... Most of my knowledge of my faith has been derived through discussions with priests and laymen."— GRADUATE STU-DENT IN ENGLISH.

"With Sunday school training through the ninth grade only, I was unprepared to defend my faith intellectually; I was still feeling the unspoken pressure in a Protestant community against the irrationality of Catholicism."— RADCLIFFE SENIOR IN FINE ARTS

"I didn't know all I could have, but I knew enough."— HARVARD FRESHMAN IN ROMANCE LANGUAGES.

"Nil—I had gone to Sunday School and Christian Doctrine classes at my parish from age 10-14, and learned nothing; had picked up a few facts and opinions (still almost my only ones) from my parents, whose religion is somewhat stamped by their personalities, but whose teaching I respect more than anyone's I have been exposed to."— RADCLIFFE JUNIOR IN SOCIAL SCIENCES.

CRISIS AND MATURITY

Dom Aelred Graham, a figure prominent in American Catholic educa-tion, has said in a speech reprinted in this issue of The CURRENT: "It is to be expected that a boy at college will have difficulties about reli-gion. If he has not, then I would suggest that he is exceptionally dull-witted, or that there is something wrong with the college." Most Harvard students are not dull-witted, nor in this respect is there any-thing wrong with the college, judging from the results of our poll. The encounter with new ideas and with persons of widely differing ex-pressing widely differing viewpoints force students here to examine their beliefs in a most fundamental way. This can be salutary, for without growing pains there is no growth, and without growth there can be no maturity. Though a sizeable and clearly defined minority of

In the summer of 1963, sixteen Harvard and Radcliffe students raised money and went to Mexico to build a dispensary, teach hygiene and child care and run educational programs at Coplico en Alto.

students reported that Harvard had no effect on their religion, most were emphatic in expressing a deep impression and some kind of transformation.

In question II of our poll, we asked how the student's religion had "been affected" by Harvard, and then in question III how his religion had "affected—helped or hindered" his life here. The trend of the answers was as follows. To question II, 67 responded that their faith was helped here, as opposed to 27 who said that it was hindered. Of the rest, 61 said that Harvard had no specific effect on their religion, and 21 reported doubtful or mixed reactions. On the other hand, to question III, 96 claimed that their faith was a positive help in their Harvard lives, 26 said that it had no effect, 40 gave doubtful or mixed responses, and 3 left the question unanswered. One of the most encouraging results of the survey was the evidence it yielded to show that for many Catholics the challenge which the university presents to their beliefs and their moral conduct stimulates a strengthening, deepening and enriching of faith. The process itself is often painful, sometimes long, but that is the price of insight. Under the heading of "crisis and maturity," then, we present some of the reactions of Harvard and Radcliffe Catholics to the stimulus of university life:

> "It is Harvard's atmosphere of questioning all values that hurt my Catholicism, then brought me back to it, so that now my faith (and some works) are in better shape than before. My beliefs have helped me at Harvard—I haven't felt 'lost'; having a foundation to build on."— HARVARD SENIOR IN HISTORY

> "I'm questioning Church doctrine more deeply; but I am more deeply confirmed when I find the answers yet—I haven't found all the answers yet, but at least I am still thinking about the problems."— HARVARD SOPHOMORE IN BIOCHEMISTRY

> "I left my religion for the first 3 1/2 years of college, although this had little effect on my moral life. It had been a matter of intellectual doubt that had already been manifest during high school years. Harvard was a fine place to let my intellectual doubt take over. I returned to practice Catholicism in spring of my senior year. My reasons for this were complex, not the least of which being my dissatisfaction with the kinds of religious experience I had tried to substitute for Catholicism."— GRADUATE STUDENT IN MUSIC.

> "Harvard has forced me to consider my stand on God, faith, and Catholicism—rather than to form a stand where there was none. The truths I had just parrotted in an unchallenged Catholic atmosphere were now examined. I think I have finally stopped being Catholic and started to live Catholicism."— HARVARD SOPHOMORE IN PSYCHOLOGY

> "My concept of God has changed."— HARVARD SOPHOMORE IN PHYSICS.

> "The Catholic at Harvard runs certain risks ... Harvard is really all the risks of life itself."— HARVARD SENIOR IN ECONOMICS.

"Harvard has been a positive good in my religious development. Through people I have met here I have found just how meaningful the whole thing is—a lesson I never learned in Catholic high school. I think after this initial baptism of fire, I can safely meet any future challenge."— HARVARD SENIOR IN HISTORY.

"The proverbial religious-intellectual crisis came during my sophomore year (undergraduate). Since then I have managed to reconcile (sidestep?) the conflicts between science and religion." — GRADUATE STUDENT IN PHYSICS.

THOSE WHO LEFT

For some, of course, religious crisis does not end in renewal of faith, but in its loss, or at least in its break with specifically Catholic belief. The number of students who answered our survey who turned away from Catholicism was relatively low; about 20 of the 176 made what we call a decisive break. (The line is not always easy to draw, however, on the basis of the answers given.) Two important factors bear upon the situation of those who lose their faith at the university. One is that, in the majority of those answering our survey, they arrived here with a background in religion which they themselves described as less than adequate. The other is that the break is likely to have been begun well before the student entered the university. It is therefore difficult—and somewhat unfounded—to place the major blame on the university itself.

Those who made the break gave various reasons, but it is not usually a simple process. Most college students are in rebellion against authority of one kind or another, and religious authority is not exempted. Among other reasons, one student admitted moral laxity as a cause for turning from his faith. Several found the Church's moral teachings on birth control and sexual conduct untenable. Intellectual difficulties were a major contributing factor. But out of fairness and because they themselves are in a position to be most articulate, we have decided to let those who left speak for themselves; we would only preface these statements by making clear that we do not intend to freeze their authors into any position "outside the fold." Like the rest of us who think seriously, they are likely still to be working hard to find their way.

"I left the Church in March of my freshman year. The social and moral environment had nothing to do with my decision. The intellectual environment had no direct effect; I did not leave the Church because a section man proved Catholicism a fraud or because I wasn't convince by Aquinas's proofs for the existence of God. That I was drawn to writers who are fundamentally atheistic I consider the effect more than the cause of the change. The intellectual environment had an indirect effect in that it created an atmosphere of crisis which focused my attention on what I was and helped to cause changes which made religion incompatible with me."— RADCLIFFE SOPHOMORE IN CHEMISTRY

"Catholicism is incompatible with my intellectual and moral beliefs and practices, it neither adds nor detracts from my social life. Recently a close friend of mine died: should I believe that he went to hell because he did not worship God?"— HARVARD SENIOR IN HISTORY AND LITERATURE.

"The Harvard atmosphere converted me from an incipient atheist to a confirmed agnostic. I think I have more sympathy for religion in general now, but less for Catholicism in particular. This, I feel, was not caused by Harvard's environment; I think that any Catholic who is going to break with the Church will do so no matter where he is."— HARVARD JUNIOR IN ENGLISH.

"I can no longer call myself Catholic, but I am not sorry to have been one. I shall try to 'bear my own cross' and content myself with the here and now."— HARVARD SOPHOMORE IN ENGLISH.

"I consider religion a balm to soothe hurts when people think they're getting a raw deal from life. It planes things away and lets people live with themselves. It's a mythology that deceives people so that life is bearable."— HARVARD JUNIOR IN SOCIAL RELATIONS.

"It seems fairly incredible to me that anyone with a reasonable I.Q. can remain a believing Catholic for even as long as I did. Theologically it reduces to illogisms [sic] and, even worse, claptrap."— HARVARD SENIOR IN PHYSICS.

THE INTELLECTUAL MILIEU

Despite the fact that in their courses many Catholics confronted questions of serious religious import with which they could not fully cope, and despite the myth of the atheist Harvard professor, the prevailing trend in the CURRENT's survey showed a favorable relationship between religion and the intellectual environment. The comments on questions II and III which related to the intellectual environment yielded the following results. 89 (over half) reported that the intellectual atmosphere exerted a positive influence on their faith; 27 said that it hindered their faith; 46 claimed that it had no effect, and 14 showed doubtful or mixed feelings. On the matter of how the student's religion affected his intellectual development, the other side of the coin, 72 responded favorably, 13 were uncertain, and 35 offered no specific comment.

The minority who found that the intellectual atmosphere had harmed their faith did not usually articulate their reasons. In the answers of a sizeable number of those who thought that the intellectual climate had aided their faith, the word "stimulate" occurred frequently. For one thing, questions raised in classes and challenges in personal discussions seem to have sent students to search for answers in reading and reflection. Undergraduates in particular remarked that courses in history (and to a lesser extent, philosophy) deepened their knowledge of the nature of the Church and of Catholicism. Conversely, many found—again, mostly in history courses—that a Catholic background was a definite advantage in understanding issues in the development

The Catholic-Protestant Colloquium of 1963 was centered on the Stillman lectures of Cardinal Bea. With him are President Pusey, Dean Samuel Miller of the Divinity School and Cardinal Cushing.

of western civilization. The next most frequently cited way in which religion helped students' intellectual activity was by giving coherence and purpose, not only to studies and thought, but to life as well.

Here then is a sampling of what the Harvard Catholic thinks of his intellectual milieu:

"Academically the social sciences and humanities courses seem to have a greater effect on religion or at least they tend to raise religious questions. Science courses tend to be amoral and consequently 'safe'.... Soc. Sci. I with its emphasis on Church history (at least in the first semester) taught me a good deal of theology in such a back-handed way that it made me eager to 'get it straight.' Humanities 5—philosophically stimulating anyway—was even more stimulating for me because I had constantly to rethink my own religiously-based philosophical position. Even when we read St. Augustine, St. Paul, and St. Thomas they were interpreted in such an un-Catholic (even un-Christian) manner that my thinking was confused. I am afraid I fought Kant, Hegel, etc. so much that I missed some of their good points." — RADCLIFFE SOPHOMORE IN BIO-CHEMISTRY

"Courses in history and philosophy have also tended to strengthen rather than weaken the Faith (Hum. 5, Soc. Sci.I)."— RADCLIFFE JUNIOR IN GOVERNMENT.

"Humanities 5 stimulated me to read some more and think about the Faith and to have discussions with non-Catholics. It made me a bit sceptical at times, but this drove me to further inquiry. Soc. Sci. I—I am being disillusioned about the Church in the Middle Ages, but not about my religion."— ANOTHER RADCLIFFE SOPHOMORE IN BIOCHEMISTRY.

"I have attended non-Catholic (private) institutions of learning since the third grade, and have always found that my Catholicism has given me a better background than my classmates (Catholic and non-Catholic) in vocabulary, literature, history, and the Bible. Catholicism has played a tremendous role in

A Catholic and Protestant pair of scripture scholars at the Colloquium: Dr. Krister Stendahl of the Harvard Divinity School and Fr. Raymond Brown, S.S.

western civilization, and can be, in fact, equated with that civilization at certain times; my Catholicism has been an excellent contribution to my understanding and awareness of history and literature."— HARVARD SENIOR IN HISTORY AND LITERATURE.

"It was valuable intellectually in creating a vivid imagination. My life would have been somewhat empty without the myths and symbols."— HARVARD JUNIOR IN PHYSICS.

"Gives me a head start when we study the Middle Ages."— HARVARD JUNIOR IN GOVERNMENT.

"It has made me distrust the interpretation of Tudor-Stuart history which is being given here."— HARVARD SOPHO-MORE IN HISTORY.

"The intellectual environment has made me want to see some sort of rational basis for the existence of religious dogmas. I find such a basis lacking." — HARVARD JUNIOR IN BIOCHEMISTRY.

"Religion gives some meaning to my intellectual pursuits, which by themselves alone at times seem to mean very little—they are so contradictory."— HARVARD FRESHMAN IN GOVERNMENT.

THE MORAL CLIMATE.
When we come to the student's morals, we arrive close to home, the place where religion most clearly touches practical life. Oddly enough, however, the answers of 79 students to question IIc, "How has your religion been affected ... by the ... moral environment?" amounted to "no effect." 43 said that their religion was helped by it, 32 said it was hindered, and another 22 offered doubtful of mixed response. On the other hand, 78 asserted that their religion was a positive help in shaping their moral lives; ten said it was a hindrance. Of the rest, 40 offered no specific answer, 17 were doubtful, and 31 found that religion had no special effect on their moral conduct.

A few distinct patterns of response to the moral climate here became clear in the survey. The most common appraisal of the state of Harvard morals was low—especially when compared with the well defined code offered by the Church to its members. But the same students who found that Harvard morality was less than it might be also thought that in this area their religion was of the most practical assistance. As a Harvard sophomore in physical sciences put it, "Religion has been perhaps the only thing that has kept me from destroying all my moral values since having arrived at Harvard. Gone were the binding school rules and the 'in person' guidance." Like the astringent intellectual atmosphere, the (to Catholics) uncertain moral climate of Harvard challenged many to greater effort and more conviction; on the moral plane it was again a matter of challenge or crisis leading towards maturity. A minority report found Harvard morals no worse than morals anywhere else, and some students had reason to be deeply edified by the conduct and ideals of their friends and associates here.

The strongest protests against the Church's position was aimed, not unexpectedly, at rigidity and alleged unreasonableness particularly on the subject of sexual morality. Acceptance and embrace of a firm moral position amidst the maelstrom of student life were, however, the more common reaction. We present representative comments:

> "The moral atmosphere is bad—either it makes you become a good Catholic or causes you to drop away completely."— HARVARD JUNIOR IN HISTORY.

> "Harvard does not seem to be especially immoral to me— although they make a lot of noise about it."— RADCLIFFE SOPHOMORE IN BIOCHEMISTRY.

> "The moral environment is far more moral than my own, predominantly Catholic, home town."— HARVARD SENIOR IN PHYSICS.

> "As to moral environment, the place can be as uplifting or as degrading as you wish it to be. The individual makes his own bed."— HARVARD SENIOR IN HISTORY.

> "Harvard morals hardly seem to coincide with Catholic morals." — HARVARD FRESHMAN IN CLASSICS.

> "My standards of conduct perhaps are not the best, but they would be the same were I here or at Notre Dame."—HARVARD SOPHOMORE IN HISTORY.

> "Morally I find my religion a substantial model for living and thinking—a model for which I owe *no one* any apologies." — STUDENT IN THE HARVARD BUSINESS SCHOOL.

> "I now endorse the idea (fact) that morals are relative and in that light see little or no right for the Catholic Church to want to impose a universal moral code."— HARVARD JUNIOR IN BIOCHEMISTRY.

John F. Kennedy, '40, was an Overseer when he was elected President and was mobbed when he returned to Harvard for meetings.

"The moral environment has made me a better Catholic because my moral code has been challenged here and my beliefs have been the only thing that has helped me to follow this code. In other words I guess my morals have been strengthened by attack or something."— HARVARD SOPHOMORE IN HISTORY.

"In the Radcliffe situation I think the greatest problem for a Catholic girl is the prevailing moral attitude. The attitude is totally alien to that in which most Catholic girls (and probably most girls) were raised... The education most Catholic girls have had does not prepare them to cope with this situation, and one just has to stubbornly insist that she is right even though she has no very coherent reasons to justify her attitude."— RADCLIFFE SENIOR IN HISTORY.

HARVARD AS WE SEE IT.
Having sketched something of what Harvard and Radcliffe Catholics think of their university, the editors claim their own turn to express a considered opinion on the same subject. The trademark of the Harvard student publication seems to be criticism of the institution, and we

*Catholic student
leaders of the late
1980's on retreat.*

would not wish to disappoint anyone; yet our appraisal of Harvard must include a general measure of approval. As we said in the opening remarks of this interpretation, we think that Catholics belong at Harvard. Not, perhaps, the Catholic of fragile conscience, unstable personality, or uncertain background in his faith. But then not every Protestant, Jew, or secularist belongs at a university like Harvard either.

The Harvard Catholic often finds himself in the minority: among Catholics, he is at Harvard; at Harvard, because he is Catholic. He must not allow himself to be swayed by any stereotype that the majority on either side may hold of him. Being at Harvard does not mean that a person is any less a Catholic; though his co-religionist may not be aware of it, he is in the Church's front line, meeting challenges where they really exist and learning the nature of the world we are so often told we must change. Being a Catholic does not mean that a person is any less devoted to the ideals of academic excellence. If the opinion of many at Harvard is that religion is for the simple-minded or that Catholicism is no more than a medieval remnant in our modern world, then perhaps Harvard too has something to learn.

In closing, we would repeat our challenge that the Catholic belongs here; in fact, we would add that he must be here if the Church is to keep up with the rapidly accelerating pace of historical change in our day. There is a sentence from Newman which is sometimes quoted as a warning to Catholics about secular education, but which can be read in exactly the opposite sense. Concluding his lecture on "Knowledge and Religious Duty," Newman made this compelling observation: "Basil and Julian were fellow students at the schools of Athens; and one became the saint and doctor of the Church, the other her scoffing and relentless foe." Too often we have been frightened away from the wisdom of the secular academy because we have thought only of Julian, whom we know as "the apostate." We might, however, ask ourselves whether we could ever have had a St. Basil, doctor of the Church, if he had not learned at the schools of Athens.

THEODORE MARIER

*Dr. Marier, a national leader in the Gregorian Chant movement, founded
the Boston Archdiocesan Choir School in 1963. He retired from St.
Paul's in 1984 after fifty years as organist and music director and is now
the Justine B. Ward Professor of Music at Catholic University.
He gave this interview in 1993.*

How did your association with St. Paul's begin?

In June of 1934 I graduated from Boston College. That same
month I was invited by Dr. Joseph Ecker, choirmaster at St. Paul's, to
audition for the post of organist. I was pleased that he offered me the
job and so my association with the parish began and lasted, as you
know, for more than fifty years. That same year also marked the beginning of my close friendship and thirty-year association with
Monsignor Augustine F. Hickey, Pastor of St. Paul's, one of the finest
priests I've ever known.

How would you describe St. Paul's in those early days?

As I recall, St. Paul's parish was alive with the many activities one would expect to find in those days stemming from normal
parish life: annual missions, Friday night devotions with Benediction of the Most Blessed Sacrament; Wednesday night services during Lent with guest preachers; Tenebrae Services during Holy Week;
an active Holy Name Society and Ladies Sodality; a parish school
with some 400 students; a boys' choir, an adult choir of about eighty
voices (that was a special institution of St. Paul's); daily and Sunday
High Masses (in Latin); the Harvard Catholic Club; upper and lower
churches—as they were called; a large gallery organ in the upper
church and a smaller reed organ in the lower church; miscellaneous
private devotions such as novenas, triduums; Saint Vincent de Paul
Society; numerous social activities. It was a busy place all taking
place during the "great depression."

I should mention here the fact that the entire parish school in
those days sang a Gregorian Chant High Mass on the important feast
days of the year such as Immaculate Conception, Corpus Christi, etc.
The children were trained by the Sisters of Saint Joseph who staffed
the school. This religious community has continued to provide teachers
for St. Paul's to this day, though fewer and fewer in number as time
went on. Many of the names come to mind as I think of the school and
its gradual demise as a parish school. There was Sister Margaret
William, Sister Agneta, Sister Kennan, Sister Margretta, and Sister
Honor, Sister Ralph, Sister Helen, all devoted teachers making their
vital contribution to the children of the parish and later to the choir
school. Sister Kathleen Berube is the last remaining Sister of Saint
Joseph on the staff of the school. The presence of these dedicated
women remains a precious memory.

Did you have any qualms about accepting the post of organist at St. Paul's?

I don't suppose I ever thought of that. I was happy to have a
large instrument to play and especially the opportunity to accompany
St. Paul's unusually fine choir, which sang great and challenging choral music. I found I had time to continue my organ studies at the New

*The choir school in
action in the 1980's.*

England Conservatory of Music with Homer Humphrey. I practiced to improve my skills, all the while playing for Requiem Masses, weddings, funerals, rehearsals in the church, with radio programs, concerts, and conducting outside of my church duties.

Did you grow up in a musical family?

Yes. Both my father and mother were very musical. My mother's sister, however, was the member of the family who had an extraordinary musical talent. I believe I was greatly influenced by her and began my piano studies with her when I might have been five or six years of age. This took place in Fall River where I was born in 1912. My family moved to Mansfield as my father's work changed and then to Dedham, perhaps around 1920. When in Dedham I soon became attached to the parish Church of St. Mary's, first as an altar boy and then as assistant organist for the Sunday School. I had my first lessons in organ playing with Ruth McMahon who was in charge of music at St. Mary's at that time. I suppose it was during those years that my future involvement with Church music was beginning to take its direction. I seemed comfortable in the environment of the church and, with the support of my family, what I was doing seemed to be the right thing for me to do.

What influenced you to choose a career in Church music?

There were many influences, as I look back, which gave impetus to what was to become my life's work. One of the most important, I suspect, was my making contact for the first time with Gregorian Chant. Interest in the chant persisted and helped me eventually to form a solid basis for the music program at St. Paul's.

In the mid-thirties, the Pius Tenth School of Liturgical Music in New York announced courses in Gregorian Chant to be held at the Sacred Heart Academy in Newton. The faculty for the courses was headed by Mother Georgia Stevens, a Religious of the Sacred Heart, and a group of her students, all from the New York School. The courses included a study of Gregorian Chant notation in the sung liturgy of the Church. We listened to recordings of the chant made by the choir of the Abbey of St. Pierre de Solesmes, France, under the direction of

John Brien preparing a trumpet part for 1963 Christmas, while Sr. M. Kennan, C.S.J., supports him at the keyboard.

Dom Joseph Gajard, O.S.B. The courses proved to be a mind-stretching experience for me and one that has lasted throughout my life. The recordings especially impressed me by the beauty of tone, the flow of the rhythm and the nuances of diction.

I was "hooked." I bought the choir's first album, produced by Victor in the early 78rpm format. (I still own this album—a treasure!) Little did I know at that time that the director of the fabulous choir and I were to become close friends 25 years later.

It seemed to me that there was nothing to do but to start my own Gregorian Chant schola. This I did just before the start of World War II. This small schola of friends and chant enthusiasts became the chant schola at St. Paul's after I took over as choirmaster in 1947. It was this schola that attracted a few Harvard students, among whom was a student named Bernard Law. Another was Father Gabriel, a Trappist monk of St. Joseph's Abbey in Spencer, Massachusetts, who as Jack Bertoniere has sung in my group. It was through him that I was privileged to meet Dom Gajard who came to Spencer to work with the monks in the area of Gregorian Chant. After that meeting we became close friends and remained so until Dom Gajard's death in France in 1972. My close relationship with the other monks of Solesmes has remained so until today.

What other influences helped shape your musical career?

As I look back over the years, there were many other influences, all of which almost inevitably seemed to be focused toward the work and development of the choir school at St. Paul's.

There was, for instance, the exhilarating experience of studying choral conducting with Dr. Archibald Davison, Director of the Harvard Glee Club, while I was preparing for my graduate degree at Harvard in the late 30's. His enthusiasm for good choral sound and his competence in teaching the disciplines of choral conducting made me want to be like him and produce as fine a choral group as his.

I often think about "Doc Davison," as he was known among his students. Stock phrases of his keep coming to mind and his image

Fr. Joseph Fratic, teacher and patron of the choir program, in front of the old school building.

appears before me whenever in my own teaching I hear myself saying: "Have the music in your head, not your head in the music!" or "Do not talk about the music, give your singers the example you want them to imitate, for one illustration is worth a thousand words!" I remember how in choral class he would sit in one of the sections of the chorus, for example among the altos or tenors, and then proceed to sing wrong notes. His purpose was to observe whether the student conductor heard the wrong notes and then listen to what the student planned to do about it. Such lessons one never forgets.

Then there was Walter Piston, whose lessons in composing techniques sparked whatever creativity I may have had in the way of music composition. His classes in harmonic analysis, fugue, and private lessons in free composition opened areas of music which might otherwise have remained a closed book to me. In addition to classroom work, there were special seminars sponsored by the music department to which Mr. Piston invited me. One was with Igor Strawinsky who was visiting professor that year. As I recall it, there were perhaps five or six would-be "composers" in his sessions which met for two hours once a week for five weeks. Each time we met, each student was expected to play one of his own pieces. Strawinsky would then make some comment about the piece just played or about the orchestration submitted for his critique. Looking over the score he would make some comment like: "Your flute player is idle here for sixteen measures. He's paid by the musicians' union, you know, so you'd better give him something to do." Then the great composer would launch into an explanation of some technical details in one of his own compositions, *Petrouschka*, or the *Rite of Spring*, revealing his mastery of the craft of orchestration. Inspiring sessions to be sure.

How did your interest in liturgy come about?
Right after the war one could hear the rumblings of changes in liturgical practice. The era of congregational participation was about to begin and Monsignor Hickey was one of the first to adopt the idea

and eventually to adapt it to his style of saying and singing the Order of the Mass. At the same time that extensive changes were being talked about, after the appearance of the *Mediator Dei* encyclical letter, Dr. Ecker decided to retire as St. Paul's choir director. Monsignor asked me to take over, which I did. It was then that my choral conducting experience and Gregorian Chant preparation were put to good use in building a program that would eventually include congregrational participation.

At first, it was the "dialogue Mass" introduced by Monsignor Hickey and ably and enthusiastically supported by his assistant, Father Joseph Collins. I seemed to be attracted to the idea and so sought out ways to learn more about papal legislation having to do with liturgy. This interest brought me into contact with leaders of the new movement, especially with members of the National Liturgical Conference including Fathers Sean Sheehan, William Leonard, S.J., Monsignor Hellriegel, Father Gerald Ellard, S.J., among others.

When Father Ellard passed away, since he had been conspicuously in the front ranks of the vanguard of reformers, a group of his friends decided to produce a book, a "festschrift" in his honor. Contributors to this book of essays were those involved in the growing liturgical movement. Father Leonard asked me to write a piece for the collection. At first I was unsure what to write until he said, "You are always talking about integrating a choir program into the curriculum of a parish school; why not write about that?" And so I tried to make more specific what had been up to that time only a vague proposal. It was here that the idea of the choir school was born.

What effect did your publishing experience have on the music program at St. Paul's?

At the conclusion of the war, in the mid-forties, I accepted a position with McLaughlin and Reilly Co., publishers of Catholic Church music. My association with this company here in Boston lasted for some fifteen years. During this period I edited many publications for the Church and became acquainted with many of the composers of Church music of the time and the details of the publishing process. When the Pius Tenth School of Liturgical Music decided to produce their own hymnal, I was put in charge of the operation. I then became acquainted with Mother Aileen Cohalan, R.S.C.J., and then with Mother Josephine Morgan, R.S.C.J., who over a period of several years succeeded each other as directors of the school, and thus wound up in charge of producing what became the very successful *Pius Tenth Hymnal*. My editorial experience with M & R Co. made the development of a hymnal especially designed for St. Paul's predictable. This book, which we now know and use, is, of course, *Hymns, Psalms and Spiritual Canticles*.

Could you say more about Monsignor Hickey?

How can I encapsulate with words the image and stature of this great priest, pastor and supremely human being? During his term of office as Pastor of St. Paul's, which began in the early 1920's and lasted until the founding of the choir school in 1963, there was order in every detail of parish management. He was strict about responsibility and punctuality. Indeed, when the chime in the tower sounded the hour, Mass began; when the clock said 7:45 on Friday night, the

This 1991 procession of saints continues a tradition of special children's liturgy.

Holy Hour began; whenever there was a question about a detail in the ritual, he always asked, "what does the book say? That is what we shall do." He was always available for a conference because he never took a day off. On Thursday mornings he went to give a course at Regis College. On Sunday afternoons he visited his brother, or, on occasion, came to our house for dinner. He did not own an automobile, preferring to make his visitation to the poor, for example, by taxi. His was a disciplined and structured life as a priest and pastor.

For all his uncompromising attitude toward efficient management of the parish, he was open to the challenge of new ideas if he felt these ideas were consonant with the teaching of the Church or for the good of the prayer life of the people. His leadership in the liturgical movement of the Archdiocese of Boston attests to this. In spite of the fact that the "liturgical movement" was unpopular with many of the archdiocesan clergy, he paid no attention and instituted the "dialogue Mass" for his own Mass at 8 o'clock Sunday mornings.

When the National Liturgical Conference held its national convention in 1948 in Boston, Monsignor Hickey was the first to offer the use of St. Paul's vestments, candles, missals, whatever was necessary for the presentations at Mechanics Hall, while many of the local clergy stayed away in droves from the scheduled events. One of the most memorable events at the convention was the presentation of the new Easter Vigil ritual, led by Monsignor Hellriegel of St. Louis, Missouri. Later this same rite was the first televised liturgical event in the Archdiocese of Boston, and it took place at St. Paul's. (That same night, outside on the sidewalk were Father Leonard Feeney's followers—their headquarters, if you remember, were across the street from the church—parading back and forth with placards in front of the church announcing "Father Hickey's midnight frolics!" taking place at that moment inside the church.)

Also in 1948, with Monsignor's permission and encouragement, a card was printed containing the musical notation for the Creed and the Mass Responses. The card was distributed in the pews. From that moment on the people were invited to take part in the singing of the Mass prayers and responses at the High Mass. Some people always seem to resent change but by repetition and insistence over a period of about 10 years (!), the resistance eventually broke down, and now congregational participation in the Mass has become the order of the day.

Another example of Monsignor Hickey's foresightedness and willingness to adjust to necessary change was his support of the project which I initiated to install an organ in the front of the church near the sanctuary. We discussed this project many times and, though hesitant at first, he finally acquiesced and allowed me to make the necessary enquiries and to formulate the plan. I proposed taking the organ console down from the gallery and wiring into it a second and smaller organ near the chancel where it stands today. In this way both the gallery and chancel organs could be played from the one console near where the choir was located. He agreed for he saw the necessity of uniting the musical forces in the front of the church where the liturgy took place and from which position a leader could involve the people in the singing more effectively.

A role model for pastors, Monsignor Hickey certainly was. I feel privileged to have known him and to have counted him among my closest friends.

What was your relationship to Cardinal Cushing?

There was another great leader of the Church, strongly opinionated, feisty on occasion and possessed of a heart of gold. I came to know him when he was Director of the Society for the Propagation of the Faith. As director of the Catholic Choral Society, I was able to offer him a vehicle for fundraising for Carney Hospital, for example, or for whatever cause he was promoting at the time.

I like to tell a few stories about him because they reveal his special character and lovable quality as a person.

Following Cardinal O'Connell's death, Bishop Cushing was made Archbishop of Boston. Early on in his new assignment he was invited by Mother Kenny, Religious Superior of the Sacred Heart Community in Newton, to officiate at the close of the summer school sessions in sacred music. Knowing of my friendship with the Archbishop, Mother Kenny invited me to accompany her to greet His Excellency when he arrived for the ceremony. I agreed. He arrived on schedule (like Monsignor Hickey, he respected promptness), and as we walked down the corridor toward the chapel where the ceremony was to take place, Mother suggested politely: "Your Excellency, we would just adore to have you intone the *Te Deum.* Would you?" He replied, "Sure, Mother, I'd be glad to—and you'll never forget it." Anyone who has been initiated to His Excellency's style of singing will understand the impact of that statement.

I remember, too, that same day when he addressed the assembled students, he began, as he often did, with a humorous anecdote. This time he ventured to ask, "What am I doing here addressing a group of music students? When I was in the seminary I was told that I was tone deaf. I thought they said that I was stone deaf! So I was sent out to the garden to pick potatoes." Then he launched into what was an improvised message without script, inspiring and from the heart, on the need to form one's heart and mind according to the Church's teaching and prayer-life. Unforgettable.

Some years later when I had worked out some of the details of the choir school program, Father Collins and I made an appointment to see the Archbishop, now Cardinal Cushing, in order to request permission to go ahead with our plan. His Eminence was definitely not in a good mood that day. After a perfunctory greeting of "Hi!" and before we could explain why we had come for our appointment, he began by saying, "Do what you want, but don't ask me for money. Everybody wants money... and I don't have it...." He was obviously having a down day. We left the episcopal residence somewhat disappointed and in silence. Finally Father Collins said, "Wasn't that a futile meeting?" I remember saying, "But, Father, he didn't say NO!" Two days later we received a personal note from His Eminence apologizing for his abruptness and including a check for $5000 with the message, "Go ahead with your plan for I know it is a good work for the Church." He continued his financial help for a few more years after that.

What influence did Justine Ward and the Ward Method have on the musical life of St. Paul's?

Here begins another story, one which is not over yet for it continues to unfold even to my present occupation as the Justine B. Ward Visiting Professor of Liturgical Music at The Catholic University of America in Washington.

Justine Ward was the author of a widely used method of teaching the elements of music to children. As a method it was designed to be an important component in the curriculum of the Catholic schools. Its music pedagogy focussed on the elements of music with a special emphasis on Gregorian Chant. Through my connection with Dom Gajard, whom I mentioned earlier, I was introduced to Mrs. Ward in 1960. Because I expressed interest in her method, uniquely designed for training Catholic children in music, she provided me with grants to study at the Abbey of Solesmes in France and to take Ward Method courses offered each year in Paris and in Cambridge, England. Upon my return from these training periods abroad, I immediately started to use the Method at St. Paul's by teaching the first, second and third grades. As it turned out, there could have been no better preparation for me in view of the plan to teach the children of the choir school.

Justine Ward began to formulate the details of her Method in the early 20's. It found its way into the schools of Holland, France and Italy. An edition in English was prepared for use in this country and it soon became widely used in many of our large dioceses. When I met her in 1960, she was in the process of revising the Method and updating some of the material. She invited me to participate in this revision but unfortunately, as age was beginning to

*Cardinal Law blesses
the new choir school on
All Saints Day in 1991.*

take its toll, she was unable to finish. Since that time I have been commissioned to continue the revision, a project which still occupies me. I am happy to say that the Ward Method has been and still is the basis of the teaching method at BACS.

Speaking of teachers, how was the staff maintained over the years?

As time went on, a host of lay teachers began to fill the ranks left vacant by the gradual withdrawal of the sisters from the staff. These lay teachers contributed significantly to the successful continuance of the choir school. Among them, as I remember were: Rita Waldron, Barbara Yeoman, Gilbert Whittemore, Micheline Vareika, Valerie Curtin, Gail Majaukas, Paul Hotin, and John Dunn, who taught math at first and assisted at the organ, then became director and principal of the school. Others as part-time teachers included Ed Haugh, Jr., Elaine Muise, Mark Nemeskal, and Mary Geiger who, though not a teacher, kept the office, ticket sales, class lists, and correspondence in efficient running order.

Any other contributing factors to the success of the choir school?

Yes. A factor no one can forget, that is, the Parents' Guild. This group of wonderfully supportive people gave unstintingly of their time and effort to the operation of the school by running flea markets, cake sales, by supplying drivers for the numerous "off-campus" engagements in which the boys were involved, such as singing for weddings, concerts, and TV programs; they acted as ushers in the church and even catered many of the social events related to the choir. Their almost 100% attendance at monthly meetings was considered by many educators as unique. I suppose this was due to the fact that their boys were happy; and they, as parents, wanted to keep them that way.

What does BACS stand for?

In this current age of acronyms, the choir school is right out front with its own. BACS stands for Boston Archdiocesan Choir School. In the beginning, the term BACS Club identified those who provided financial support to our tuition-free school. The idea to form such a group as the BACS Club was suggested by my friend and member of our advisory board, G. Wallace Woodworth, Director of the Harvard-Radcliffe Choral Society. We were having a rough time in those early days, and I expressed to him my concern for some sort of financial equilibrium in the management of the school. He said, "Ted, why don't you ask the people who know you and like what you are doing to support the program by contributing financially to its support? No harm in asking."

And so we did. The response exceeded my expectations, as one can readily observe by the size and enthusiasm of the BACS Club membership today. How right "Woody" was and how grateful we have been for his suggestion.

The term BACS has become a choir school logo. Some of the parents even had bumper stickers made ("I love BACS") and sold them to realize a small profit for the school. The hymnal in the pews, too, is published by the BACS Publishing Company, which I set up to provide us with books and, at the same time, to provide some income for the benefit of the school. Our hopes for the success of the book have not, unhappily, been realized.

What about the term "Boston Boy Choir"?

In order to enhance the outreach of the choir into the area of the non-church-oriented music world, a simpler title than Boston Archdiocesan Choir School was needed (many people had a problem pronouncing Archdiocesan) and so the term Boston Boy Choir was adopted. Under this title the choir became known especially to the audiences of the Boston Symphony Orchestra over a period of fifteen years or more. During those years the choir was privileged to sing under the baton of such eminent conductors as Arthur Fiedler, John Williams, Seiji Ozawa, Sir Colin Davis, Claudio Abado, among others, in performances at Symphony Hall in Boston, Carnegie Hall in New York and Tanglewood. A close association also developed over the years with the music program at Harvard. Elliot Forbes and John Ferris frequently asked the choir to participate in concerts at Sanders Theater and Memorial Church.

What is the meaning of the choir school motto?

Repleatur os meum laude tua means "let my mouth be filled with your praise." It is the first line of an antiphon proposed by Pope Pius XII as a unifying chant for all the choirs of the world. I thought this a singularly appropriate motto for the choir school and asked Gerard Rooney, the artist for the *Pilot,* to prepare a design that would incorporate this motto. Today, every choirboy has to memorize the entire antiphon and to sing it before Mass each day. Gerry Rooney's design appears on the BACS stationery and publications.

Any thoughts on the church building itself?

One of the contributing factors to the success of the choir program has been and is the church building. Its location on the edge of Harvard Square makes it accessible to choir boys from some thirty or more parishes of the Archdiocese by public transportation. In addition to its favorable location, the architectural design of the building is awesome and inspiring as an environment for religious services and, in addition, acoustically ideal for music. I have always felt that the singing of the choir was greatly enhanced by the building's spatial design.

*William Alfred,
Harvard professor and
Broadway playwright,
lent his poetic skills to
translation work for the
St. Paul's hymnal. For
forty years he has been
a model for Catholic
students.*

Would you care to add a personal note about your own family?

Yes. I would like to close these reminiscences about St. Paul's, where I feel I devoted the best years of my musical life, on a personal note.

Shortly after I came to St. Paul's in 1934, I met a Radcliffe student by the name of Edith Alice Hickey. Our courtship lasted until our marriage in 1939. As I look back, I think this was the most important event of my life. She was perfect for me. Only a loving, understanding and sympathetic wife, as she was, could have adjusted to and supported the various aspects of my somewhat eclectic career. Our first child, Suzanne, was born just before the outbreak of the war, and the twin boys, Robert and Vincent, were born during the days of the war when I was working in a war plant "for the duration." Through good times and not-so-good, she was always present to the children and to me, as a mother and wife. During the choir school years she came to know the boys of the school and their parents intimately, offering comfort and encouragement to both when needed. She was a real "mother" to the choir until she died in 1977, on the Feast of the Sacred Heart. After she died, there was such an outpouring of sympathy and condolences that a fund was started to make the present choir stalls possible: a memorial to her.

Although she was unable to share in the celebrations that have taken place recently that have given witness to the success of the choir program, I know very well that her share in these festivities has been real, for without the encouragement, inspiration and domestic tranquility which she provided year in and year out, I could not have attained the goals for which we both strove. How often she said when storm clouds seemed to gather on the horizon, "Don't worry, this program will succeed because it is God's work." And so it has and so she was right.

REMEMBERING THE ST. THOMAS MORE BOOKSHOP

For fifty years, Harvard Square enjoyed one of the finest Catholic bookstores in the country. Within the St. Thomas More Bookshop could be found both a deep collection of Catholic literature and a warm home for Catholic conversation.

Evangeline Mercier credits the Holy Spirit with the inspiration for a Catholic bookshop in Harvard Square. Her parents, Zoé and Louis J. A. Mercier of the Harvard faculty, strongly felt the need for a Catholic presence near the university and as she frequented the Personal Bookshop in the Square, she had noticed the lack of Catholic books or books by Catholics. She had asked herself: should there not be a *Catholic* bookshop? Joining her in the enterprise were two other recent graduates of Emmanuel College, Martha B. Doherty and Mary Stanton (who was doing graduate work at Radcliffe at the time).

The St. Thomas More Lending Library and Bookshop opened its doors in January 1936 at 33 Church Street in Harvard Square. The hours were from 10:30 a.m. to 3:30 p.m. The space was small and shaped like a piece of pie, narrow at the front and wide toward the back. A distinctive gold and blue sign, designed by Graham Carey, hung from a bracket attached to the outside brick wall. The shop bore the name of the recently canonized lay saint Thomas More, and a bookplate with his image designed by Ade Bethune was placed on the inside front cover of each book to be borrowed. Many priests of the archdiocese were very supportive of the endeavor. Christopher Griffin, a seminarian at St. John's Seminary wrote a letter of congratulations, and Fr. Francis Barry was a frequent visitor.

By October of that same year, Mary Stanton and Evangeline Mercier had entered the Carmel (now Sr. Mary Elizabeth of the Trinity, O.C.D. and Sr. Evangeline of Jesus, O.C.D.). Martha Doherty remained to manage the shop, assisted by Jeannette Roman, a recent convert from Judaism and a graduate of Wellesley, until the latter too entered the Carmel.

In 1939, Doherty reported that the bookshop had 900 volumes of fiction, essays, biography, church liturgy and doctrine, philosophy and the social sciences. Those who came in largest numbers were professors and students, but lawyers, housewives, artists, doctors, writers and columnists, political appointees, and private scholars also frequented the shop.[1] Biography was most popular. For about a year, a French language section was managed by Helena Leonard, who also became a religious.

In the early years, when the bookshop was on Church Street, lectures were given by prominent Catholics, such as the novelist Frances Parkinson Keyes, Fr. Gerald Fitzgerald, author and founder of the Servants of the Paraclete. Christopher Huntington, then a dean at Harvard, introduced the speakers and lectured himself. Soon the location became too crowded (capacity only 30), and no doubt this caused the search for what eventually became the St. Benedict Center at 23 Arrow Street across from St. Paul Church. Madeleine Mercier Crist remembers when Avery Dulles, before his conversion to Catholicism came into the bookshop to purchase a Missal so that he might follow the Catholic liturgy at St. Paul's during Holy Week. She recalls that he took quite a long time deciding on one, but finally chose the St. Andrew Missal. He asked for recommendations and frequently left with dozens of borrowed books.

From the beginning there was a guest book designed by Eric Gill. The scholar Etienne Gilson was the first to inscribe his name in it. Others included Leonard Feeney, S.J., Louis J. A. Mercier, Helen C. White, Jesuits John LaFarge and Francis P. LeBuffe of *America* magazine, Frank Sheed, Martin D'Arcy, S.J., Señorita del Valle and the Baroness de Hueck. There was a steady clientele of over one thousand, though there was no front window in which to display books. The bookshop was aptly described by Alba I. Zizzamia: "If you visit it, you will be charmed not only with St. Thomas and his business associates—you will be delighted and refreshed by the Catholicity of its clientele. It is all pervading."[2]

The Stanton and Mercier families continued to take care of the bookshop and eventually the Stanton family became the sole owners at which time (1940) Catherine Clarke became manager. The Stantons then turned over the bookshop to Agnes Bourneuf (1958) and her sister who later moved the store from its original location to Holyoke Street. For the twenty years Agnes Bourneuf owned the Thomas More Book Shop, it was no longer combined with a lending library but it maintained its role as a gathering place for the Catholic community of Cambridge and Boston. Miriam Donovan then acquired the store for two years before selling it to The Seabury Press who sold it to the Massachusetts Bible Society who closed the store in 1986, then in the Holyoke Center arcade. Would that it would open its doors again.

---

[1] "Do People Read Religious Books?" *Publishers Weekly* (March 25, 1939).

[2] "St. Thomas More—Bookseller", *The Catholic Transcript* (March 24, 1938).

Louise M. Des Marais is a Cambridge writer and editor.

PEGGY ELLSBERG

Peggy R. Ellsberg teaches in the English Department at Barnard College in New York City. She was interviewed in 1991 about Agnes Bourneuf and the Thomas More Bookstore.

The first time I ever walked into the Thomas More Bookstore, it was late on a Saturday afternoon in December. The Cambridge sky was gunmetal grey, and a light snow was falling. The store was then a small, square, brightly-lit, room on Holyoke Street and Agnes was serving tea and cookies. I found out on that occasion that tea and cookies were served every day at 3:30, at which moment every customer became a guest.

I was dazzled to discover in that small, cozy space the whole mainstream of Christian tradition, and I feel that when the Thomas More Bookstore left Harvard Square Cambridge lost touch with something timeless and profoundly significant. As the years went by, and turned into decades, I visited the Thomas More Bookstore and Agnes often. It was usual to find visiting scholars, bishops, university professors, cleaning ladies, sisters in habits, college students, and every imaginable kind of person congregating for conversation and browsing among the books, cards, and small religious objects that Agnes collected and sold. Agnes gave Catholic bookstores a good name. She created a total, Catholic environment which was a high-toned addition to the rectory, the Catholic student center and the parish church, It was a modest, quiet and constant reminder of the beauty of the Word and of the wisdom of the Church. Agnes performed her ministry in a steady, reliable way. As a lay woman, she carved out her own vocation in the Church and it was ecumenical, intellectual, literary and aesthetic. There was something about her that reminded me of Dorothy Day. Educated Catholics and Catholics in the process of getting an education alike needed a home and Agnes provided one. You could walk into her shop with any concern or any need—not just for books—and she could help. I often had the feeling she knew everything about everything.

I also often had the feeling she knew everyone. The Thomas More Bookstore was the kind of place where you could strike up a conversation with a stranger and then discover it was an old friend of Agnes. Every customer became her friend. The first time the bookstore nearly went under financially, President Derek Bok got letters supporting the bookstore from all over the world. After Agnes left, there was a brief time when her mood and her agenda continued to shed its light on the shop, but eventually it became just a business.

Agnes grew up in a convent school and never married. She worked as a secretary for an architects' firm for a long time. Meanwhile, she learned a lot about investments. Somehow—and I don't know exactly how—she stumbled upon this opportunity to run a bookshop. The space was on Church Street at that time. Later she moved it to Holyoke Street. By the time I met Agnes, Mim Donovan owned the store and Agnes managed the book department for her. I remember that Agnes used to borrow a book from the shop inventory and take it home with her overnight and bring it back the next morning read thoroughly and all the way through.

During the day, she could speak with real authority about the books on the shelves and make proper recommendations to scholars and beginning readers alike.

Once a year, Agnes would travel and she would buy religious articles, rosaries, statuary, icons, wallhangings, cards and so on. And so the store was always stocked with tasteful and often beautiful devotional objects. It was a wonderful place to buy Christmas presents and also Christmas cards.

Agnes was very quiet about her personal life. Few people knew that she had cancer. She never discussed it. My friend Sally Fitzgerald liked Agnes enormously and told me she couldn't understand why Agnes retired from the bookstore. Sally felt the bookstore was a sacred vocation—I think a lot of us felt that. But of course Sally didn't know that Agnes was dying and I think very few people knew that Agnes was actually in her eighties. She seemed so young and vital and full of quiet stamina.

Agnes must have had a daring character when you think of what a risk it had been for her to buy the shop to begin with. She began a whole new career and a whole new life in her late fifties and early sixties when most people can think only of their retirement. In what could have become just a small business there flourished a spiritual and literary center.

My friend Sally Fitzgerald always remembers that Agnes decorated the shop with a fantastic painting of the Spanish court with St. Michael depicted carrying a rifle. "I was looking for *Art and Scholasticism*, " Sally told me, "which I had lost when we had moved either to or from Italy. I had been unable to find it anywhere in Boston or New York, but of course Agnes had it the first time I walked in. I was sold from that moment on. The shop also carried gorgeous Italian *crêches*, which were non-existent in Harvard Square at that time." My husband Robert Ellsberg remembers talking to Agnes about an uproar regarding a recent papal encyclical and Agnes said to him, "When you've been a Catholic for as long as I have, you've seen popes come and you've seen popes go. I am not worried in the least." And when the Episcopalian Seabury Press bought the shop, Agnes said to Robert, in real horror, "But aren't they the very ones who murdered St. Thomas More."

I met my husband Robert Ellsberg at the Thomas More Bookstore. And soon after our engagement, Agnes threw a big book-signing party for his *By Little and By Little: The Selected Writings of Dorothy Day*, and that was another one of Agnes' ministries. Every time a local Catholic published a book, she turned it into a festive event. It was worth the trouble of writing a book in order to have a party in your honor at Agnes' store.

Remembering John Leary '81

In 1983, an anonymous donor funded an annual social service fellowship for Harvard-Radcliffe students in memory of John Leary.

"John Leary, aged 24, died suddenly of cardiac arrest in the late afternoon of August 31, 1982. He had finished his full day of work at the Pax Christi USA Center for Conscience and War and was jogging back to Boston's Haley House, a Catholic Worker soup kitchen where he lived and served the needs of the homeless poor and elderly. Later that evening he was to have attended the regular planning session at Sojourner's House, a recently opened haven for deserted or displaced families. Following that there was to have been a practice session with the Ailanthus Singers in preparation for Sunday liturgy. A fairly normal schedule of activity for him; if anything a lighter day than most."

Gordon Zahn
John Timothy Leary:
A Different Sort of Hero (1983).

"I am proud to say that I was one of his teachers here, but John Timothy Leary of the class of 1981, taught me more than I taught him, and thus I mourned with hundreds of others when this ordinary boy of extraordinary grace and courage died of a heart attack at the age of twenty-four just before the fall term began. In the crowd that populates Harvard College and Harvard Square, John Leary did not stand out; he had neither wings nor halo. But the difference with John was that he discovered that life had no purpose, no meaning, no direction, and no focus apart from the purpose and focus of God. And for an attractive, able secular to discover that in the 20th century is a minor miracle. The major miracle is that he oriented his life to act upon that discovery. He became in his short life the complete total man for others, and those who knew and loved him testify to the love of Christ that shone in and through him and illumined the prisons where he worked as a P.B.H. volunteer, the street hostels in the South End, the derelicts to whom he gave shelter and support, his fellow activists in the peace movement, to whom he gave moral courage, and even those who disagreed with his conscientious support of the life of the unborn. And when this working class Irish Catholic boy of no profession or fame died, hundreds of us filled a great church in Jamaica Plain to thank God that in this fellow we have seen something of the light of the world."

—The Reverend Peter J. Gomes
Sermon for September 26, 1983

John Leary (left) at Haley House, a Catholic Worker soup kitchen in Boston.

PETER J. GOMES

*Rev. Peter J. Gomes is Minister in the Memorial Church and Plummer
Professor of Christian Morals at Harvard. He contributed this anecdotal
recollection in October, 1990.*

When I came to Harvard Divinity School, now twenty-five years ago
this past autumn, it was without any thought or impression of the
presence of the Roman Church here. Harvard was Protestant turf,
modified slightly by the Boston heresy of Unitarianism, but still in its
culture and form Protestant. And no place was this more so than in
the Divinity School, where the presence of the Charles Chauncey
Stillman *Visiting* (emphasis mine) Professor of Roman Catholic Theological Studies only added to the exotic and foreign nature of matters
Roman. We understood him to be to us as was the ambassador of Islam
in the Center of World Religions, or the occasional Buddhist or Hindu,
compliments or condiments, if you will, to our reformed mutton. Father
Joseph Fichter, the Stillman Professor of the day, in his genial, non-di-
dactic way, was a domesticated Roman presence in our midst, the
House Catholic, if you will.

But this was to change. The opening convocation of my first
year, September, 1965, had as the preacher the Hollis Professor of Divinity, George Hunston Williams, an accredited Visitor to the Second
Vatican Council in Rome from which he had just returned, full of grace
and truth. He preached to us on the renewal of the Catholic Church,
and here he was, a Protestant's Protestant, in the Memorial Church,
speaking of his intimate observances of the Roman Church in Council,
his impeccable Latin allowing him a greater participation, alas, than
most of the prelates voting and present.

In our senior year, 1967-8, the winds of change had reached
even to the Archdiocesan seminary of St. John at Brighton, where several seminarians had been expelled for demanding that at least one
service a week be said in English. The expelled students enrolled in
Harvard Divinity School and came to live in Divinity Hall where I came
to know them all well. They were, we thought, a strange lot: men
professed to a life of holy obedience and chastity, decidedly un-Protes-
tant causes, and who were now made to suffer for their faith. They
were as heroic martyrs to us. With a slightly renegade Jesuit priest-
graduate student as their celebrant, these Catholics began to hold daily
mass in our chapel, a decidedly unconsecrated place, known as the
scene of Emerson's Divinity School address of 1838. We were impressed, so much so, that we wrote of their doings in the school
newspaper, envious of their sense of community and purpose.
Unbeknownst to us, our paper was routinely circulated to donors
and friends of the school, chief among whom was none other than
Richard Cardinal Cushing, Archbishop of Boston, friend of President
Pusey and Dean Miller.

Our student Catholic friends were summoned to the Archepiscopal
presence in Brighton for an audience of the Cardinal. As they told the story
afterwards, they were prepared to confront the old boy and tell him their
view of what was wrong with him and his church, but as they were made
to cool their heels in ante-chamber after ante-chamber, their resolve began
to cool. Finally a monsignor admitted them into the presence. The

Fr. John MacInnis, Plummer Professor Peter Gomes, Sr. Mary Karen Powers and Fr. John Boles after a guest homily of Gomes at the St. Paul's student liturgy.

Cardinal, not well, was propped up on many pillows in a great chair, coughing and hacking. The men fell to their knees and kissed the Cardinal's ring. He demanded to know what they were doing at Harvard, of all places. The designated spokesman, a handsome, articulate, young man began to speak. The Cardinal cut him off with the question, "Who are you? What's your name" The young man gave his full baptismal name. "What kind of a name is that?" roared the Cardinal. "Polish, your eminence," replied the young man. "Polish, Polish: you do this to me after all I've done for the Poles?" The rest of the interview was not vouchsafed to us back in Divinity Hall, but the clandestine masses ceased.

Many years later I had the honor to invite the new Cardinal to preach in the Memorial Church, the first Roman prelate to do so. (The first Roman Catholic to do so was John Courtney Murray, at the invitation of my predecessor, George A. Buttrick, in the 1950's). Three incidents remind me of that happy visit. The first of these occurred in the robing room just before the service was to begin. The Cardinal, resplendent in his scarlet, was nonetheless nervous, and I tried the clerical small talk, universal before church, to put him at ease. As if for the first time, he noticed my name: "Gomes, Gomes," he said in his Portuguese-accented English, "is that not a Portuguese name?" I replied, "It is, your Eminence. My father was born and baptized a Catholic on the Island of Brava, and I was baptized a Catholic here in St. Peter's, Cambridge." "Ah," he said, "and where did we go wrong?" I took the "we" to refer not to the corporate me but to the Roman Church, and before I had time to answer, the bell summoned us to divine service.

The second incident occurred after the service. Two Cambridge ladies of a certain age, the sort described by e.e. cummings as living in "furnished souls," were chatting about the service in the narthex. One said, "How lovely of the Cardinal to wear his crimson for the occasion." "Oh no, my dear," said the other. "That is scarlet, not crimson, the colour of a college slightly older than our own."

Finally, there was lunch given by The Most Catholic Master of Adams, Professor Robert Kiely, in Apthorp house, the Master's elegant lodgings and once the rectory of the Reverend East Apthorp, rector of Christ Church, Cambridge. (So pretentious was he and grand his house that it was known as "The Bishop's Palace.") No one could be less at ease in such a place than the humble Cardinal Medeiros. The usual characters had assembled for sherry and then were escorted into the dining room where all stood behind their chairs waiting for the Cardinalate Blessing, but no cardinal was to be found. The discreet silence that followed was based on the almost universal assumption that he had gone to the loo and was still there. Time passed, the Most Catholic Master and his lady looked concerned, when suddenly the door to the butler's pantry opened and there entered the Cardinal. He had been in the kitchen giving his blessing to the Irish cooks, maids, and assembled household staff. It was not an uncharacteristic detour.

My final tale has more to do with what did NOT happen rather than with what did, but is true nonetheless. Sometime in the late summer of 1976 of a late Thursday afternoon, late enough in fact to count as the beginning of the weekend, I ran into the Hollis Professor

Bernard Law (the Archbishop of Boston) and Robert Runcie (the Archbishop of Canterbury) meet on neutral turf—Sparks House at Harvard.

Krakow Archbishop Karol Wojtyla, after lecturing during the 1976 Harvard summer session, speaks with Dean Krister Stendahl and Stillman Professor George MacRae, S.J.

of Divinity, Professor George Williams. He was full of agitation as he had a guest coming to lecture in the Harvard Summer School, and he wanted me to give a dinner party in honor of his guest on the following Monday evening. My respect and affection for my former teacher notwithstanding, I was annoyed at so importunate a request. I explained that "no one entertained in Cambridge on a Monday night in August," that my cook was on holiday, and my house shut up, and that I in fact was on my way to Plymouth and would not be back for days. Professor Williams, crestfallen but persistent, asked if I had any suggestions. To end this prolonged conversation, I suggested that he try the Dean of the Divinity School, whose house was larger than mine and who just might have his establishment on call. Professor Williams took the diverting suggestion; but as a polite, but insincere, expression of interest, I asked who his guest was. He replied that he was the Cardinal Archbishop of Krakow, an old friend from Vatican II days, who was here to lecture on some medieval form of Polish mysticism in the Summer School. I counted myself fortunate to have gotten out of an evening of such dismal prospects, and merrily went on my way. There stands now on the desk of Krister Stendahl a silver-framed photograph of three very familiar figures on the steps of Jewitt House, the Dean's residence. Professor Williams, Dean Stendahl, and in the middle, the then Cardinal Archbishop of Krakow, known to the rest of us as Pope John Paul II. Whenever I read Hebrews 13:2, all of this comes back to mind in painfully vivid detail: "Do not forget to entertain strangers, for by so doing some people have entertained angels without knowing it."

PRIESTS OF ST. PAUL'S PARISH, CAMBRIDGE

From 1923 to 1965, in the heyday of Boston urban parishes, St. Paul's was assigned five priests. By 1984, the parish had returned to its original staffing of pastor plus assistant, although the Harvard-Radcliffe chaplains are no longer counted in this number.

1875-1907: Rev. William Orr, Pastor

1877 Rev. Timothy Hannigan			
1877-78 Rev. James H. Conlon			
1878-79 Rev. Daniel J. Splain			
1879-80 Rev. Martin J. Lee			
1880-81 Rev. John Gilday			
1881-86 Rev. Daniel J. Gleason			
1886-88 Rev. John J. Moore			
1888-97 Rev. John C. Coan	1889-1907 Rev. John J. Ryan		
1897-99 Rev. William J. Barry	"		
1899-1907 Rev. John J. Farrell	"		

1907-1925: Rev. John J. Ryan, Pastor

1907-11 Rev. Jos. F. McGlinchey	1908-13 Rev. Charles A. Finn	1907-15 Rev. John J. Buckley	
1911-14 Rev. Irving L. Gifford	1913-26 Rev. Denis A. O'Brien	1916-18 Rev. John B. Mullin	
1915-25 Rev. Denis F. Murphy	"	1918-37 Rev. William G. Gunn	1923-46 Rev. Dennis J. Fitzpatrick

1925-1965: Msgr. Augustine F. Hickey, Pastor

1925-30 Rev. Richard S. McShane	1927-41 Rev. Daniel J. Golden	"	"
1930-31 Rev. Jeremiah F. Minihan	"	"	"
1931 Rev. Arthur J. Riley	"	"	"
1932-43 Rev. Francis J. Greene	1942-46 Rev. Donald Whalen	1937-46 Rev. Edward J. Haynes	"
1946-65 Rev. Joseph I. Collins	1946-61 Rev. John E. Kenney	1946-54 Rev. John J. Sullivan	1947-60 Rev. Charles B. Murphy
"	1961-68 Rev. David P. Noonan	1954-67 Rev. Charles I. Sheehy	1960-65 Rev. John B. Scorzoni

1965-1971: Rev. Joseph I. Collins, Pastor

1965-67 Rev. William J. Chevalier	"	"	
1967-69 Rev. John K. Connell	1968-74 Rev. Richard J. Shmaruk		
1969-70 Rev. Joseph M. Carney	"		
1970-71 Rev. John P. Galvin	"		

1971-1974: Msgr. Edward G. Murray, Pastor

1974-1992: Rev. John P. Boles, Pastor

1971-84 Rev. Joseph P. Fratic	1973-83 Rev. Paul W. Hurley
1983-89 Rev. Gerald J. Osterman	
1990— Rev. James A. Field	

1992— Rev. J. Bryan Hehir, Pastor

PRINCIPALS OF ST. PAUL'S SCHOOL, CAMBRIDGE

From the founding of St. Paul's parish school in 1889 until the graduation of its last class in 1974, over 220 women of the Congregation of the Sisters of St. Joseph served the school in some capacity. For the first eighty years, the parish provided a convent for their residence and the community superior generally also held the position of principal.

1889-1893	Sister Mary Comer, C.S.J.	1930-1936	Sister Estelle Howard, C.S.J.
1893-1894	Sister Mary John McLaughlin, C.S.J.	1936-1937	Sister Helen Eugenius Murphy, C.S.J.
1894-1897	Sister Mgt. Mary Alocoque Morgan, C.S.J.	1937-1939	Sister Leo Clement Fallon, C.S.J.
1897-1906	Sister Clara Agnes Perley, C.S.J.	1939-1945	Sister Edgar Halliden, C.S.J.
1906-1917	Sister Mary Genevieve Martin, C.S.J.	1945-1951	Sister Stella Vincent Keyes, C.S.J.
1917-1918	Sister Mary Paul Condrin, C.S.J.	1951-1957	Sister Corita Tomei, C.S.J.
1918-1920	Sister Hildegarde O'Brien, C.S.J.	1957-1963	Sister William Clare Walsh, C.S.J.
1920-1923	Sister Benignus Buckley, C.S.J.	1963-1969	Sister Margretta Tuohy, C.S.J.
1923-1924	Sister Pauline Hogan, C.S.J.	1969-1974	Sister Honor Dougherty, C.S.J.
1924-1930	Sister Mary Camilla O'Connor, C.S.J.		

Catholic Chaplains at Harvard

In 1898-1899, Rev. Thomas I. Gasson, S.J. of Boston College gave talks and spiritual direction.

1901-1907	Rev. John J. Farrell	[*Assistant at St. Paul's*]
1908-1913	Rev. Charles A. Finn, D.D.	[*Assistant at St. Paul's*]
1913-1925	Rev. John J. Ryan	[*Pastor*]
1925-1930	Rev. Augustine F. Hickey	[*Pastor*]
1930-1931	Rev. Jeremiah F. Minihan, S.T.D.	
1931-1932	Rev. Arthur J. Riley	
1932-1943	Rev. Francis J. Greene	[*Assistant. at St. Paul's*]
1943-1947	Rev. Dennis J. Fitzpatrick	[*Assistant at St. Paul's*]
1947-1950	Rev. John J. Sullivan	[*Assistant at St. Paul's*]
1950-1952	Rev. Lawrence J. Riley, S.T.L.	[*Professor at St. John's Seminary*]
1952-1954	Rev. Vincent McQuade, O.S.A.	[*President of Merrimack College*]
1954-1960	Rev. William Porras	[*Priest of Opus Dei*]

Catholic Chaplains at Radcliffe

1906-1923	Rev. John J. Ryan	[*Pastor*]
1923-1936	Rev. William W. Gunn	[*Assistant at St. Paul's*]
1936-1937	Rev. Francis J. Greene	[*Assistant at St. Paul's*]
1940?-1941	Rev. Daniel J. Golden	[*Assistant at St. Paul's*]
1940s	Rev. Donald Whelan	[*Assistant at St. Paul's*]
1946-1960	Rev. Joseph I. Collins	[*Assistant at St. Paul's*]

Catholic Chaplains at Harvard-Radcliffe

1960-1966	Rev. Joseph I. Collins		
1962-1965	Rev. Thomas W. Buckley		
1966	Rev. George Hagmaier		
1967-1968	Rev. Frederick J. Collins		
1968-1975	Rev. Richard Griffin, S.J.	1969-1975	Sr. Ann Kelley, O.P.
1971-1974	Rev. Edward Murray [*Pastor*]		
1974-1992	Rev. John P. Boles [*Pastor*]		
1975-1986	Rev. Thomas F. Powers	1975-1986	Sr. Evelyn Ronan, S.N.D.
1981-1990	Rev. John E. MacInnis	1986—	Sr. Mary Karen Powers, R.S.M.
1990—	Rev. Richard J. Malone		
1992—	Rev. J. Bryan Hehir [*Pastor*]		
1992—	Rev. George Salzmann		

Notes

Introduction (3-18)

[1]S.B. Sutton, *Cambridge Reconsidered* (1976). 56.

[2]For the nineteenth-century history of the Catholic Churches in Cambridge, see Charles J. McIntire, "The Catholics and their Churches", 244-252, in Arthur Gilman, ed., *The Cambridge of 1896* (Cambridge, 1896); Wm. A. Leahy, "Archdiocese of Boston", 208-216, in Wm. Byrne, et al., *History of the Catholic Church in New England* (Boston, 1899); James S. Sullivan, *One Hundred Years of Progress. A Graphic, Historical and Pictorial Account of the Catholic Church of New England, Archdiocese of Boston* (Boston, 1894). Especially for later events, see also the relevant sections of the official archdiocesan history: Robert H. Lord, John E. Sexton, Edward T. Harrington, *History of the Archdiocese of Boston* (Boston, 1945) in three volumes, afterwards abbreviated *HAB*. The Archives of the Archdiocese of Boston (afterwards AAB) hold the relevant parish records. The extensive files of the Cambridge Historical Commission are particularly useful for architectural data and newspaper clippings. Occasionally correspondence in the Harvard University Archives (afterwards HUA) mentions the affairs of local Catholics.

[3]J. S. Sullivan, *The Catholic Church of New England*, 533.

[4]S.B. Sutton, *Cambridge Reconsidered*, 57. *HAB*, vol. 2, 223-4.

[5]J.L. Sibley in his private journals, 35-6, HUA.

[6]*Pilot*, Jan. 29, Feb. 5, 1848.

[7]J. S. Sullivan, *The Catholic Church of New England*, 545ff. The architect and sculptor Henry Greenough may have designed the original building. See Bainbridge Bunting and R. H. Nylander, *Survey of Architectural History in Cambridge, Report Four: Old Cambridge* (Cambridge), 137, although the date of demolition should be the late 1920's, not 1915.

[8]St. Paul Parish records, AAB.

[9]J. S. Sullivan, *The Catholic Church of New England*, 548. *HAB* II. 270.

[10]Taken from remarks to his classmates on the occasion of their 45th anniversary in June, 1946. John LaFarge papers, Box 22, Folder 5, Georgetown University Special Coll.

[11]For the early history of the buildings, see entries on Ford and St. Paul's in the files of the Cambridge Historical Commission.

[12]J. S. Sullivan, *The Catholic Church of New England*, 536.

[13]B.A. Mandelbaum and M.K. FitzSimons, "Edward Waldo Forbes: City Planner" in *Edward Waldo Forbes: Yankee Visionary* (Fogg Art Museum, Cambridge 1971), 49-91; Ryan to O'Connell, Sept. 28, 1907, AAB; Although Eliot did see Fr. Orr at least once in 1900, in 1902 Eliot wrote to Ford that Orr's "proposal, that the line on Holyoke Street rather than on De Wolfe Street should be used, is not at all tenable," since it was blocked by heavy and expensive buildings, concluding that "De Wolfe Street is much the cheaper and most desirable route." Ford papers (HUG 4403.5), HUA; Olmstead to Ford, Dec. 31, 1901, ibid.

[14]Fr. Ryan's remarks in the dedication booklet of St. Paul's Church, Oct 13, 1924, page 39, AAB.

[15]Convent day book, Archives of C.S.J., Mt. St. Joseph, Brighton.

[16]Wm. Cardinal O'Connell, *Sermons and Addresses*, vol. 5 (Boston, 1922), 186.

[17]For Graham, see the files of Camb. Hist. Commission and the Harvard-Radcliffe Catholic Student Center photo archives. St. Paul's is quite similar to Graham's St. Mary's Church in Akron, Ohio, illustrated in the *Brickbuilder* (also called *The Architectural Forum*), vol. 27, 1914.

[18]Ryan to O'Connell, sometime in spring 1924, AAB.

[19]Hickey to Minihan, Dec. 1, 1938; Chancery to Hickey, Dec. 2, 1938, AAB.

[20]St. Paul's card file. AAB. The method for collecting this data varied over the years, so individual years may vary in their accuracy.

[21]June 21, August 20, Nov. 17, 1914. Convent Day Book, St. Paul's, Archives of the Sisters of St. Joseph, Brighton.

[22]*A Brief Historical Review of the Archdiocese of Boston, 1907-1923* (1925), 79-174.

The Immigrant Community (19-38)

[1] Thomas H. O'Connor, *Fitzpatrick's Boston: 1846-1866* (Boston, 1984), 3-5. Mary E. Daly, *The Famine in Ireland* (Dublin, 1986), 21-25. Kirby A. Miller, *Emigrants and Exiles: Ireland and the Irish Exodus to North America* (New York, 1985).

[2] Mary E. Daly, ibid., 2. Mary E. Daly, ibid., 44-45.

[3] Thomas H. O'Connor, ibid., 9. David Fitzpatrick, *Irish Emigration: 1801 - 1921* (Dublin, 1984), 33.

[4] Kirby A. Miller, ibid., 281-282.

[5] Mary E. Daly, ibid., 99. Kirby A. Miller, ibid., 282, 286, 291-2.

[6] David Fitzpatrick, ibid., 34.

[7] Letter of Peter Roak, ca 1850. Harney family letters, Billerica, Mass.

[8] Henry C. Binford, *The First Suburbs: Residential Communities on the Boston Periphery, 1815 - 1860*. (Chicago, 1985), 38-39.

[9] Henry C. Binford, ibid., 49, 163.

[10] Oscar Handlin, *Boston's Immigrants: A Study in Acculturation* (Cambridge, Mass., 1979), 247.

[11] Henry C. Binford, ibid., 163.

[12] J.L. Sibley in his private journals, 829 (April 24, 1869), 749 (July 17, 1866), 913 (April 12, 1871), and 579 (Aug. 11, 1861), Harv. Univ. Archives.

[13] *Cambridge Tribune*, Aug. 30, 1890, page 5.

[14] *HAB*, 387.

[15] *Cambridge Chronicle, 1846-1946*, 36.

[16] The material in this section on the history of Houghton Mifflin is drawn from Ellen B. Ballou, *The Building of the House: Houghton Mifflin's Formative Years* (Boston, 1970).

[17] Charles A. Rheaut, Jr., *The Riverside Press, 1852-1971* (Boston, 1979).

[18] *A Brief Description of the Riverside Press* (Cambridge, 1899).

[19] Charles A. Rheaut, Jr., *The Riverside Press, 1852-1971* (Boston, 1979).

[20] Charles A. Rheaut, Jr., *The Riverside Press, 1852-1971* (Boston, 1979).

[21] The quotations in this section and what little else can be documented about the early history of St. Paul's School are to be found in the archives of the Sisters of St. Joseph, Brighton.

The Mission Community (39-44)

[1] The traditional historical division of the three periods of Catholic missions are the Apostolic period to the time of Constantine; the National period, which included the missions to "nations:" Cyril and Methodius, Boniface, Columban, Augustine of Canterbury; and the Modern period, which began at the time of the Catholic Reformation with the missions of the Franciscans, Dominicans, and Jesuits. The choice of Saint Columban as the "national" missioner depicted in the mural, highlights the mainly Irish congregation during the period under Fr. John J. Ryan when the Church was built. Next to the mission murals is the altar (with statue and two paintngs) of St. Patrick, the patron of the heavily Irish diocese.

[2] Father Celestine Roddan, C.P., was from Randolph, Massachusetts. He was the Superior of the Passionist Fathers' first mission to Hunan, China in 1921. Fr. Paul F. Rooney, O.F.M., Harvard A.B. 1898, labored among Indians in Oklahoma and Baja, California where he died in 1906. A number of his letters to Mrs. LaFarge (mother of his friend John LaFarge) demonstrate the use of college ties for fundraising and raising mission awareness, (Georgetown Univ. Spec. Coll., LaFarge collection).

[3] James A. Walsh, "Duty of American Catholics Toward the Foreign Missions," in *Report of the Proceedings and Addresses of the 16th Annual Meeting of the Catholic Educational Association, 1919* (Cincinnati: Catholic Educational Association, 1919), 506.

[4] Mary Josephine Rogers, a graduate of Smith College, helped Walsh at the Propagation of the Faith office in Boston. Another parish connection with Maryknoll is the mention by Bishop Raymond Lane, Maryknoll missioner in China, that "Father Willie Orr, the famous North of Ireland Pastor in Cambridge" had married Lane's parents. Raymond A. Lane, M.M. *The Early Days of Maryknoll* (New York, 1951): 43.

[5] *Field Afar* 2 (October, 1908), 3.

[6] Joseph McGlinchey, "Address," *Second American Catholic Missionary Congress* (Chicago, 1909), 65.

[7] Other participants at the Congress from St. Paul and from Cambridge were James H. Corcoran, Mrs. George F. Doherty, Mrs. John Doyle, Miss Mary E. Duffy, Miss M. Dwyer, Mrs. J.C. Fay, Vincent Fox, Miss A. Fox, B.J. Hally, Mary C. Healey, M. and P. La Rose, Miss Agness G. Purcell, Mrs. Francis Rohde; Miss Mary Rohde, Mrs. May Rachen, Mr. and Mrs. John T. Shea, James N. Vallely, Bernard B. Welch.

[8] During the first thirty years of the twentieth century, many mission periodicals sprang up to arouse the Catholics of America to the needs of home and foreign missions. Among the more well known of these were *Field Afar* (more recently called *Maryknoll*), *Catholic Missions* (published by the national office of the Society for the Propagation of the Faith) *Catholic Extension, Far East* (Society of St. Columban), *The Sign* (Passionist Fathers).

[9] Henry McGlinchey's biography was written by a confrere of his who composed the work largely from McGlinchey's letters home and to friends, as well as the author's own memories of McGlinchey: Neil Boyton, SJ, *Yankee Xavier: Henry P. McGlinchey, SJ* (New York, 1937). James A. Walsh wrote the introduction.

[10] James A. Walsh, M.M., *Discourses of James A. Walsh* (N.Y.: Maryknoll, n.d.), 269-70.

[11] In D.J. O'Sullivan, *An American Girl in the Foreign Missions: The Life of Mother Mary Lawrence, F.M.M.* (Boston: Society for the Propagation of the Faith, 1919), 4-5. Roman authorities were also of the mind that Americans, especially women, were not strong enough for foreign mission work. It was only after World War I when Europeans saw the service that women had rendered in the War Effort that the Constitutions for the Maryknoll Sisters were finally approved.

The University Community: Harvard (53-102)

[1] This chapter and the following are adapted from a larger book project (tentatively entitled *Ecumenical Pioneers: Catholic Intellectuals and Protestant Educators*) on the experience of Catholics in Ivy League colleges.

[2] Morison, *Harvard College in the Seventeenth Century* (Cambridge, 1936), 276, 279n5. When Ezekiel Rogers of Rowley bequeathed his library to Harvard in 1660, he excepted Aquinas' *Summa*, as the Library already had a copy. S. E. Morison, *The Founding of Harvard College* (Cambridge, 1935), 264-7.

[3] Cotton Mather, *Magnalia Christi Americana*, vol. 1, 69. As often, "Jesuit" here is a general term for a Catholic priest.

[4] Morison on the anti-Catholicism of 1695: "there is significance in that date, in the midst of New England's *decennium luctuosum*, the decade of warfare and frontier raids by the French and Indians." *Harv. Coll. in the Seventeenth Cent.*, 279. Commencement titles from Morison, *Harvard in the Seventeenth Century*, vol. 2, App. B.

[5] In his anti-Catholic "Dissertation on the Canon

and Feudal Law", in Charles Francis Adams, ed., *The Works of John Adams* (Boston, 1851), vol. 3, 456. Although colonial Harvard was neither tolerant nor tolerable to Catholics, an alumnus may have married a Catholic, if Morison is right in identifying the Maryland Puritan Richard Bennett, Jr., as the Mr. Bennett of the Class of 1659. S.E. Morison, "Virginians and Marylanders at Harvard College in the Seventeenth Century", *Wm. and Mary Quart.* vol. 13 (1933), 1-9.

[6] Josiah Quincy, *Figures of the Past* (1882), 311-2.

[7] Walter Muir Whitehill, *A Memorial to Bishop Cheverus with a catalogue of the books given by him to the Boston Athenaeum*(1951), xiv. Whitehill's preface to the catalogue offers an excellent example of what might be called the Harvard view of Cheverus.

[8] Charles Francis Adams, ed., *The Works of John Adams* (Boston, 1851), vol. 3, 453; Whitehill, ibid., x.

[9] For accounts of Brosius see *Am. Cath. Hist. Res.* 5 (1888), 155-9, *HAB*, 647-9 and Annabelle Melville, *Cheverus* (Milwaukee, 1958), 163-4.; Feb. 21, 1814, HUA, Corp. Rec. vol. 5, p. 144. Several Frenchmen had taught their native language at the college before this period, but they appear to be Hugenots. Whatever his original sympathies, Paul Joseph Guerard de Nancrède, Instructor in French from 1787 to 1800, apparently leaned towards Rousseau, Helvétius, and 'l'humanitarisme sentimental'; cf. his *DAB* entry.

[10] March 18, 1814, quoted by Melville, *Cheverus*, 163.

[11] April 14, 1815, in the Mass. Hist. Soc. Sexton (*HAB*, 767) similarly reports the welcoming effect of a letter of introduction from Fr. Matignon for a Brookline minister visiting Montreal.

[12] Cheverus to Litta, Feb. 7, 1817. Copy from Arch. Prop. Fide, AAB. For more on Cheverus' concerns about Unitarianism, see Melville, *Cheverus*, 143f.

[13] Father Matignon to Bishop Carroll, (June 18, 1804). Archdiocese of Balt. Archives.

[14] Faculty Records, Vol. 8, 44. (Apr. 7, 1807); Corp. Rec., Vol. 4, 130f. (March 6, 1807), HUA. Edmund Jennings Lee, *Lee of Virginia, 1642-1892* (Philadelphia, 1895), 393, describes Col. John Lee (as he was later called) thus, "In religion he was a Roman Catholic and a sincere worshipper at its ancient altars." After the Revolution, Christ Church was in disarray and often without clergy or communion, so its services would have been even less threatening to a Catholic.

[15] Fac. Rec., Vol 8, 49 (July 6, 1807), HUA.

[16] Effie G. Bowie, *Across the Years in Prince George's County*(1947), 525f.

[17] S.E. Morison, *Three Centuries of Harvard* (1936), 199.

[18] Faculty Rec. vol. 9, 245f. (Feb., 1821), HUA.

[19] Cheverus to Archbishop Maréchal, Sept. 1, 1820. ABA. The translation is that of *HAB*.

[20] Cheverus to Maréchal, Dec. 6, 1820, ABA.

[21] Cheverus to Maréchal, Dec. 10, 1819 and March 26, 1821. ABA. My translation.

[22] Fac. Rec. X. 62, X. 81, HUA.

[23] Useful and fairly comprehensive treatments of the anti-popery lecture are: M. Augustina Ray, *American Opinion*. 126-138; Douglas C. Stange, "The Third Lecture: One Hundred and Fifty Years of Anti-Popery at Harvard", *Harv. Lib. Bull.* 16 (1968), 354-369; *HAB*, vol. 1, see index.

[24] For the interactions of these two bodies in the first-half of the nineteenth century, see Ronald Story, *The Forging of an Aristocracy*, (Middletown, 1980), 135ff.

[25] Francis Callay Gray, *Letter to Gov. Lincoln in Relation to Harvard University* (1831), 2nd ed. HUA.

[26] Andrew Peabody, *Harvard Reminiscences* (Boston, 1888), 203; see also his accounts of the above individuals. So also Edward Everett Hale, *James Russell Lowell and His Friends* (1899), reprinted 1980, 15, "In this college they studied Latin, Greek, and mathematics chiefly. But on 'modern language days,' which were Monday, Wednesday, and Friday, there appeared teachers of French, Italian, Spanish, German, and Portuguese; and everybody not a freshman must take his choice in these studies."

Gray's mathematics has sometimes been quoted out of context to illustrate the quick infiltration of Catholics at Harvard—variously seen either as a scandal or a sign of Unitarian tolerance. Although some sense of Unitarian tolerance can be seen here, the purpose of Gray's clever argumentation is to disguise the fact that the majority faith of Massachusetts, Calvinist congregationalism, was held by only one member of the faculty. Only by counting the Janitor and the Assistant Steward and by discounting the endowed professorships, can Gray claim his Trinitarian majority. Moreover, Congregationalists were completely locked out of the ruling Harvard Corporation. In profiling the university of that day in detail, Ronald Story found that of the thirty-six men elected to the Harvard Corporation between 1800 and 1860, all but three (who were Episcopalians) were Unitarians. See Ronald Story, *The Forging of an Aristocracy* (Middletown, Conn. 1980), 35.

[27] Fitzpatrick to Walker, Nov. 8, 1845, thanking him for his "kind letter of 30th ult." Coll. Pap. 2nd ser., vol. 13, 100, HUA.

[28] Gray, ibid.

[29] Ronald Story, *The Forging of an Aristocracy*, 66.

[30] For sources on the nineteenth century Dudleian lectures, see Douglas C. Stange, "The Third Lecture: One Hundred and Fifty Years of Anti-Popery at Harvard", *Harv. Lib. Bull.* 16 (1968), 354-369.

[31] George W. Burnap, "The Errors and Superstitions of the Church of Rome", *The Christian Examiner and Religious Miscellany*, LV (1853), 48. Burnap is also aware of provincial councils of bishops and the fact "that an American bishop would travel to Rome to make his submission at the chair of St. Peter!"

[32] See his biographical file at HUA.

[33] A memorial notice in his biographical file at HUA.

[34] Thomas H. O'Connor, *Fitzpatrick's Boston, 1846-1866* (Boston, 1984), 61; *HAB*, vol. 2, 406-7.

[35] Technically the honorary degree to Abbé Correa earlier in the century was the first.

[36] Corp. Rec. vol. 10, 230, 241, HUA. The brief nature of the Corporation Records gives no clue whether Fitzpatrick was passed over the first time or declined before the name was forwarded to the Board of Overseers. Amos A. Lawrence diary, June 20, 1861, Lawrence Papers, MHS, quoted from O'Connor, 197. Does Lawrence imply that Harvard was afraid to anoint a gentleman of "character and learning," to use Felton's phrase, while Know-Nothingism ran rampant?

[37] Bishop Fitzpatrick to Pres. Felton, July 21, 1861, AAB, quoted from *HAB* vol 2, 755. O'Connor suggests that the telescope imagery looks back to the tour of the observatory President Everett gave Fitzpatrick and some visiting Jesuits in the 1840's. If the dates are correct, Pres. Felton speedily wrote to Fitzpatrick the next day announcing the conferral and stating that the diploma will be forwarded. Pres. Felton Papers, 207.

[38] O'Connor, 198. *HAB*, vol. 2, 756.

[39] Senator Alexander Twombly, a Republican from Suffolk, made the proposal in Feburary, 1862. Fitzpatrick tactfully explained that he was prevented by his other duties from accepting the appointment. O'Connor, 198-9. *HAB*, vol. 2, 756.

[40] D.C. Stange, *Harv. Lib. Bull.* 16 (1968), 362.

[41] Fac. Rec. 5, 240, 246, 254, and 272. HUA.

[42] A biography of Greene can be found in William L. Lucey, S.J., *The Catholic Church in Maine* (Francestown, N.H., 1958), 245-50, but the Harvard data there is slightly incorrect. A major source is "Correspondence Between Henry Clarke Bowen Green, M.D. and Very Rev. William Taylor, 1824-25", *U.S. Cath. Hist. Mag.*, 3 (1890), 369-391.

[43] The most complete accounts of Haskins' life are Wm. D. Kelly, *The Life of Father Haskins*, (Boston, 1899), quoted here from 151; *HAB*, vol. 2, *passim*; and Thomas J. O'Donnell, "For Bread and Wine", *The Woodstock Letters* 80 (1951) pp. 116-125. On his work see Peter C. Holloran, *Boston's Wayward Children: Social Services for Homeless Children, 1830-1930* (Rutherford, 1989).

[44] O'Connor, 115-6; *HAB*, ibid.

[45] Fortunately we have Shaw's diary edited in 1965 with a fine introduction by Walter J. Meagher, S.J., *A Proper Bostonian, Priest, Jesuit: Diary of Fr. Joseph Coolidge Shaw, S.J. (1821-1851)*.

[46] V. A. Lapomarda, *The Jesuit Heritage in New England* (Worcester, 1977), 83.

[47] R. Emmett Curran, S.J., ed., *American Jesuit Spirituality: The Maryland Tradition, 1634-1900* (New York, 1988), 38.

[48] For Searle, see his articles on him in *Catholic World* (Feb. 1898), vol. 66, 714-6; (Aug. 1904), vol. 79, 677-9; and (1918), vol 107, 713-6.

[49] *HAB*, 411. Stone's life, with several letters, is told in Walter George Smith and Helen Grace Smith, *Fidelis of the Cross: James Kent Stone* (New York, 1926).

[50] Edward I. Devitt, S.J., "Father Francis J. O'Neill, S.J.", *Stylus* 18 (March, 1905), 14.

[51] Entry by W. R. Dimmock in *Harvard Memorial Biographies* (1866), II, 48-9.

[52] In his entry in the *Reports of the Class of 1859*.

[53] Wm. D. Kelly,*The Life of Father Haskins* (Boston, 1899), 73.

[54] *Harv. Mem. Biog.* II, 54. Clipping from a Boston paper, N. B. Shurtleff's biographical file, HUA. Probably through his influence, his sister also became a Catholic.

[55] William Stetson Merrill's story of his conversion in Georgina Pell Curtis, *Some Roads to Rome in America* (St. Louis, 1909), 335-41.

[56] *HAB*, Vol. 2, 427, relating the *Pilot* and the *Boston Transcript*. No mention of such considerations appear in the Harvard records, but it is probable that these were not formal offers, but preliminary ones sounding out the disposition of the prospective recipient.

[57] *HAB*, 402, 429.

[58] *HAB*, 401, citing M. Curran, *Life of Patrick A. Collins*(Norwood, 1906); For examples of other Harvard Irish-Americans, see the biographies in James Bernard Cullen, *The Story of the Irish in Boston* (Boston, 1889).

[59] *Quinquennial Catalogue of the Law School of Harvard University, 1817-1934* (Cambridge, 1935). Evans, like most students, left no declaration of their religion, but his correspondence to Mt. St. Mary's indicates a Catholic family background. I am grateful to Kelly Fitzpatrick, the archivist at "the Mountain", for research into several early graduates.

[60] Anderson Humphreys, *Semmes America* (1989), 365-71.

[61] J. B. Bishop, *Charles Joseph Bonaparte* (New York, 1922), 32. For his political career, see Eric F. Goldman, *Charles J. Bonaparte: Patrician Reformer* (Baltimore, 1943).

[62] Feb. 18, 1871, J. B. Bishop, *Bonaparte*, 40.

[63] J. B. Bishop, *Bonaparte*, 34.

[64] J. B. Bishop, *Bonaparte*, 39.

[65] J. B. Bishop, *Bonaparte*, 42.

[66] J. B. Bishop, *Bonaparte*, 81-2. Harvard Catholic Club papers, HUA.

[67] E. Goldman, 55-6.

[68] However, for distaste against Catholics, see Marcia Graham Synnott, *The Half-Opened Door: Discrimination and Admissions at Harvard, Yale, and Princeton, 1900-1970* (Westport, 1979), 40-44.

[69] *The Christian Register*, vol. 69 (1890), 695-6. Keane also spoke at Harvard on Feb. 10, 1892 on the topic "Principles Taught by History" and received an honorary degree in 1893. See Patrick H. Ahern, *The Life of John J. Keane: Educator and Archbishop, 1839-1918* (Milwaukee, 1955), 105.

[70] *Opportunities for Religious Worship* (1895), a pamphlet in HUA (HUD 895.64).

[71] *Pilot*, March 10, 1894. For this period of O'Connell's life, see *HAB* 452-64 or the forthcoming

Militant and Triumphant(1992) by James M. O'Toole.

72 "Apologetic Harvard", an article in the file of P. J. O'Callaghan '88, HUA.

73 "Catholics at Harvard", *The Catholic Family Annual for 1895*, 74-80.

74 Unnamed source quoted in Walter George Smith and Helen Grace Smith, *Fidelis of the Cross: James Kent Stone* (New York, 1926), 326-9.

75 H. James, *Charles William Eliot* (1930), vol. 1, 141.

76 For Eliot's relations with Catholic leaders, see Hugh Hawkins, *Between Harvard and America*, 184ff.

77 *Opportunities for Religious Worship* (1895), a pamphlet in HUA (HUD 895.64). Italics added.

78 The most documented study of Eliot's controversy with the Jesuits is to be found in Hugh Hawkins, *Between Harvard and America: The Educational Leadership of Charles W. Eliot* (New York, 1971), 186-190. For a Catholic version, see David R. Dunigan, *A History of Boston College* (Milwaukee, 1947), 168-172.

79 Mullan to Eliot, Jan. 11, 1900, Eliot Papers, HUA. See Fr. Ryan's summary of the Catholic view ("It was no longer a question of education divorced from religion; it became one of education versus religion.") in his article, "The St. Paul's Catholic Club", *Harv. Alum. Bull.* 17 (1914-5), 264-7. For Catholic enrolments, I have used the reports of the graduating classes here.

80 LaFarge had put out a general notice seeking books, St. Paul Catholic Club Scrapbook, HUA.

81 "Catholic Club Report 1905-6", PBHA files, HUA.

82 John Whitney Evans, "John LaFarge, *America*, and the Newman Movement", *The Catholic Historical Review* (vol. 64, Oct., 1978), 614-643. The original of LaFarge's "Report on the Condition of Catholic Students at Harvard University" is now at Georgetown Univ. Spec. Coll.

83 Evans, 615; John LaFarge, *The Manner is Ordinary* (New York, 1954), 65.

84 Evans, 615-7; John LaFarge, 65-6.

85 See the paper delivered by Francis B. Cassilly, S.J. at the Cath. Educ. Assn. 3rd Annual Meeting (July, 1906), entitled "Catholic Students at State Universities", and poignantly subtitled "A Growing Educational Problem". Most of these numbers are approximations and Harvard's leadership here may be only a reporting phenomenon.

86 Evans, 618-620.

87 Wm. Elliot Norton to Walter Tibbetts of PBH, Nov. 13, 1925. HUA.

88 Doherty's and Tierney's comments come from answers to questionnaires by the HRCSC in 1964.

89 John J. Sullivan, "The First Olympic Champion", *Columbia*, Jan. 1956, 4. My thanks to the staff of the Gallery of Living Catholic Authors at Georgetown Univ. Spec. Coll. for bringing Jim Connolly's file to my attention.

90 "The St. Paul's Catholic Club", *Harvard Alumni Bulletin* 17 (1914-5), 265.

91 Of this group Brickley was particularly distinguished, Captain of the 1915 football team and winning letters in track and baseball too. J.A. Blanchard, *The H Book of Harvard Athletics: 1852-1922* (1923), 424ff.

92 Entry in *The American Catholic Who's Who 1938-39*.

93 SPCC report of 1913-1914. Religious Societies files, (UA 5.688.25), HUA.

94 Lowell to Byrne, Feb. 1920; Morgan to Lowell, March 2, 1920; and Lowell to Morgan, March 3, 1920, ALL, #448 Byrne, James, HUA.

95 Lowell to Morgan, ibid. For the Jewish situation, see Nitza Rosovsky, ed., *The Jewish Experience at Harvard and Radcliffe* (Cambridge, 1986), 8-33.

96 Ryan to O'Connell, Jan. 14, 1915, AAB. Woods phrased the plan as part of "the scheme of Pres. Lowell to have Harvard the *great National University*," but Ryan, who seemed eager about the interest by Harvard, also understood Wood's move as "an indication of the effort being made to placate Catholics that have been scared off by Pres. Eliot's utterances."

97 For several amusing episodes and some indication of the mutual respect held unspoken by the two institutions, see the chapter "Cardinals at Harvard" in Dorothy G. Wayman, *Cardinal O'Connell of Boston* (New York, 1955), 241-254. The honorary degree came the year *after* the many given for the Harvard Tercentennial and may be connected with the fact that on June 27, 1937, three days after his honorary degree, "the Cardinal presided at the first Mass ever celebrated in Harvard Stadium, a memorial service for the war dead" (p. 255).

98 Ryan to Chancery, July, 1918. AAB.

99 Ryan to Arthur Beane, Sept. 27, 1917, PBHA files, HUA.

100 Ryan to Chancery, June 13, 1921. AAB.

101 Hickey to O'Connell, May 14, 1930. St. Paul's Church files. AAB.

102 For G. H. Shaw, see various newspaper clippings in the file on him at the Univ. of Notre Dame Archives (Laetare file) or HUA.

103 The classic apologia for the St. Benedict's Center is Catherine Goddard Clarke, *The Loyolas and the Cabots* (Boston, 1950). For further, see Robert Connor, *Walled In* (1979) and George B. Pepper, *The Boston Heresy Case in View of the Secularization of Religion: A Case Study in the Sociology of Religion* [Studies in Religion and Society, vol. 18] (New York, 1988). Perhaps the best portrait of Fr. Feeney by someone who knew him is Mary Clare Vincent's introduction to the St. Bede's reprint of his *Survival to Seventeen* (Still River, Mass., 1980), ix-xxx.

104 *The Center Review* (Spring 1978).

105 In a discussion with students at the Elmbrook University Center, Oct. 13, 1989.

106 Porras to Rev. John McCabe, May 16, 1955.

107 Christina Scott, *A Historian and His World* (1984), 180.

108 Scott, 189.

The University Community: Radcliffe (103-116)

[1] For a history of Radcliffe, see Dorothy Ella Howells, *A Century to Celebrate: Radcliffe College, 1879-1979* (Cambridge, 1978). Sources for the individual accounts included in this section are usually to be found in the Radcliffe Archives, where extant alumnae surveys and memorial biographies are collected. Sometimes religion is only to be deduced from yearbook information and obituaries. For the history of the Radcliffe Catholic Club, the Radcliffe Yearbooks are most useful, often giving activities and a listing of Catholic Club members or at least the officers. The Radcliffe Archives also have some relevant files. The interviews with Gertrude E. Myles and Marie Scollard Degnan were conducted at a reception for Radcliffe Catholics on the occasion of the Radcliffe Centennial in 1979.

[2] Biographical information from her 1942 Memorial Biography and 1928 alumna survey. Rad. Arch.

[3] The words of her sister Blanche McIntyre in her Memorial Biog. Rad. Arch.

[4] The only substantial account of Miss Cary's life is that in Annette S. Driscoll, *Literary Convert Women* (Manchester, N.H. 1928), 54-5; see also William Cardinal O'Connell's "A Life Lived for God" in his *Sermons and Addresses* (Boston, 1922), vol. 6, 122-9; her own brief story of her conversion is found in Georgina P. Curtis' volumes *Some Roads to Rome* (1909), 71-4 and *Beyond the Road to Rome* (1914), 81-2. See also Paula Kane, *Boston Catholics and Modern American Culture, 1900-1920* (Yale Diss. 1987), 197-200.

[5] Amalie M. Kass, "Harriet Ryan Albee: Charity Begins at the Channing Home," *Harvard Medical School Bulletin*, Winter 1989, 48-53.

[6] Her article "Who Should Go to Prison?", *Catholic World* 49 (April, 1889), 68-74, argues for distinguishing between hardened criminals and minor juvenile offenders.

[7] Letter Nov. 11, 1920. Rad Arch.

[8] Nov. 1918. Rad. Arch. RG II Ser. 2; Dec. 3, 1918 and Jan. 16, 1919. Rad. Arch.

[9] Recollection of Marie Scollard Degnan '17 in 1979. The most useful collections on Helen C. White are the files in the archives of Notre Dame (her Laetare Medal file), Radcliffe, and the Univ. of Wisconsin. See also the *Catholic Library World* 1939-40.

[10] *Catholic Library World* 1939-40; Part of an anecdote concerning a Harvard lecturer's "comparative table of the great ages of history with regard to one simple touchstone—one's chance of dying *quietly* in one's bed," to be found in her commencement address at St. Mary's College in 1948, Univ. of Notre Dame Archives, UDIS Box 134, folder 26.

[11] AAB, Ryan to O'Connell, May 18, 1915.

[12] AAB, Chancery to Emma Forbes Cary, Nov. 27, 1915.

[13] A few tacit restrictions, however, may have existed for Jewish students. See Nitza Rosovsky, ed., *The Jewish Experience at Harvard and Radcliffe* (Cambridge, 1986), 38-40.

[14] Radcliffe Archives.

[15] The recollection of Genevieve Mathison, archives of the HRCSC. Florence Hunter Russell '32, who was also in attendance, remembers Margaret Driscoll '29 of Brookline and Mary Carr Baker ('29 or '30) being present.

In Their Own Words (117-203)

[1] See John LaFarge, *The Manner is Ordinary* (New York, 1954) and a LaFarge manuscript (now at G.U.S.C.) quoted in John Whitney Evans, "John LaFarge, *America*, and the Newman Movement," *Cath. Hist. Rev.* (Oct. 1978), 614ff; Christopher Huntington, "The Voice of Authority," in John A. O'Brien, ed., *The Road to Damascus*, vol. 3 (London, 1954), 105-125; John Cort, in Dan O'Neill, *The New Catholics* (New York, 1987), 1-19, adapted into "Discovering the Church in Harvard Yard," *The New Oxford Review* (Nov. 1987), 6-16; and the partial recollections of Michael Novak and others in *Generation of the Third Eye*, ed. Daniel Callahan (New York, 1965). Perhaps the best portrait of Fr. Feeney by someone who knew him is Mary Clare Vincent's introduction to the St. Bede's reprint of his *Survival to Seventeen* (Still River, Mass., 1980), ix-xxx.

[2] Cardinal O'Connell also seems to have thwarted Professor Lowell's invitation to Hippolyte Delehaye to lecture at Harvard; see George Hunston Williams, *The Harvard Divinity School: Its Place in Harvard University and American Culture* (Boston, 1954), 203n.58.